RACING & FOOTBALL OUTLOOK

FOOTBALL

Annual 2002-2003

RACING & FOOTBALL OUTLOOK
FOOTBALL ANNUAL 2002-2003

Editor Sean Gollogly
Contributors Chris Cook, Steve
Cook, Alex Deacon, Steve Hughes,
Steve Jones, Nigel Speight.

Published in 2002 by Raceform
High Street, Compton, Newbury, Berkshire, RG20 6NL
Tel: 01635 578080. Fax: 01635 578101
Raceform Ltd is a wholly owned subsidiary of MGN Ltd

Copyright © Raceform Ltd 2002

ISBN 1-901100-44-8

A catalogue record for this book is available from the
British Library.

Printed by Cox and Wyman

Cover photo: Jermain Dafoe breaks through Ipswich
Town's defence to score West Ham's third
goal in Cctober 2001

Sponsored by Stan James

RACING & FOOTBALL
Outlook

Contents

Sponsored by Stan James

Tough times, more profits

The balance of power is swinging in favour of the punter as the major bookmakers have finally bowed to the inevitable and have abolished the much-hated minimum treble rule on non-live football.

Ladbrokes and Hills have accepted that their Canute-like stance against unrestricted singles could not be maintained. They will now accept single bets on all matches bar the Aussie's leagues. Did I say all? Coral have stubbornly refused to extend the availability of singles beyond the Premiership, though they have stated that this position remains under review.

On the playing front, the hegemony of Manchester United was challenged for the first time in four seasons, as the defensive frailties of the Red Devils finally came home to haunt them. Arsenal and Liverpool, who had been struggling to bridge the class gap, looked the equal of Fergie's boys.

Sponsored by Stan James

Outlook

Introduction
by Sean Gollogly
RFO Football Editor

Sir Alex Ferguson has once again broken the bank to secure Rio Ferdinand and, while that will undoubtedly make United more formidable than ever, this is no one-horse race. Remember Fergie's mammoth spending last season was not enough to secure a single trophy.

Arsenal, in particular, rose to the United challenge and were by the end of the season simply awesome, capturing the domestic double, the first success of any kind since their double year of 1998.

Houllier is back in the manager's chair at Anfield and, in his ante-post analysis, Figaro has stated the case for Liverpool to land a first Championship since 1989/90. They have been busy in the transfer market and there can be no doubting their ambition.

Money is as ever the major factor in success or failure but this season could be a watershed year for clubs large and small, as they come to terms with the reckless spending of the boom years.

A cold wind is blowing through football as the likes of Chelsea and Leeds face up to the realities of roaring football inflation. The BSkyB money is still in place for the Premiership but the Nationwide has been ripped asunder in the wake of the collapse of the ITV Digital television deal.

Clubs have had to tighten belts drastically and even then former Premiership clubs like Watford and Bradford have been forced into administration; you can almost feel the dominoes teetering. Whilst the Sky deal will bring some welcome relief, the amount of money on the table is now significantly less than was expected. The implication of this is that the playing field in the Na-

tionwide could be levelled and there will be surprises in all three divisions. The relegated Premiership teams will have their Sky parachute money but, with their spiralling debts and heavy wage bills, they could also find themselves in trouble.

There has never been a more important time to have the tools that the RFO provides close to hand. The unique RFO Index allows cross-divisional and national league comparison from which the study and analysis of domestic and European clubs can be undertaken, with full home and away ratings as well as current Index trend figures.

The Index enables true odds to be calculated and allows out-of-line bookmaker quotes to be highlighted and punished. Our own supremacy and total goals forecasts can be used together with our fixed odds analysis, expert opinion and wealth of statistical data to ensure that the layers are kept honest.

This season, the Outlook will be expanding its European coverage to take in the French Championnat, giving readers a comprehensive in-depth coverage of all four major European Leagues

Always have an Outlook and keep ahead of the crowd.

Sponsored by Stan James

6

AUGUST
02 Start of the French Championnat
03 Start of the Scottish League programme
10 Start of the Nationwide League programme
10 Start of the Bundesliga
11 FA Community Shield: **Arsenal v Liverpool**
13 Champions League Third Qualifying Round first leg
13 UEFA Cup: First Qualifying Round 1st leg
14 Champions League Third Qualifying Round first leg
15 UEFA Cup: First Qualifying Round 1st leg
17 Start of the Barclaycard Premier League programme
24 FA Cup Extra Premliminary Round
27 Champions League Third Qualifying Round second leg
28 Champions League Third Qualifying Round second leg
29 UEFA Cup First Qualifying Round 2nd leg
31 FA Cup Premliminary Round

SEPTEMBER
01 Start of the Spanish Primera Liga
07 European Championship Qualifying
   Faroe Islands v Scotland
   Finland v Wales
   Russia v Rep of Ireland
08 Italian Serie A, TBC
09 Worthington Cup First Round
14 FA Cup First Round Qualifying
17 Champions League First Group Stage matches
18 Champions League First Group Stage matches
19 UEFA Cup First Round 1st leg
24 Champions League First Group Stage matches
25 Champions League First Group Stage matches
28 FA Cup Second Round Qualifying
30 Worthington Cup Second Round

OCTOBER
01 Champions League First Group Stage matches
02 Champions League First Group Stage matches
03 UEFA Cup First Round 2nd leg
12 FA Cup Third Round Qualifying
12 European Championship Qualifying
   Iceland v Scotland
   Spain v Northern Ireland
   Slovakia v England
16 European Championship Qualifying
   Northern Ireland v Ukraine
   England v FYR Macedonia
   Wales v Italy
   Rep of Ireland v Switzerland

Sponsored by Stan James

22 Champions League First Group Stage matches
23 Champions League First Group Stage matches
26 FA Cup Fourth Round Qualifying
29 Champions League First Group Stage matches
30 Champions League First Group Stage matches
31 UEFA Cup Second Round 1st leg

NOVEMBER

04 Worthington Cup Third Round
12 Champions League First Group Stage matches
13 Champions League First Group Stage matches
14 UEFA Cup Second Round 2nd leg
16 FA Cup First Round
20 European Championship Qualifying
   Azerbaijan v Wales
26 Champions League Second Group Stage matches
27 Champions League Second Group Stage matches
28 UEFA Cup Third Round1st leg

DECEMBER

02 Worthington Cup Fourth Round
07 FA Cup Second Round
10 Champions League Second Group Stage matches
11 Champions League Second Group Stage matches
12 UEFA Cup Third Round 2nd leg
16 Worthington Cup Fifth Round

JANUARY

04 FA Cup Third Round
06 Worthington Cup semi-finals first legs
20 Worthington Cup semi-finals second legs
25 FA Cup Fourth Round

FEBRUARY

15 FA Cup Fifth Round
18 Champions League Second Group Stage matches
19 Champions League Second Group Stage matches
20 UEFA Cup Fourth Round1st leg
25 Champions League Second Group Stage matches
26 Champions League Second Group Stage matches
27 UEFA Cup Fourth Round 2nd leg

MARCH

02 Worthington Cup Final
08 FA Cup Sixth Round
11 Champions League Second Group Stage matches
12 Champions League Second Group Stage matches

Sponsored by Stan James

13 UEFA Cup Fifth Round 1st leg
18 Champions League Second Group Stage matches
19 Champions League Second Group Stage matches
20 UEFA Cup Fifth Round 2nd leg
29 European Championship Qualifying
    Scotland v Iceland
    Armenia v Northern Ireland
    Liechtenstein v England
    Wales v Azerbaijan
    Georgia v Rep of Ireland

APRIL

02 European Championship Qualifying
    Lithuania v Scotland
    Northern Ireland v Greece
    England v Turkey
    Yugoslavia v Wales
    Albania v Rep of Ireland
08 Champions League quarter-finals first legs
09 Champions League quarter-finals first legs
10 UEFA Cup semi-finals 1st leg
13 FA Cup semi-finals
22 Champions League quarter-finals second legs
23 Champions League quarter-finals second legs
24 UEFA Cup semi-finals 2nd leg

MAY

06 Champions League semi-finals first legs
07 Champions League semi-finals first legs
13 Champions League semi-finals second legs
14 Champions League semi-finals second legs
17 FA Cup Final
21 UEFA Cup Final
24 26 Nationwide Division Three Play-Off Final
25 26 Nationwide Division Two Play-Off Final
26 Nationwide Division One Play-Off Final
28 Champions League Final

JUNE

07 European Championship Qualifying
    Scotland v Germany
    Rep of Ireland v Albania
11 European Championship Qualifying
    Northern Ireland v Spain
    Englandv Slovakia
    Rep of Ireland v Georgia

Sponsored by Stan James

Fixture list 2002-03

SATURDAY 3RD AUGUST 2002

BANK OF SCOTLAND SCOTTISH PREMIER DIVISION

Home	v	Away						Last year
Celtic	v	Dunfermline	5-1/4-2	1-2/5-1	5-0/5-0	-	3-1	3-1/5-0/5-0
Dundee	v	Hearts	-	-	1-0/2-0	1-0/0-0	1-1/0-0	1-1
Hibernian	v	Aberdeen	0-1/3-1	2-2/1-1	-	2-0/1-0	0-2	2-0/3-4
Kilmarnock	v	Rangers	1-4/1-1	0-3/1-1	1-3/0-5	1-1/0-2	2-4/1-2	2-2
Livingston	v	Motherwell	-	-	-	-	-	3-1
Partick	v	Dundee Utd.	-	-	-	-	-	-

BELL'S SCOTTISH FIRST DIVISION

Home	v	Away						Last year
Arbroath	v	Ross County	3-1/2-1	2-2/1-1	-	0-1/1-2	-	2-1/1-1
Ayr	v	Falkirk	-	1-2/1-3	4-2/1-2	1-1/3-3	5-2/6-0	2-2/0-0
Inv. CT	v	Alloa	1-0/3-1	-	3-2/1-1	-	2-1/2-0	-
Queen of Sth	v	Clyde	0-2/0-1	4-3/0-0	2-1/2-1	1-1/3-0	-	
St Mirren	v	St Johnstone	0-3/2-1	-	-	-	0-1/1-0	-

BELL'S SCOTTISH SECOND DIVISION

Home	v	Away						Last year
Airdrie Utd.	v	Forfar	-	-	-	-	-	-
Brechin	v	Berwick	3-2/3-1	-	1-1/0-3	0-3/1-2	-	
Cowdenbeath	v	Hamilton	-	-	-	-	2-0/1-1	2-1/2-1
Raith	v	Stranraer	-	-	2-0/3-2	-	-	
Stenhsmuir	v	Dumbarton	0-1/1-4	-	0-3/0-2	-	-	

BELL'S SCOTTISH SECOND DIVISION

Home	v	Away						Last year
E. Stirling	v	Montrose	1-3/4-2	4-1/1-2	3-1/2-1	2-0/1-0	1-2/0-1	0-1/2-1

How to read the results

Alongside each fixture are the results for the corresponding league match over the last six seasons. The most recent result (ie 2001-2002) is on the right. Where Scottish clubs have met more than once in the same season each result is divided by an oblique stroke, the most recent of the matches appearing to the right. Please note that SKY television coverage (details pages 88-89) and weather conditions will cause alterations to the fixture list. The Scottish Premier League will also spilt into top and bottom six sections later in the season. These fixtures cover the period until that split.

Fixtures are reproduced under copyright licence no print/coun/7009. Copyright © The FA Premier League/The Scottish Premier League/The Football League/The Scottish Football League Limited 2002. These fixtures are copyright of The Football Data Co Ltd and must not be reproduced in whole or part without consent of The Football DataCo and without the acquisition of a copyright licence.

New Member	v	Morton	-	-	-	-	-	-
Peterhead	v	East Fife	-	-	-	-	0-0/2-1	1-3/1-1
Queen's Park	v	Elgin	-	-	-	-	-	0-0/3-0
Stirling	v	Albion	-	-	-	-	-	2-2/0-3

SATURDAY 10TH AUGUST 2002

NATIONWIDE LEAGUE DIVISION I

Bradford	v	Wolves	2-1	2-0	2-1	-	-	0-3
Burnley	v	Brighton	-	-	-	-	-	-
Coventry	v	Sheff. Utd.	-	-	-	-	-	1-0
Derby	v	Reading	-	-	-	-	-	-
Leicester	v	Watford	-	-	-	1-0	-	-
Millwall	v	Rotherham	2-0	-	-	-	4-0	1-0
Norwich	v	Grimsby	2-1	-	3-1	3-0	2-1	1-1
Portsmouth	v	Nottm F.	-	0-1	-	2-1	0-2	3-2
Preston	v	Crystal Pal.	-	-	-	-	2-0	2-1
Sheff. Weds.	v	Stoke	-	-	-	-	-	-
Walsall	v	Ipswich	-	-	-	0-1	-	-
Wimbledon	v	Gillingham	-	-	-	-	4-4	3-1

NATIONWIDE LEAGUE DIVISION II

Bristol C.	v	Blackpool	0-1	2-0	-	5-2	-	2-1
Cheltenham	v	Wigan	-	-	-	-	-	-
Colchester	v	Stockport	-	-	-	-	-	-
Huddersfield	v	Brentford	-	-	-	-	-	1-1
Luton	v	Peterboro	3-0	-	-	-	3-2	-
Mansfield	v	Plymouth	-	-	2-0	2-2	0-0	0-3
Northampton	v	Crewe	-	-	-	-	-	-
Notts Co.	v	Wycombe	1-2	-	1-0	2-1	0-2	0-1
Oldham	v	Cardiff	-	-	-	1-2	-	1-7
Port Vale	v	Tranmere	2-1	0-1	2-2	1-0	-	1-1
QPR	v	Chesterfield	-	-	-	-	-	0-0
Swindon	v	Barnsley	3-0	-	1-3	1-2	-	-

NATIONWIDE LEAGUE DIVISION III

Boston	v	Bournemouth	-	-	-	-	-	-
Cambridge U.	v	Darlington	5-2	1-0	2-1	-	-	-
Carlisle	v	Hartlepool	1-0	-	2-1	0-3	2-3	0-2
Hull	v	Southend	-	-	1-1	0-0	1-1	0-0
Kidderminstr	v	Lincoln	-	-	-	-	1-3	1-1
Macclesfield	v	York	-	-	1-2	1-1	0-1	2-1
Oxford Utd	v	Bury	-	1-1	0-1	1-1	1-0	-
Rochdale	v	Leyton O.	1-0	0-2	2-1	1-4	3-1	3-0
Scunthorpe	v	Wrexham	-	-	-	0-2	-	-

Sponsored by Stan James

Shrewsbury	v	Exeter	-	1-1	1-1	1-4	2-0	0-1
Swansea	v	Rushden & D	-	-	-	-	-	0-0
Torquay	v	Bristol R.	-	-	-	-		2-1

BANK OF SCOTLAND SCOTTISH PREMIER DIVISION

Aberdeen	v	Celtic	2-2/1-2	0-2/0-1	3-2/1-5	0-5/0-6	1-1/0-1	2-0/0-1
Dundee Utd.	v	Kilmarnock	0-0/2-0	1-2/1-1	0-2/0-0	0-0/2-2	0-1	0-2/0-2
Dunfermline	v	Livingston	-	-	-	3-0/4-1	-	1-2/1-0
Hearts	v	Hibernian	0-0/1-0	2-0/2-2	-	0-3/2-1	0-0/1-1	1-1
Motherwell	v	Partick	-	-	-	-	-	-
Rangers	v	Dundee	-	-	1-0/6-1	1-2/3-0	0-2	2-0/2-1

BELL'S SCOTTISH FIRST DIVISION

Alloa	v	Arbroath	1-1/0-2	3-0/3-1	1-1/1-2	0-0/2-1	-	-
Clyde	v	Ayr	2-3/1-1	-	-	-	0-1/2-2	2-2/2-2
Falkirk	v	St Mirren	1-1/1-1	3-1/2-2	1-1/1-0	3-1/2-0	-	3-2/0-0
Ross County	v	Queen of Sth	-	-	-	1-1/2-0	-	-
St Johnstone	v	Inv. CT	-	-	-	-	-	-

BELL'S SCOTTISH SECOND DIVISION

Berwick	v	Raith	-	-	-	-	-	-
Dumbarton	v	Brechin	1-1/1-2	-	1-2/2-0	1-3/2-1	0-2/1-0	1-2/2-1
Forfar	v	Stenhsmuir	-	1-1/0-1	-	-	2-2/7-0	1-2/2-0
Hamilton	v	Airdrie Utd.	-	0-0/0-2	1-1/0-2	-	-	-
Stranraer	v	Cowdenbeath	-	-	-	-	-	3-0/2-1

BELL'S SCOTTISH THIRD DIVISION

Albion	v	Peterhead	-	-	-	-	0-0/0-1	1-0/2-1
East Fife	v	E. Stirling	-	-	-	1-0/3-1	3-1/4-1	0-4/1-0
Elgin	v	New Member	-	-	-	-	-	-
Morton	v	Stirling	3-2/1-1	1-3/1-0	-	-	-	-
Montrose	v	Queen's Park	3-2/1-1	1-3/4-3	1-0/3-0	2-1/0-2	-	3-1/3-1

TUESDAY 13TH AUGUST 2002

NATIONWIDE LEAGUE DIVISION I

Brighton	v	Coventry	-	-	-	-		-
Crystal Pal.	v	Bradford	3-1	-	1-0	-	-	2-0
Gillingham	v	Derby	-	-	-	-		-
Grimsby	v	Wimbledon	-	-	-	-	1-1	6-2
Reading	v	Sheff. Weds.	-	-	-	-	-	-
Rotherham	v	Norwich	-	-	-	-	-	1-1
Sheff. Utd.	v	Portsmouth	1-0	2-1	2-1	1-0	2-0	4-3
Watford	v	Millwall	0-2	0-1	-	-	-	1-4
Wolves	v	Walsall	-	-	-	1-2	-	3-0

Sponsored by Stan James

NATIONWIDE LEAGUE DIVISION II

Barnsley	v	Cheltenham	-	-	-	-	-	-
Blackpool	v	Luton	0-0	1-0	1-0	3-3	-	-
Brentford	v	Bristol C.	0-0	1-4	-	2-1	2-1	2-2
Cardiff	v	Port Vale	-	-	-	-	-	1-0
Chesterfield	v	Swindon	-	-	-	-	-	4-0
Crewe	v	Notts Co.	3-0	-	-	-	-	-
Peterboro	v	Oldham	-	-	-	-	0-0	2-2
Plymouth	v	Huddersfield	-	-	-	-	-	-
Stockport	v	QPR	-	2-0	0-0	3-3	2-2	-
Tranmere	v	Colchester	-	-	-	-	-	0-0
Wigan	v	Mansfield	2-0	-	-	-	-	-
Wycombe	v	Northampton	-	0-0	1-2	-	1-0	2-1

NATIONWIDE LEAGUE DIVISION III

Bournemouth	v	Kidderminstr	-	-	-	-	-	-
Bristol R.	v	Hull	-	-	-	-	-	1-1
Bury	v	Cambridge U.	-	-	-	0-2	0-1	2-2
Darlington	v	Swansea	4-1	3-2	2-2	1-1	-	0-0
Exeter	v	Scunthorpe	0-1	2-3	2-2	-	2-1	0-4
Hartlepool	v	Boston	-	-	-	-	-	-
Leyton O.	v	Macclesfield	-	1-1	-	0-0	2-1	2-0
Lincoln	v	Rochdale	0-2	2-0	-	1-1	1-1	1-1
Rushden & D	v	Torquay	-	-	-	-	-	0-0
Southend	v	Carlisle	-	1-1	0-1	2-0	1-1	3-2
Wrexham	v	Oxford Utd	-	-	-	1-0	5-3	-
York	v	Shrewsbury	0-0	-	-	1-0	2-1	1-1

WEDNESDAY 14TH AUGUST 2002

NATIONWIDE LEAGUE DIVISION I

Nottm F.	v	Preston	-	-	-	-	3-1	1-1
Stoke	v	Leicester	-	-	-	-	-	-

SATURDAY 17TH AUGUST 2002

FA BARCLAYCARD PREMIER DIVISION

Arsenal	v	Birmingham	-	-	-	-	-	-
Aston Villa	v	Liverpool	1-0	2-1	2-4	0-0	0-3	1-2
Blackburn	v	Sunderland	1-0	-	-	-	-	0-3
Charlton	v	Chelsea	-	-	0-1	-	2-0	2-1
Everton	v	Tottenham	1-0	0-2	0-1	2-2	0-0	1-1
Fulham	v	Bolton	-	-	-	1-1	1-1	3-0
Leeds	v	Man. City	-	-	-	-	1-2	-

Sponsored by Stan James

Man. Utd.	v	WBA	-	-	-	-	-	-
Newcastle	v	West Ham	1-1	0-1	0-3	2-2	2-1	3-1
Southampton	v	Middlesbro	4-0	-	3-3	1-1	1-3	1-1

NATIONWIDE LEAGUE DIVISION I

Brighton	v	Norwich	-	-	-	-	-	-
Crystal Pal.	v	Portsmouth	1-2	-	4-1	4-0	2-3	0-0
Gillingham	v	Millwall	2-3	1-3	1-1	2-0	-	1-0
Grimsby	v	Derby	-	-	-	-	-	-
Ipswich	v	Leicester	-	-	-	-	2-0	2-0
Nottm F.	v	Sheff. Weds.	0-3	-	2-0	-	0-1	0-1
Reading	v	Coventry	-	-	-	-	-	-
Rotherham	v	Preston	0-1	-	-	-	-	1-0
Sheff. Utd.	v	Walsall	-	-	-	1-1	-	0-1
Stoke	v	Bradford	1-0	2-1	-	-	-	-
Watford	v	Wimbledon	-	-	-	2-3	3-1	3-0
Wolves	v	Burnley	-	-	-	-	1-0	3-0

NATIONWIDE LEAGUE DIVISION II

Barnsley	v	QPR	1-3	-	1-0	1-1	4-2	-
Blackpool	v	Swindon	-	-	-	-	-	1-0
Brentford	v	Oldham	-	2-1	-	2-0	1-1	2-2
Cardiff	v	Northampton	2-2	-	-	-	-	2-0
Chesterfield	v	Port Vale	-	-	-	-	-	1-1
Crewe	v	Colchester	-	-	-	-	-	-
Peterboro	v	Huddersfield	-	-	-	-	-	1-2
Plymouth	v	Luton	3-3	0-2	-	-	-	2-1
Stockport	v	Notts Co.	0-0	-	-	-	-	-
Tranmere	v	Cheltenham	-	-	-	-	-	-
Wigan	v	Bristol C.	-	0-3	-	2-1	0-0	1-2
Wycombe	v	Mansfield	-	-	-	-	-	-

NATIONWIDE LEAGUE DIVISION III

Bournemouth	v	Cambridge U.	-	-	-	2-1	1-1	2-2
Bristol R.	v	Rochdale	-	-	-	-	-	0-2
Bury	v	Swansea	-	-	-	-	3-0	-
Darlington	v	Oxford Utd	-	-	-	-	-	1-0
Exeter	v	Hull	0-0	3-0	3-0	1-0	0-1	1-3
Hartlepool	v	Macclesfield	-	0-0	-	1-4	2-2	1-2
Leyton O.	v	Scunthorpe	0-1	1-0	1-0	-	1-1	0-0
Lincoln	v	Carlisle	1-1	-	-	5-0	1-1	3-1
Rushden & D	v	Kidderminstr	1-1	4-1	1-1	5-3	-	0-2
Southend	v	Shrewsbury	-	-	2-1	3-2	0-0	0-2
Wrexham	v	Boston	-	-	-	-	-	-
York	v	Torquay	-	-	-	2-2	3-2	1-1

Sponsored by Stan James

BANK OF SCOTLAND SCOTTISH PREMIER DIVISION

Celtic	v	Dundee Utd.	1-0/3-0	4-0/1-1	2-1/2-1	4-1/2-0	2-1		5-1/1-0
Dunfermline	v	Dundee	-	-	2-0/2-0	-	1-0		1-0/2-0
Hibernian	v	Rangers	2-1/1-2	3-4/1-2	-	0-1/2-2	1-0/0-0		0-3
Kilmarnock	v	Motherwell	2-4/1-0	2-1/4-1	0-0/0-1	0-1/0-2	3-2/1-2		2-0/1-4

BELL'S SCOTTISH FIRST DIVISION

Arbroath	v	Clyde	-	-	0-0/0-3	2-1/1-1	-		2-1/2-0
Ayr	v	Ross County	-	-	-	-	1-0/0-2		2-0/0-0
Inv. CT	v	Falkirk	-	-	-	2-3/0-3	2-3/1-1		1-2/3-2
Queen of Sth	v	St Johnstone	-	-	-	-	-		-
St Mirren	v	Alloa	-	-	-	-	-		-

BELL'S SCOTTISH SECOND DIVISION

Airdrie Utd.	v	Stranraer	-	-	3-2/2-0	-	-		-
Brechin	v	Hamilton	0-2/0-1	-	-	-	0-0/3-4		-
Cowdenbeath	v	Forfar	1-3/1-2	-	-	0-3/4-1	-		3-2/1-2
Raith	v	Dumbarton	-	-	-	-	-		-
Stenhsmuir	v	Berwick	1-1/1-1	-	1-2/1-1	-	2-0/0-2		3-0/1-3

BELL'S SCOTTISH THIRD DIVISION

E. Stirling	v	Albion	0-1/1-4	1-0/2-0	0-1/4-1	4-3/3-1	1-1/1-0		1-2/1-2
New Member	v	Montrose	-	-	-	-	-		-
Peterhead	v	Morton	-	-	-	-	-		-
Queen's Park	v	East Fife	-	-	-	0-1/1-0	-		1-2/2-0
Stirling	v	Elgin	-	-	-	-	-		0-1/3-1

SUNDAY 18TH AUGUST 2002

BANK OF SCOTLAND SCOTTISH PREMIER DIVISION

Aberdeen	v	Hearts	4-0/0-0	1-4/2-2	2-0/2-5	3-1/1-2	1-1/1-0		3-2/2-3
Partick	v	Livingston	-	-	1-3/1-1	-	-		-

SATURDAY 24TH AUGUST 2002

FA BARCLAYCARD PREMIER DIVISION

Birmingham	v	Blackburn	-	-	-	1-0	0-2		-
Bolton	v	Charlton	4-1	-	-	0-2	-		0-0
Chelsea	v	Man. Utd.	1-1	0-1	0-0	5-0	1-1		0-3
Liverpool	v	Southampton	2-1	2-3	7-1	0-0	2-1		1-1
Man. City	v	Newcastle	-	-	-	-	0-1		-
Middlesbro	v	Fulham	-	-	-	-	-		2-1
Sunderland	v	Everton	3-0	-	-	2-1	2-0		1-0
Tottenham	v	Aston Villa	1-0	3-2	1-0	2-4	0-0		0-0
WBA	v	Leeds	-	-	-	-	-		-
West Ham	v	Arsenal	1-2	0-0	0-4	2-1	1-2		1-1

Sponsored by Stan James

NATIONWIDE LEAGUE DIVISION I

Bradford	v	Grimsby	3-4	-	3-0	-	-	3-2
Burnley	v	Sheff. Utd.	-	-	-	-	2-0	2-0
Coventry	v	Crystal Pal.	-	1-1	-	-	-	2-0
Derby	v	Wolves	-	-	-	-	-	-
Leicester	v	Reading	-	-	-	-	-	-
Millwall	v	Ipswich	-	-	-	-	-	-
Norwich	v	Gillingham	-	-	-	-	1-0	2-1
Portsmouth	v	Watford	-	-	1-2	-	1-3	0-1
Preston	v	Stoke	-	-	3-4	2-1	-	-
Sheff. Weds.	v	Rotherham	-	-	-	-	-	1-2
Walsall	v	Nottm F.	-	-	-	0-2	-	2-0
Wimbledon	v	Brighton	-	-	-	-	-	-

NATIONWIDE LEAGUE DIVISION II

Bristol C.	v	Wycombe	3-0	3-1	-	0-0	1-2	0-1
Cheltenham	v	Plymouth	-	-	-	2-0	5-2	0-0
Colchester	v	Brentford	-	-	-	0-3	3-1	1-1
Huddersfield	v	Crewe	-	2-0	0-0	3-0	3-1	-
Luton	v	Barnsley	-	-	-	-	-	-
Mansfield	v	Chesterfield	-	-	-	-	0-1	-
Northampton	v	Blackpool	-	2-0	0-0	-	-	1-3
Notts Co.	v	Wigan	-	-	0-1	0-2	2-2	1-3
Oldham	v	Tranmere	1-2	-	-	-	-	1-1
Port Vale	v	Stockport	-	2-1	1-1	1-1	-	-
QPR	v	Peterboro	-	-	-	-	-	1-0
Swindon	v	Cardiff	-	-	-	-	-	0-3

NATIONWIDE LEAGUE DIVISION III

Boston	v	Lincoln	-	-	-	-	-	-
Cambridge U.	v	Leyton O.	2-0	1-0	1-0	-	-	-
Carlisle	v	Bristol R.	-	3-1	-	-	-	1-0
Hull	v	Bury	-	-	-	-	-	-
Kidderminstr	v	Exeter	-	-	-	-	0-0	3-1
Macclesfield	v	Wrexham	-	-	0-2	-	-	-
Oxford Utd	v	Southend	5-0	-	-	-	-	2-0
Rochdale	v	Darlington	2-0	5-0	0-0	0-0	1-1	3-1
Scunthorpe	v	York	-	-	-	-	4-0	1-0
Shrewsbury	v	Rushden & D	-	-	-	-	-	0-2
Swansea	v	Bournemouth	-	-	-	-	0-3	-
Torquay	v	Hartlepool	0-1	1-0	3-0	0-0	1-0	1-0

BANK OF SCOTLAND SCOTTISH PREMIER DIVISION

Dundee	v	Hibernian	-	-	-	3-4/1-0	1-2/0-2	2-1/1-0
Hearts	v	Dunfermline	2-0/1-1	3-1/2-0	2-1/2-0	-	2-0/7-1	1-1/2-0

Sponsored by Stan James

Livingston	v	Kilmarnock	-	-	-	-	-		0-1
Partick	v	Celtic	-	-	-	-	-		-

BELL'S SCOTTISH FIRST DIVISION

Alloa	v	Falkirk	-	-	-	-	3-2/0-1	-
Arbroath	v	St Johnstone	-	-	-	-	-	-
Clyde	v	St Mirren	-	-	-	-	-	1-1/3-1
Inv. CT	v	Ross County	2-0/3-0	-	-	-	0-1/3-3	3-0/1-1
Queen of Sth	v	Ayr	1-2/1-3	-	-	-	-	-

BELL'S SCOTTISH SECOND DIVISION

Brechin	v	Forfar	-	2-0/1-1	-	0-2/1-0	-		-
Cowdenbeath	v	Raith	-	-	-	-	-		-
Dumbarton	v	Airdrie Utd.	-	-	-	-	-		-
Hamilton	v	Berwick	4-2/4-1	-	-	-	-		0-1/3-1
Stenhsmuir	v	Stranraer	0-1/4-0	3-0/0-1	-	1-1/1-1	1-2/2-2		0-0/0-0

BELL'S SCOTTISH THIRD DIVISION

East Fife	v	Montrose	-	-	-	0-0/2-0	3-1/1-0	1-2/2-0
Elgin	v	Peterhead	-	-	-	-	1-3/0-1	4-1/0-3
Morton	v	Queen's Park	-	-	-	-	-	-
New Member	v	Albion	-	-	-	-	-	-
Stirling	v	E. Stirling	-	-	-	-	-	1-1/1-0

SUNDAY 25TH AUGUST 2002

BANK OF SCOTLAND SCOTTISH PREMIER DIVISION

Dundee Utd.	v	Motherwell	1-1/2-0	4-0/1-0	2-2/0-3	0-2/1-2	1-1/2-0/1-0	1-1/1-0
Rangers	v	Aberdeen	2-2/4-0	3-3/2-0	2-1/3-1	3-0/5-0	3-1/1-0	2-0/2-0

MONDAY 26TH AUGUST 2002

NATIONWIDE LEAGUE DIVISION I

Brighton	v	Walsall	-	-	-	-	-	-
Crystal Pal.	v	Leicester	-	0-3	-	-	-	-
Gillingham	v	Preston	1-1	0-0	1-1	0-2	4-0	5-0
Grimsby	v	Portsmouth	0-1	-	1-1	1-0	2-1	3-1
Ipswich	v	Bradford	3-2	2-1	3-0	-	3-1	-
Nottm F.	v	Wimbledon	1-1	-	0-1	-	1-2	0-0
Reading	v	Burnley	-	-	1-1	0-0	-	-
Rotherham	v	Derby	-	-	-	-	-	-
Sheff. Utd.	v	Millwall	-	-	-	-	-	3-2
Stoke	v	Norwich	1-2	2-0	-	-	-	-
Watford	v	Coventry	-	-	-	1-0	-	3-0
Wolves	v	Sheff. Weds.	-	-	-	-	1-1	0-0

Sponsored by Stan James

NATIONWIDE LEAGUE DIVISION II

Barnsley	v	Notts Co.	-	-	-	-	-	-
Blackpool	v	Oldham	-	2-2	3-0	1-2	-	0-2
Brentford	v	Swindon	-	-	-	-	0-1	2-0
Cardiff	v	Luton	-	-	-	1-3	-	-
Chesterfield	v	Northampton	-	2-1	0-0	-	-	2-2
Crewe	v	Cheltenham	-	-	-	-	-	-
Peterboro	v	Colchester	-	3-2	-	-	3-1	3-1
Plymouth	v	Bristol C.	0-0	2-0	-	-	-	-
Stockport	v	Mansfield	-	-	-	-	-	-
Tranmere	v	Huddersfield	1-1	1-0	2-3	1-0	2-0	1-0
Wigan	v	Port Vale	-	-	-	-	1-0	0-1
Wycombe	v	QPR	-	-	-	-	-	1-0

NATIONWIDE LEAGUE DIVISION III

Bournemouth	v	Oxford Utd	-	-	-	4-0	4-3	-
Bristol R.	v	Swansea	-	-	-	-	1-0	4-1
Bury	v	Shrewsbury	2-0	-	-	-	-	-
Darlington	v	Carlisle	2-1	-	1-1	3-1	1-0	2-2
Exeter	v	Torquay	1-1	1-1	1-1	3-2	1-1	0-0
Hartlepool	v	Hull	1-1	2-2	1-0	2-0	0-1	4-0
Leyton O.	v	Kidderminstr	-	-	-	-	0-0	1-3
Lincoln	v	Macclesfield	-	1-1	1-0	1-1	1-2	1-0
Rushden & D	v	Scunthorpe	-	-	-	-	-	0-0
Southend	v	Cambridge U.	-	-	0-1	-	-	-
Wrexham	v	Rochdale	-	-	-	-	-	-
York	v	Boston	-	-	-	-	-	-

TUESDAY 27TH AUGUST 2002

FA BARCLAYCARD PREMIER DIVISION

Arsenal	v	WBA	-	-	-	-	-	-
Charlton	v	Tottenham	-	-	1-4	-	1-0	3-1
Leeds	v	Sunderland	3-0	-	-	2-1	2-0	2-0

WEDNESDAY 28TH AUGUST 2002

FA BARCLAYCARD PREMIER DIVISION

Aston Villa	v	Man. City	-	-	-	-	2-2	-
Blackburn	v	Liverpool	3-0	1-1	1-3	-	-	1-1
Everton	v	Birmingham	-	-	-	-	-	-
Fulham	v	West Ham	-	-	-	-	-	0-1
Man. Utd.	v	Middlesbro	3-3	-	2-3	1-0	2-1	0-1
Newcastle	v	Bolton	-	2-1	-	-	-	3-2
Southampton	v	Chelsea	0-0	1-0	0-2	1-2	3-2	0-2

Sponsored by Stan James

SATURDAY 31ST AUGUST 2002

FA BARCLAYCARD PREMIER DIVISION

Birmingham	v	Leeds	-	-	-	-	-	-
Bolton	v	Aston Villa	-	0-1	-	-	-	3-2
Chelsea	v	Arsenal	0-3	2-3	0-0	2-3	2-2	1-1
Liverpool	v	Newcastle	4-3	1-0	4-2	2-1	3-0	3-0
Man. City	v	Everton	-	-	-	-	5-0	-
Middlesbro	v	Blackburn	2-1	-	2-1	-	-	1-3
Sunderland	v	Man. Utd.	2-1	-	-	2-2	0-1	1-3
Tottenham	v	Southampton	3-1	1-1	3-0	7-2	0-0	2-0
WBA	v	Fulham	-	-	-	0-0	1-3	-
West Ham	v	Charlton	-	-	0-1	-	5-0	2-0

NATIONWIDE LEAGUE DIVISION I

Bradford	v	Rotherham	-	-	-	-	-	3-1
Burnley	v	Crystal Pal.	-	-	-	-	1-2	1-0
Coventry	v	Nottm F.	0-3	-	4-0	-	-	0-0
Derby	v	Stoke	-	-	-	-	-	-
Leicester	v	Gillingham	-	-	-	-	-	-
Millwall	v	Grimsby	-	0-1	-	-	-	3-1
Norwich	v	Watford	-	-	1-1	-	2-1	3-1
Portsmouth	v	Brighton	-	-	-	-	-	-
Preston	v	Ipswich	-	-	-	-	-	-
Sheff. Weds.	v	Sheff. Utd.	-	-	-	-	1-2	0-0
Walsall	v	Reading	-	-	0-2	-	2-1	-
Wimbledon	v	Wolves	-	-	-	-	1-1	0-1

NATIONWIDE LEAGUE DIVISION II

Bristol C.	v	Tranmere	-	-	1-1	-	-	2-0
Cheltenham	v	Cardiff	-	-	-	-	3-1	-
Colchester	v	Wigan	3-1	-	2-1	2-2	0-2	2-2
Huddersfield	v	Blackpool	-	-	-	-	-	2-4
Luton	v	Chesterfield	0-1	3-0	1-0	1-1	-	-
Mansfield	v	Crewe	-	-	-	-	-	-
Northampton	v	Barnsley	-	-	-	-	-	-
Notts Co.	v	Brentford	1-1	-	-	0-1	2-2	0-0
Oldham	v	Wycombe	-	0-1	0-0	2-2	2-0	2-0
Port Vale	v	Peterboro	-	-	-	-	5-0	4-1
QPR	v	Plymouth	-	-	-	-	-	-
Swindon	v	Stockport	-	1-1	2-3	1-1	-	-

NATIONWIDE LEAGUE DIVISION III

Boston	v	Bury	-	-	-	-	-	-
Cambridge U.	v	Rushden & D	-	-	-	-	-	-
Carlisle	v	Exeter	2-0	-	1-3	0-0	0-1	1-0

Sponsored by Stan James

Hull	v	Leyton O.	3-2	3-2	0-1	2-0	1-0	1-1
Kidderminstr	v	Darlington	-	-	-	-	0-0	1-0
Macclesfield	v	Bournemouth	-	-	2-2	-	-	-
Oxford Utd	v	Hartlepool	-	-	-	-	-	1-2
Rochdale	v	Southend	-	-	1-0	2-0	0-1	0-1
Scunthorpe	v	Bristol R.	-	-	-	0-2	-	1-2
Shrewsbury	v	Lincoln	-	0-2	-	1-2	3-2	1-1
Swansea	v	York	-	-	-	1-0	-	0-1
Torquay	v	Wrexham	-	-	-	-	-	-

BANK OF SCOTLAND SCOTTISH PREMIER DIVISION

Dundee Utd.	v	Dundee	-	-	0-1/0-2	2-1/1-0	0-2	2-2/1-0
Dunfermline	v	Rangers	2-5/0-3	0-0/2-3	0-2/0-3	-	0-0	1-4/2-4/1-1
Hearts	v	Kilmarnock	3-2/2-0	5-3/1-1	2-1/2-2	2-2/0-0	0-2/3-0	2-0
Motherwell	v	Hibernian	1-1/2-1	1-1/6-2	-	2-2/2-0	1-3	1-3/4-0

BELL'S SCOTTISH FIRST DIVISION

Ayr	v	Arbroath	-	-	-	-		0-1/0-0
Falkirk	v	Queen of Sth	-	-	-	-		-
Ross County	v	Clyde	-	-	2-0/2-2	0-2/2-0		4-0/2-1
St Johnstone	v	Alloa	-	-	-	-		-
St Mirren	v	Inv. CT	-	-	3-2/2-0	-		1-1/0-0

BELL'S SCOTTISH SECOND DIVISION

Airdrie Utd.	v	Cowdenbeath	-	-	-	-		
Berwick	v	Dumbarton	3-1/0-3	5-3/1-1	3-1/0-1	0-1/0-0	-	
Forfar	v	Hamilton	-	-	-			3-0/1-4
Raith	v	Stenhsmuir	-	-	-	-		
Stranraer	v	Brechin	0-1/0-1	4-0/0-2	-	-		

BELL'S SCOTTISH THIRD DIVISION

Albion	v	East Fife	-	-	-	1-3/3-1	0-1/1-2	3-0/2-1
E. Stirling	v	Morton	-	-	-	-		-
Montrose	v	Elgin	-	-	-	-	0-0/2-1	0-2/1-0
Peterhead	v	Stirling	-	-	-	-		3-3/5-1
Queen's Park	v	New Member	-	-	-	-		

SUNDAY 1ST SEPTEMBER 2002

BANK OF SCOTLAND SCOTTISH PREMIER DIVISION

Aberdeen	v	Partick	-	-	-	-	-
Celtic	v	Livingston	-	-	-	-	3-2/5-1

SATURDAY 7TH SEPTEMBER 2002

NATIONWIDE LEAGUE DIVISION I

Bradford	v	Coventry	-	-	-	1-1	2-1	2-1

Derby	v	Burnley	-	-	-	-	-	-
Gillingham	v	Portsmouth	-	-	-	-	1-1	2-0
Grimsby	v	Ipswich	2-1	-	0-0	2-1	-	-
Millwall	v	Brighton	-	-	-	-	-	-
Norwich	v	Sheff. Utd.	1-1	2-1	1-1	2-1	4-2	2-1
Rotherham	v	Reading	-	-	-	-	1-3	-
Sheff. Weds.	v	Crystal Pal.	-	1-3	-	-	4-1	1-3
Stoke	v	Nottm F.	-	1-1	-	-	-	-
Watford	v	Walsall	1-0	1-2	-	-	-	2-1
Wimbledon	v	Leicester	1-3	2-1	0-1	2-1	-	-
Wolves	v	Preston	-	-	-	-	0-1	2-3

NATIONWIDE LEAGUE DIVISION II

Blackpool	v	Tranmere	-	-	-	-	-	1-1
Brentford	v	Luton	3-2	2-2	-	2-0	2-2	-
Bristol C.	v	Northampton	-	0-0	-	-	2-0	1-3
Colchester	v	Cheltenham	-	-	-	-	-	-
Crewe	v	Chesterfield	1-2	-	-	-	-	-
Huddersfield	v	Barnsley	0-0	-	0-1	2-1	1-1	-
Mansfield	v	QPR	-	-	-	-	-	-
Notts Co.	v	Oldham	-	-	0-1	0-1	1-0	0-2
Plymouth	v	Cardiff	-	-	1-1	-	2-1	-
Stockport	v	Peterboro	0-0	-	-	-	-	-
Swindon	v	Port Vale	1-1	4-2	1-1	2-1	0-1	3-0
Wigan	v	Wycombe	-	5-2	0-0	2-1	2-1	0-0

NATIONWIDE LEAGUE DIVISION III

Bury	v	York	4-1	-	-	-	-	-
Cambridge U.	v	Hull	1-0	0-1	2-0	-	-	-
Carlisle	v	Rochdale	3-2	-	0-1	1-2	1-2	1-2
Darlington	v	Wrexham	-	-	-	-	-	-
Exeter	v	Bournemouth	-	-	-	-	-	-
Kidderminstr	v	Boston	-	-	-	-	-	-
Lincoln	v	Scunthorpe	2-0	1-1	-	-	1-1	3-2
Macclesfield	v	Bristol R.	-	-	3-4	-	-	2-1
Oxford Utd	v	Torquay	-	-	-	-	-	1-1
Rushden & D	v	Southend	-	-	-	-	-	0-1
Shrewsbury	v	Leyton O.	-	1-2	1-1	1-0	1-1	1-0
Swansea	v	Hartlepool	2-2	0-2	1-0	2-1	-	0-1

TUESDAY 10TH SEPTEMBER 2002

FA BARCLAYCARD PREMIER DIVISION

Arsenal	v	Man. City	-	-	-	-	5-0	-
Middlesbro	v	Sunderland	0-1	3-1	-	1-1	0-0	2-0

Sponsored by Stan James

WEDNESDAY 11TH SEPTEMBER 2002

FA BARCLAYCARD PREMIER DIVISION

Aston Villa	v	Charlton	-	-	3-4	-	2-1	1-0
Blackburn	v	Chelsea	1-1	1-0	3-4	-	-	0-0
Fulham	v	Tottenham	-	-	-	-	-	0-2
Liverpool	v	Birmingham	-	-	-	-	-	-
Man. Utd.	v	Bolton	-	1-1	-	-	-	1-2
Newcastle	v	Leeds	3-0	1-1	0-3	2-2	2-1	3-1
Southampton	v	Everton	2-2	2-1	2-0	2-0	1-0	0-1
West Ham	v	WBA	-	-	-	-	-	-

BANK OF SCOTLAND SCOTTISH PREMIER DIVISION

Aberdeen	v	Dundee Utd.	3-3/1-1	1-1/1-0	0-3/0-4	1-2/3-1	4-1/1-2	2-1/4-0
Dundee	v	Livingston	-	-	-	-	-	1-0/2-0
Hibernian	v	Dunfermline	0-0/1-0	5-2/1-0	-	-	3-0	5-1/1-1
Kilmarnock	v	Partick	-	-	-	-	-	-
Motherwell	v	Celtic	2-1/0-1	2-3/1-1	1-2/1-7	3-2/1-1	3-3	1-2/0-4
Rangers	v	Hearts	3-0/0-0	3-1/2-2	3-0/0-0	1-0/1-0	1-0/2-0	3-1/2-0

SATURDAY 14TH SEPTEMBER 2002

FA BARCLAYCARD PREMIER DIVISION

Birmingham	v	Aston Villa	-	-	-	-	-	-
Bolton	v	Liverpool	-	1-1	-	-	-	2-1
Charlton	v	Arsenal	-	-	0-1	-	1-0	0-3
Chelsea	v	Newcastle	1-1	1-0	1-1	1-0	3-1	1-1
Everton	v	Middlesbro	1-2	-	5-0	0-2	2-2	2-0
Leeds	v	Man. Utd.	0-4	1-0	1-1	0-1	1-1	3-4
Man. City	v	Blackburn	-	-	-	2-0	-	-
Sunderland	v	Fulham	-	-	-	-	-	1-1
Tottenham	v	West Ham	1-0	1-0	1-2	0-0	1-0	1-1
WBA	v	Southampton	-	-	-	-	-	-

NATIONWIDE LEAGUE DIVISION I

Brighton	v	Gillingham	-	-	-	-	-	-
Burnley	v	Stoke	-	-	0-2	1-0	-	-
Coventry	v	Grimsby	-	-	-	-	-	0-1
Crystal Pal.	v	Wolves	2-3	-	3-2	1-1	0-2	0-2
Ipswich	v	Norwich	2-0	5-0	0-1	0-2	-	-
Leicester	v	Derby	4-2	1-2	1-2	0-1	2-1	0-3
Nottm F.	v	Watford	-	-	-	-	0-2	0-0
Portsmouth	v	Millwall	-	-	-	-	-	3-0
Preston	v	Sheff. Weds.	-	-	-	-	2-0	4-2
Reading	v	Wimbledon	-	-	-	-	-	-

Sponsored by Stan James

Sheff. Utd.	v	Rotherham	-	-	-	-	-	2-2
Walsall	v	Bradford	-	-	-	-	-	2-2

NATIONWIDE LEAGUE DIVISION II

Barnsley	v	Plymouth	-	-	-	-	-	-
Cardiff	v	Stockport	-	-	-	-	-	-
Cheltenham	v	Bristol C.	-	-	-	-	-	-
Chesterfield	v	Wigan	-	2-3	1-1	1-1	-	1-2
Luton	v	Notts Co.	2-0	-	0-1	2-2	0-1	-
Northampton	v	Huddersfield	-	-	-	-	-	0-3
Oldham	v	Mansfield	-	-	-	-	-	-
Peterboro	v	Crewe	2-2	-	-	-	-	-
Port Vale	v	Colchester	-	-	-	-	3-1	3-1
QPR	v	Swindon	1-1	1-2	4-0	2-1	-	4-0
Tranmere	v	Brentford	-	-	-	-	-	1-0
Wycombe	v	Blackpool	1-0	2-1	2-2	0-2	-	1-4

NATIONWIDE LEAGUE DIVISION III

Boston	v	Oxford Utd	-	-	-	-	-	-
Bournemouth	v	Bury	1-1	-	-	1-1	1-0	3-2
Bristol R.	v	Exeter	-	-	-	-	-	0-0
Hartlepool	v	Darlington	1-2	2-2	2-3	2-0	2-1	1-2
Hull	v	Carlisle	0-1	-	1-0	2-1	2-1	0-1
Leyton O.	v	Lincoln	2-3	1-0	-	2-3	1-0	5-0
Rochdale	v	Shrewsbury	-	3-1	1-0	2-1	1-7	1-0
Scunthorpe	v	Kidderminstr	-	-	-	-	2-0	1-0
Southend	v	Macclesfield	-	-	-	1-0	3-1	3-0
Torquay	v	Cambridge U.	0-1	0-3	0-1	-	-	-
Wrexham	v	Swansea	-	-	-	-	1-0	-
York	v	Rushden & D	-	-	-	-	-	0-1

BANK OF SCOTLAND SCOTTISH PREMIER DIVISION

Celtic	v	Hibernian	5-0/4-1	5-0/0-0	-	4-0/1-1	3-0/1-1	3-0
Dundee Utd.	v	Dunfermline	1-1/2-1	0-0/2-2	1-1/1-1	-	3-2/1-0	3-2/0-2
Hearts	v	Motherwell	1-1/4-1	2-0/1-1	3-0/0-2	1-1/0-0	3-0/3-0	3-1
Kilmarnock	v	Aberdeen	3-0/1-1	1-0/2-1	4-0/4-2	2-0/1-0	1-0/0-0	3-1
Livingston	v	Rangers	-	-	-	-	-	0-2/2-1
Partick	v	Dundee	0-0/2-2	0-3/1-2	-	-	-	-

BELL'S SCOTTISH FIRST DIVISION

Arbroath	v	St Mirren	-	-	-	-	-	0-2/0-3
Ayr	v	St Johnstone	-	-	-	-	-	-
Clyde	v	Alloa	-	-	2-1/0-1	0-1/0-0	0-0/1-1	-
Queen of Sth	v	Inv. CT	-	2-1/1-0	2-2/1-1	-	-	-
Ross County	v	Falkirk	-	-	-	0-2/4-1	1-2/4-2

Sponsored by Stan James

BELL'S SCOTTISH SECOND DIVISION

Berwick	v	Stranraer	1-2/2-0	-	-	-	1-1/0-2	2-2/4-1
Brechin	v	Cowdenbeath	-	-	2-1/1-1	2-0/1-2	0-0/2-0	-
Dumbarton	v	Forfar	-	-	-	3-3/0-0	-	-
Raith	v	Airdrie Utd.	-	1-1/1-1	1-3/0-1	1-1/2-0	1-1/5-0	2-2/2-1
Stenhsmuir	v	Hamilton	0-1/3-1	-	-	0-0/0-1	-	2-0/0-3

BELL'S SCOTTISH THIRD DIVISION

Elgin	v	East Fife	-	-	-	-	1-3/1-3	1-1/2-0
Morton	v	Albion	-	-	-	-	-	-
New Member	v	Peterhead	-	-	-	-	-	-
Queen's Park	v	E. Stirling	3-3/3-0	0-1/0-2	0-4/2-1	2-1/0-1	-	2-3/1-0
Stirling	v	Montrose	-	-	-	-	-	1-1/0-1

TUESDAY 17TH SEPTEMBER 2002

NATIONWIDE LEAGUE DIVISION I

Burnley	v	Millwall	1-0	1-2	2-1	4-3	-	0-0
Crystal Pal.	v	Derby	-	3-1	-	-	-	-
Ipswich	v	Wolves	0-0	3-0	2-0	1-0	-	-
Portsmouth	v	Wimbledon	-	-	-	-	2-1	1-2
Preston	v	Watford	1-1	2-0	-	-	3-2	1-1
Reading	v	Norwich	2-1	0-1	-	-	-	-
Sheff. Utd.	v	Grimsby	3-1	-	3-2	0-0	3-2	3-1
Walsall	v	Rotherham	1-1	-	-	-	1-1	3-2

NATIONWIDE LEAGUE DIVISION II

Barnsley	v	Blackpool	-	-	-	-	-	-
Cardiff	v	Brentford	-	-	4-1	1-1	-	3-1
Cheltenham	v	Swindon	-	-	-	-	-	-
Chesterfield	v	Stockport	0-1	-	-	-	-	-
Luton	v	Mansfield	-	-	-	-	-	5-3
Northampton	v	Colchester	2-1	-	3-3	-	2-0	2-3
Oldham	v	Bristol C.	-	1-2	-	1-1	0-0	0-1
Peterboro	v	Plymouth	0-0	-	0-2	2-0	-	-
Port Vale	v	Notts Co.	-	-	-	-	2-3	4-2
QPR	v	Huddersfield	2-0	2-1	1-1	3-1	1-1	3-2
Tranmere	v	Wigan	-	-	-	-	-	1-2
Wycombe	v	Crewe	2-0	-	-	-	-	-

NATIONWIDE LEAGUE DIVISION III

Bournemouth	v	Rushden & D	-	-	-	-	-	-
Bristol R.	v	Bury	4-3	-	-	0-0	2-0	-
Hartlepool	v	Lincoln	2-1	1-1	-	2-0	1-0	1-1
Hull	v	Macclesfield	-	0-0	-	2-3	0-0	0-1

Sponsored by Stan James

Leyton O.	v	Oxford Utd	-	-	-	-	-	3-0
Rochdale	v	Cambridge U.	3-0	2-0	0-2	-	-	-
Scunthorpe	v	Carlisle	0-0	-	3-1	-	3-0	2-1
Southend	v	Kidderminstr	-	-	-	-	1-1	1-0
Torquay	v	Shrewsbury	-	3-0	0-3	3-1	0-0	2-1
Wrexham	v	Exeter	-	-	-	-	-	-
York	v	Darlington	-	-	-	0-0	2-0	2-0

WEDNESDAY 18TH SEPTEMBER 2002

NATIONWIDE LEAGUE DIVISION I

Brighton	v	Stoke	-	-	-	-	-	1-0
Coventry	v	Sheff. Weds.	0-0	1-0	1-0	4-1	-	2-0
Leicester	v	Bradford	-	-	-	3-0	1-2	-
Nottm F.	v	Gillingham	-	-	-	-	0-1	2-2

NATIONWIDE LEAGUE DIVISION III

Boston	v	Swansea	-	-	-	-	-	-

SATURDAY 21ST SEPTEMBER 2002

FA BARCLAYCARD PREMIER DIVISION

Arsenal	v	Bolton	-	4-1	-	-	-	1-1
Aston Villa	v	Everton	3-1	2-1	3-0	3-0	2-1	0-0
Blackburn	v	Leeds	0-1	3-4	1-0	-	-	1-2
Fulham	v	Chelsea	-	-	-	-	-	1-1
Liverpool	v	WBA	-	-	-	-	-	-
Man. Utd.	v	Tottenham	2-0	2-0	2-1	3-1	2-0	4-0
Middlesbro	v	Birmingham	-	3-1	-	-	-	-
Newcastle	v	Sunderland	1-1	-	-	1-2	1-2	1-1
Southampton	v	Charlton	-	-	3-1	-	0-0	1-0
West Ham	v	Man. City	-	-	-	-	4-1	-

NATIONWIDE LEAGUE DIVISION I

Bradford	v	Burnley	-	-	-	-	-	2-3
Derby	v	Preston	-	-	-	-	-	-
Gillingham	v	Sheff. Utd.	-	-	-	-	4-1	0-1
Grimsby	v	Nottm F.	-	-	-	4-3	0-2	0-0
Millwall	v	Walsall	1-0	0-1	1-2	-	2-0	2-2
Norwich	v	Portsmouth	1-0	2-0	0-0	2-1	0-0	0-0
Rotherham	v	Brighton	-	0-0	2-1	1-3	-	-
Sheff. Weds.	v	Leicester	2-1	1-0	0-1	4-0	-	-
Stoke	v	Ipswich	0-1	1-1	-	-	-	-
Watford	v	Crystal Pal.	-	-	2-1	-	2-2	1-0
Wimbledon	v	Coventry	2-2	1-2	2-1	1-1	-	0-1
Wolves	v	Reading	0-1	3-1	-	-	-	-

Sponsored by Stan James

NATIONWIDE LEAGUE DIVISION II

Blackpool	v	Port Vale	-	-	-	-	-	4-0
Brentford	v	Wycombe	0-0	1-1	-	0-0	0-0	1-0
Bristol C.	v	QPR	-	-	0-0	-	-	2-0
Colchester	v	Oldham	-	-	2-2	0-1	1-1	2-1
Crewe	v	Tranmere	-	2-1	1-4	0-2	3-1	-
Huddersfield	v	Luton	-	-	-	-	-	-
Mansfield	v	Cheltenham	-	-	-.	0-1	2-1	2-1
Notts Co.	v	Cardiff	-	3-1	-	2-1	-	0-0
Plymouth	v	Chesterfield	0-3	1-1	-	-	3-0	-
Stockport	v	Barnsley	-	-	0-1	1-3	2-0	1-3
Swindon	v	Northampton	-	-	-	-	1-1	2-1
Wigan	v	Peterboro	-	-	-	-	1-0	2-1

NATIONWIDE LEAGUE DIVISION III

Bury	v	Hartlepool	-	-	-	-	-	-
Cambridge U.	v	York	-	-	-	-	-	-
Carlisle	v	Boston	-	-	-	-	-	-
Darlington	v	Bournemouth	-	-	-	-	-	-
Exeter	v	Leyton O.	3-2	2-2	1-1	1-3	2-3	0-0
Kidderminstr	v	Rochdale	-	-	-	-	0-0	4-1
Lincoln	v	Southend	-	-	-	1-0	3-0	0-1
Macclesfield	v	Scunthorpe	-	2-0	-	-	0-1	4-3
Oxford Utd	v	Hull	-	-	-	-	-	1-0
Rushden & D	v	Wrexham	-	-	-	-	-	-
Shrewsbury	v	Bristol R.	2-0	-	-	-	-	0-1
Swansea	v	Torquay	2-0	2-0	0-0	2-1	-	2-2

BANK OF SCOTLAND SCOTTISH PREMIER DIVISION

Dundee	v	Celtic	-	-	1-1/0-3	1-2/0-3	1-2	0-4/0-3
Dunfermline	v	Motherwell	1-1/3-1	0-2/2-1	1-1/1-2	-	1-2/1-2	5-2/3-1
Hearts	v	Dundee Utd.	1-0/1-2	2-1/2-0	0-1/4-1	3-0/1-2	3-1	1-2/1-2
Hibernian	v	Kilmarnock	1-2/0-1	4-0/0-1	-	0-3/2-2	1-1/1-1	2-2/2-2
Livingston	v	Aberdeen	-	-	-	-	-	2-2/0-0

BELL'S SCOTTISH FIRST DIVISION

Alloa	v	Ayr	-	-	-	-	1-1/0-2	-
Falkirk	v	Clyde	-	-	-	-	3-2/1-1	1-1/1-6
Inv. CT	v	Arbroath	2-0/4-1	-	2-1/2-0	-	-	5-1/3-2
St Johnstone	v	Ross County	-	-	-	-	-	-
St Mirren	v	Queen of Sth	-	-	-	-	-	-

BELL'S SCOTTISH SECOND DIVISION

Airdrie Utd.	v	Brechin	-	-	-	-	-	-
Cowdenbeath	v	Stenhsmuir	-	-	0-2/0-2	-	-	1-1/2-4
Forfar	v	Berwick	-	-	-	1-1/2-0	3-5/0-1	2-1/0-0

Sponsored by Stan James

| Hamilton | v | Raith | - | 2-0/1-4 | 3-2/1-2 | - | - | - |
| Stranraer | v | Dumbarton | 2-0/1-0 | - | - | - | - | - |

BELL'S SCOTTISH THIRD DIVISION

Albion	v	Elgin	-	-	-	-	1-1/0-1	4-4/2-2
East Fife	v	Stirling	2-2/1-3	-	2-3/1-0	-	-	1-1/1-1
E. Stirling	v	New Member	-	-	-	-	-	-
Montrose	v	Morton	-	-	-	-	-	-
Peterhead	v	Queen's Park	-	-	-	-	-	2-1/1-2

SUNDAY 22ND SEPTEMBER 2002

BANK OF SCOTLAND SCOTTISH PREMIER DIVISION

| Rangers | v | Partick | - | - | - | - | - | - |

TUESDAY 24TH SEPTEMBER 2002

NATIONWIDE LEAGUE DIVISION I

| Ipswich | v | Burnley | - | - | - | - | - | - |

SATURDAY 28TH SEPTEMBER 2002

FA BARCLAYCARD PREMIER DIVISION

Birmingham	v	Newcastle	-	-	-	-	-	-
Bolton	v	Southampton	-	0-0	-	-	-	0-1
Charlton	v	Man. Utd.	-	-	0-1	-	3-3	0-2
Chelsea	v	West Ham	3-1	2-1	0-1	0-0	4-2	5-1
Everton	v	Fulham	-	-	-	-	-	2-1
Leeds	v	Arsenal	0-0	1-1	1-0	0-4	1-0	1-1
Man. City	v	Liverpool	-	-	-	-	1-1	-
Sunderland	v	Aston Villa	1-0	-	-	2-1	1-1	1-1
Tottenham	v	Middlesbro	1-0	-	0-3	2-3	0-0	2-1
WBA	v	Blackburn	-	-	-	2-2	1-0	-

NATIONWIDE LEAGUE DIVISION I

Brighton	v	Grimsby	-	-	-	-	-	-
Burnley	v	Wimbledon	-	-	-	-	1-0	3-2
Coventry	v	Millwall	-	-	-	-	-	0-1
Crystal Pal.	v	Gillingham	-	-	-	-	2-2	3-1
Ipswich	v	Derby	-	-	-	-	0-1	3-1
Leicester	v	Wolves	-	-	-	-	-	-
Nottm F.	v	Rotherham	-	-	-	-	-	2-0
Portsmouth	v	Bradford	3-1	1-1	2-4	-	-	0-1
Preston	v	Norwich	-	-	-	-	1-0	4-0
Reading	v	Stoke	2-2	2-0	2-1	1-0	3-3	1-0

Sponsored by Stan James

Sheff. Utd.	v	Watford	-	-	3-0	-	0-1	0-2
Walsall	v	Sheff. Weds.	-	-	-	-	-	0-3

NATIONWIDE LEAGUE DIVISION II

Barnsley	v	Wigan	-	-	-	-	-	-
Cardiff	v	Crewe	-	-	-	-	-	-
Cheltenham	v	Notts Co.	-	-	-	-	-	-
Chesterfield	v	Blackpool	0-0	1-1	1-2	0-0	2-1	2-1
Luton	v	Swindon	-	-	-	-	2-3	-
Northampton	v	Mansfield	3-0	-	-	1-0	-	-
Oldham	v	Huddersfield	1-2	-	-	-	-	1-1
Peterboro	v	Brentford	0-1	-	2-4	-	1-1	1-1
Port Vale	v	Bristol C.	-	-	3-2	-	1-2	1-0
QPR	v	Colchester	-	-	-	-	-	2-2
Tranmere	v	Stockport	-	3-0	1-1	0-0	2-1	
Wycombe	v	Plymouth	2-1	5-1	-	-	-	-

NATIONWIDE LEAGUE DIVISION III

Boston	v	Cambridge U.	-	-	-	-	-	-
Bournemouth	v	Carlisle	-	3-2	-	-	-	-
Bristol R.	v	Kidderminstr	-	-	-	-	-	2-1
Hartlepool	v	Rushden & D	-	-	-	-	-	5-1
Hull	v	Swansea	1-1	7-4	0-2	2-0	-	2-1
Leyton O.	v	Darlington	0-0	2-0	3-2	2-1	1-0	0-0
Rochdale	v	Macclesfield	-	2-0	-	0-1	2-2	1-1
Scunthorpe	v	Shrewsbury	-	1-1	3-0	-	2-0	3-1
Southend	v	Exeter	-	-	0-0	1-2	1-1	3-1
Torquay	v	Lincoln	2-1	3-2	-	5-2	1-1	2-0
Wrexham	v	Bury	1-1	-	-	1-0	0-1	1-0
York	v	Oxford Utd	-	-	-	-	-	1-0

BANK OF SCOTLAND SCOTTISH PREMIER DIVISION

Aberdeen	v	Dunfermline	3-0/0-2	1-2/2-0	2-1/3-1	-	0-0/1-0	3-2/1-0
Celtic	v	Kilmarnock	6-0/0-0	4-0/4-0	1-1/1-0	5-1/4-2	2-1/6-0	1-0
Dundee Utd.	v	Rangers	1-0/0-1	2-1/1-2	0-0/1-2	0-4/0-2	1-1	1-6/0-1
Hibernian	v	Livingston	-	-	-	-	-	0-3
Motherwell	v	Dundee	-	-	2-1/1-2	0-2/0-3	0-2/0-3	4-2/2-1
Partick	v	Hearts	-	-	-	-	-	-

BELL'S SCOTTISH FIRST DIVISION

Ayr	v	St Mirren	-	0-2/2-2	1-1/2-2	0-3/1-2	-	4-2/4-1
Clyde	v	Inv. CT	-	4-3/1-6	4-1/1-1	-	1-1/2-2	1-1/1-0
Falkirk	v	St Johnstone	2-0/1-4	-	-	-	-	-
Queen of Sth	v	Arbroath	-	-	0-0/3-0	2-3/1-0	1-1/1-0	-
Ross County	v	Alloa	1-2/3-1	2-4/0-2	-	1-0/3-4	1-0/2-3	-

BELL'S SCOTTISH SECOND DIVISION

Berwick	v	Cowdenbeath	-	2-1/0-2	3-1/2-1	0-2/0-0	-	2-5/1-0
Dumbarton	v	Hamilton	1-3/0-3	-	-	-	2-3/1-2	-
Raith	v	Brechin	-	-	-	-	-	-
Stenhsmuir	v	Airdrie Utd.	-	-	-	-	-	-
Stranraer	v	Forfar	-	2-2/4-0	-	-	2-0/3-1	2-0/0-3

BELL'S SCOTTISH THIRD DIVISION

E. Stirling	v	Elgin	-	-	-	-	0-2/1-0	2-1/0-3
Morton	v	East Fife	0-0/2-0	-	-	-	-	-
Montrose	v	Peterhead	-	-	-	-	0-2/2-2	0-3/2-1
New Member	v	Stirling	-	-	-	-	-	-
Queen's Park	v	Albion	1-1/0-0	5-1/2-4	0-0/0-0	2-0/0-1	-	1-2/0-3

SATURDAY 5TH OCTOBER 2002

FA BARCLAYCARD PREMIER DIVISION

Arsenal	v	Sunderland	2-0	-	-	4-1	2-2	3-0
Aston Villa	v	Leeds	2-0	1-0	1-2	1-0	1-2	0-1
Blackburn	v	Tottenham	0-2	0-3	1-1	-	-	2-1
Fulham	v	Charlton	-	-	-	2-1	-	0-0
Liverpool	v	Chelsea	5-1	4-2	1-1	1-0	2-2	1-0
Man. Utd.	v	Everton	2-2	2-0	3-1	5-1	1-0	4-1
Middlesbro	v	Bolton	-	-	-	-	-	1-1
Newcastle	v	WBA	-	-	-	-	-	-
Southampton	v	Man. City	-	-	-	-	0-2	-
West Ham	v	Birmingham	-	-	-	-	-	-

NATIONWIDE LEAGUE DIVISION I

Bradford	v	Preston	-	-	-	-	-	0-1
Derby	v	Walsall	-	-	-	-	-	-
Gillingham	v	Coventry	-	-	-	-	-	1-2
Grimsby	v	Reading	2-0	-	-	-	-	-
Millwall	v	Nottm F.	-	-	-	-	-	3-3
Norwich	v	Leicester	-	-	-	-	-	-
Rotherham	v	Portsmouth	-	-	-	-	-	2-1
Sheff. Weds.	v	Burnley	-	-	-	-	2-0	0-2
Stoke	v	Crystal Pal.	2-2	-	-	-	-	-
Watford	v	Brighton	-	-	-	-	-	-
Wimbledon	v	Ipswich	-	-	-	-	-	-
Wolves	v	Sheff. Utd.	1-2	0-0	2-1	1-0	0-0	1-0

NATIONWIDE LEAGUE DIVISION II

Blackpool	v	Cheltenham	-	-	-	-	2-2	-
Brentford	v	Barnsley	-	-	-	-	-	-

Sponsored by Stan James

29

Bristol C.	v	Chesterfield	2-0	1-0	-	3-0	-	3-0
Colchester	v	Wycombe	-	-	2-1	1-0	0-0	2-2
Crewe	v	QPR	-	2-3	0-2	2-1	2-2	-
Huddersfield	v	Port Vale	0-1	0-4	2-1	2-2	-	2-1
Mansfield	v	Tranmere	-	-	-	-	-	-
Notts Co.	v	Peterboro	0-0	2-2	-	-	3-3	1-0
Plymouth	v	Northampton	-	1-3	-	2-1	-	-
Stockport	v	Luton	1-1	-	-	-	-	-
Swindon	v	Oldham	1-0	-	-	-	3-0	0-2
Wigan	v	Cardiff	0-1	-	-	2-0	-	4-0

NATIONWIDE LEAGUE DIVISION III

Bury	v	Southend	-	-	-	-	-	-
Cambridge U.	v	Wrexham	-	-	-	3-4	2-3	0-2
Carlisle	v	Torquay	5-1	-	3-0	0-0	1-0	2-0
Darlington	v	Bristol R.	-	-	-	-	-	1-0
Exeter	v	York	-	-	-	2-1	3-1	2-1
Kidderminstr	v	Hull	-	-	-	-	2-2	3-0
Lincoln	v	Bournemouth	-	-	2-1	-	-	-
Macclesfield	v	Boston	-	-	-	-	-	-
Oxford Utd	v	Scunthorpe	-	-	-	2-0	-	0-1
Rushden & D	v	Leyton O.	-	-	-	-	-	1-0
Shrewsbury	v	Hartlepool	-	1-0	0-1	0-0	1-1	1-3
Swansea	v	Rochdale	2-1	3-0	1-1	1-0	-	0-1

BANK OF SCOTLAND SCOTTISH PREMIER DIVISION

Dundee	v	Kilmarnock	-	-	1-1/2-1	0-0/1-2	0-0/2-2/2-1	1-2/2-0
Dunfermline	v	Partick	-	-	-	-	-	-
Hibernian	v	Dundee Utd.	1-1/2-0	1-3/1-2	-	3-2/1-0	3-0/1-0	0-1
Livingston	v	Hearts	-	-	-	-	-	2-1/2-0
Motherwell	v	Aberdeen	2-2/2-2	1-2/1-2	2-2/1-1	5-6/1-0	1-1/0-1/0-2	3-2

BELL'S SCOTTISH FIRST DIVISION

Alloa	v	Queen of Sth	-	-	2-1/3-5	3-1/6-1	-	2-0/4-1
Arbroath	v	Falkirk	-	-	-	-	-	1-0/0-1
Inv. CT	v	Ayr	-	-	-	1-1/1-1	7-3/1-0	3-1/1-1
St Johnstone	v	Clyde	-	-	-	-	-	-
St Mirren	v	Ross County	-	-	-	-	-	1-0/1-1

BELL'S SCOTTISH SECOND DIVISION

Airdrie Utd.	v	Berwick	-	-	-	-	-	-
Brechin	v	Stenhsmuir	0-0/1-1	1-1/4-3	1-0/0-2	-	-	-
Cowdenbeath	v	Dumbarton	-	0-2/2-0	0-2/2-1	0-2/1-2	1-1/2-2	-
Forfar	v	Raith	-	-	-	-	-	-
Hamilton	v	Stranraer	4-0/2-1	-	1-2/1-0	2-1/2-0	-	0-1/2-0

Sponsored by Stan James

BELL'S SCOTTISH THIRD DIVISION

Albion	v	Montrose	1-2/2-1	3-2/4-2	4-1/0-0	1-3/0-2	3-2/2-1	0-0/0-0
East Fife	v	New Member	-	-	-	-	-	-
Elgin	v	Morton	-	-	-	-	-	-
Peterhead	v	E. Stirling	-	-	-	-	2-4/1-2	3-2/2-1
Stirling	v	Queen's Park	-	-	-	-	0-1/0-2	0-0/3-2

SUNDAY 6TH OCTOBER 2002

BANK OF SCOTLAND SCOTTISH PREMIER DIVISION

Celtic	v	Rangers	0-1/0-1	1-1/2-0	5-1/0-3	1-1/0-1	6-2/1-0	2-1/1-1

SATURDAY 12TH OCTOBER 2002

NATIONWIDE LEAGUE DIVISION I

Bradford	v	Derby	-	-	-	4-4	2-0	-
Burnley	v	Walsall	2-1	2-1	0-0	-	-	5-2
Coventry	v	Norwich	-	-	-	-	-	2-1
Crystal Pal.	v	Reading	3-2	-	-	-	-	-
Ipswich	v	Sheff. Weds.	-	-	-	-	-	-
Millwall	v	Wimbledon	-	-	-	-	-	0-1
Nottm F.	v	Brighton	-	-	-	-	-	-
Preston	v	Leicester	-	-	-	-	-	-
Rotherham	v	Gillingham	1-2	-	-	-	-	3-2
Sheff. Utd.	v	Stoke	1-0	3-2	-	-	-	-
Watford	v	Grimsby	-	0-0	1-0	-	4-0	2-0
Wolves	v	Portsmouth	0-1	2-0	2-0	1-1	1-1	2-2

NATIONWIDE LEAGUE DIVISION II

Barnsley	v	Bristol C.	-	-	2-0	-	-	-
Cardiff	v	Wycombe	-	-	-	2-2	-	1-0
Chesterfield	v	Tranmere	-	-	-	-	-	0-2
Huddersfield	v	Notts Co.	-	-	-	-	-	2-2
Luton	v	Cheltenham	-	-	-	-	-	2-1
Northampton	v	Brentford	-	4-0	-	-	1-1	1-0
Peterboro	v	Mansfield	-	1-1	1-0	1-0	-	-
Plymouth	v	Wigan	-	3-2	-	-	-	-
Port Vale	v	Oldham	3-2	-	-	-	0-0	3-2
QPR	v	Blackpool	-	-	-	-	-	2-0
Stockport	v	Crewe	1-0	0-1	1-1	2-1	3-0	0-1
Swindon	v	Colchester	-	-	-	-	0-0	1-0

NATIONWIDE LEAGUE DIVISION III

Boston	v	Torquay	-	-	-	-	-	-
Bournemouth	v	Hartlepool	-	-	-	-	-	-

Sponsored by Stan James

Bristol R.	v	Lincoln	-	-	3-0	-	-	1-2
Bury	v	Darlington	-	-	-	-	-	-
Carlisle	v	Shrewsbury	-	-	2-1	1-1	1-0	0-1
Exeter	v	Rushden & D	-	-	-	-	-	1-1
Hull	v	Rochdale	1-1	0-2	2-1	2-2	3-2	3-1
Kidderminstr	v	Macclesfield	0-0	-	-	-	2-1	0-1
Oxford Utd	v	Swansea	-	-	-	-	3-1	2-1
Scunthorpe	v	Cambridge U.	3-2	3-3	3-2	0-3	-	-
Southend	v	York	-	4-4	-	0-0	1-0	0-1
Wrexham	v	Leyton O.	-	-	-	-	-	-

SATURDAY 19TH OCTOBER 2002

FA BARCLAYCARD PREMIER DIVISION

Aston Villa	v	Southampton	1-0	1-1	3-0	0-1	0-0	2-1
Blackburn	v	Newcastle	1-0	1-0	0-0	-	-	2-2
Charlton	v	Middlesbro	-	3-0	1-1	-	1-0	0-0
Everton	v	Arsenal	0-2	2-2	0-2	0-1	2-0	0-1
Fulham	v	Man. Utd.	-	-	-	-	-	2-3
Leeds	v	Liverpool	0-2	0-2	0-0	1-2	4-3	0-4
Man. City	v	Chelsea	-	-	-	-	1-2	-
Sunderland	v	West Ham	0-0	-	-	1-0	1-1	1-0
Tottenham	v	Bolton	-	1-0	-	-	-	3-2
WBA	v	Birmingham	2-0	1-0	1-3	0-3	1-1	1-0

NATIONWIDE LEAGUE DIVISION I

Brighton	v	Sheff. Utd.	-	-	-	-	-	-
Derby	v	Nottm F.	0-0	-	1-0	-	-	-
Gillingham	v	Watford	3-1	2-2	-	-	0-3	0-0
Grimsby	v	Rotherham	-	-	-	-	-	0-2
Leicester	v	Burnley	-	-	-	-	-	-
Norwich	v	Millwall	-	-	-	-	-	0-0
Portsmouth	v	Coventry	-	-	-	-	-	1-0
Reading	v	Ipswich	1-0	0-4	-	-	-	-
Sheff. Weds.	v	Bradford	-	-	-	2-0	-	1-1
Stoke	v	Wolves	1-0	3-0	-	-	-	-
Walsall	v	Preston	1-0	1-1	1-0	-	-	1-2
Wimbledon	v	Crystal Pal.	-	0-1	-	-	1-0	1-1

NATIONWIDE LEAGUE DIVISION II

Blackpool	v	Cardiff	-	-	-	2-2	1-0	1-1
Brentford	v	Port Vale	-	-	-	-	1-1	2-0
Bristol C.	v	Swindon	-	-	3-1	-	0-1	3-1
Cheltenham	v	QPR	-	-	-	-	-	-
Colchester	v	Chesterfield	-	-	1-0	1-0	-	1-2

Sponsored by Stan James

Crewe	v	Plymouth	3-0	-	-	-	-	-
Mansfield	v	Huddersfield	-	-	-	-	-	-
Notts Co.	v	Northampton	-	-	3-1	-	2-0	0-3
Oldham	v	Luton	-	2-1	1-1	2-1	2-0	-
Tranmere	v	Barnsley	1-1	-	3-0	2-2	2-3	-
Wigan	v	Stockport	-	-	-	-	-	-
Wycombe	v	Peterboro	2-0	-	-	-	2-0	3-0

NATIONWIDE LEAGUE DIVISION III

Cambridge U.	v	Oxford Utd	-	-	-	2-0	1-0	-
Darlington	v	Boston	-	-	-	-	-	-
Hartlepool	v	Wrexham	-	-	-	-	-	-
Leyton O.	v	Bournemouth	-	-	-	-	-	-
Lincoln	v	Exeter	2-3	2-1	-	1-0	3-1	0-0
Macclesfield	v	Carlisle	-	-	-	2-1	1-0	1-1
Rochdale	v	Scunthorpe	1-2	2-0	2-2	-	3-2	2-2
Rushden & D	v	Bury	-	-	-	-	-	-
Shrewsbury	v	Kidderminstr	-	-	-	-	1-0	4-0
Swansea	v	Southend	-	-	3-1	3-1	-	3-2
Torquay	v	Hull	1-1	5-1	2-0	0-1	1-1	1-1
York	v	Bristol R.	2-2	0-1	1-0	-	-	3-0

BANK OF SCOTLAND SCOTTISH PREMIER DIVISION

Aberdeen	v	Dundee	-	-	2-2/1-2	0-2/0-1	0-2/0-2	0-0
Dundee Utd.	v	Livingston	-	-	-	-	-	0-0
Hearts	v	Celtic	2-2/1-2	1-2/1-1	2-1/2-4	1-2/1-0	2-4/0-3	0-1/1-4
Kilmarnock	v	Dunfermline	2-2/2-1	2-1/3-0	0-0/0-0	-	2-1/2-1	0-0
Partick	v	Hibernian	-	-	-	-	-	-
Rangers	v	Motherwell	5-0/0-2	2-2/1-0	2-1/2-1	4-1/6-2	2-0	3-0/3-0

BELL'S SCOTTISH FIRST DIVISION

Alloa	v	Inv. CT	0-2/1-0	-	1-1/1-4	-	1-4/1-1	-
Clyde	v	Queen of Sth	0-2/2-1	0-0/3-1	2-0/2-1	3-0/3-1	-	-
Falkirk	v	Ayr	-	2-1/4-0	1-0/3-0	2-1/1-0	3-0/1-2	1-2/0-2
Ross County	v	Arbroath	2-0/1-0	0-0/1-0	-	2-0/1-1	-	0-2/0-1
St Johnstone	v	St Mirren	4-0/1-0	-	-	-	2-0/2-2	-

BELL'S SCOTTISH SECOND DIVISION

Airdrie Utd.	v	Hamilton	-	0-0/3-2	3-2/1-0	-	-	-
Brechin	v	Dumbarton	2-1/0-3	-	0-0/3-3	0-2/1-2	3-1/1-0	3-2/0-1
Cowdenbeath	v	Stranraer	-	-	-	-	-	2-2/1-1
Raith	v	Berwick	-	-	-	-	-	-
Stenhsmuir	v	Forfar	-	1-4/2-2	-	-	2-0/0-1	1-1/0-0

BELL'S SCOTTISH THIRD DIVISION

E. Stirling	v	East Fife	-	-	-	0-2/1-0	2-5/1-0	2-1/1-2
New Member	v	Elgin	-	-	-	-	-	-

Sponsored by Stan James

33

Peterhead	v	Albion	-	-	-	-	1-2/1-1	0-0/0-2
Queen's Park	v	Montrose	0-2/0-1	1-1/0-2	3-0/1-2	2-1/1-1	-	2-2/0-1
Stirling	v	Morton	1-3/4-3	1-3/2-2	-	-	-	-

SATURDAY 26TH OCTOBER 2002

FA BARCLAYCARD PREMIER DIVISION

Arsenal	v	Blackburn	1-1	1-3	1-0	-	-	3-3
Birmingham	v	Man. City	2-0	2-1	-	0-1	-	1-2
Bolton	v	Sunderland	-	-	0-3	-	-	0-2
Chelsea	v	WBA	-	-	-	-	-	-
Liverpool	v	Tottenham	2-1	4-0	3-2	2-0	3-1	1-0
Man. Utd.	v	Aston Villa	0-0	1-0	2-1	3-0	2-0	1-0
Middlesbro	v	Leeds	0-0	-	0-0	0-0	1-2	2-2
Newcastle	v	Charlton	-	-	0-0	-	0-1	3-0
Southampton	v	Fulham	-	-	-	-	-	1-1
West Ham	v	Everton	2-2	2-2	2-1	0-4	0-2	1-0

NATIONWIDE LEAGUE DIVISION I

Bradford	v	Norwich	0-2	2-1	4-1	-	-	0-1
Burnley	v	Portsmouth	-	-	-	-	1-1	1-1
Coventry	v	Walsall	-	-	-	-	-	2-1
Crystal Pal.	v	Brighton	-	-	-	-	-	-
Ipswich	v	Gillingham	-	-	-	-	-	-
Millwall	v	Derby	-	-	-	-	-	-
Nottm F.	v	Leicester	0-0	-	1-0	-	-	-
Preston	v	Reading	-	-	4-0	2-2	-	-
Rotherham	v	Stoke	-	-	-	-	2-1	-
Sheff. Utd.	v	Wimbledon	-	-	-	-	0-1	0-1
Watford	v	Sheff. Weds.	-	-	-	1-0	1-3	3-1
Wolves	v	Grimsby	1-1	-	2-0	3-0	2-0	0-1

NATIONWIDE LEAGUE DIVISION II

Barnsley	v	Wycombe	-	-	-	-	-	-
Cardiff	v	Tranmere	-	-	-	-	-	1-1
Chesterfield	v	Notts Co.	1-0	-	3-0	2-1	-	2-1
Huddersfield	v	Colchester	-	-	-	-	-	2-1
Luton	v	Wigan	-	1-1	0-4	1-1	0-2	-
Northampton	v	Cheltenham	-	-	-	3-2	-	-
Peterboro	v	Bristol C.	3-1	-	-	-	2-1	4-1
Plymouth	v	Blackpool	0-1	3-1	-	-	2-0	-
Port Vale	v	Crewe	-	2-3	1-0	1-0	-	-
QPR	v	Oldham	0-1	-	-	-	-	1-1

Sponsored by Stan James

| Stockport | v | Brentford | 1-2 | - | - | - | - |
| Swindon | v | Mansfield | - | - | - | - | - |

NATIONWIDE LEAGUE DIVISION III

Boston	v	Rochdale	-	-	-	-	-
Bournemouth	v	York	1-1	0-0	2-1	-	-
Bristol R.	v	Leyton O.	-	-	-	-	5-3
Bury	v	Macclesfield	-	-	-	-	-
Carlisle	v	Swansea	4-1	-	1-2	2-0	-	3-1
Exeter	v	Darlington	3-2	1-0	0-0	1-4	1-1	4-2
Hull	v	Rushden & D	-	-	-	-	-	2-1
Kidderminstr	v	Cambridge U.	-	-	-	-	-
Oxford Utd	v	Shrewsbury	-	-	-	-	0-1
Scunthorpe	v	Torquay	1-0	2-0	2-0	-	3-0	1-0
Southend	v	Hartlepool	-	-	1-1	2-1	2-1	0-0
Wrexham	v	Lincoln	-	-	2-1	-	-	-

BANK OF SCOTLAND SCOTTISH PREMIER DIVISION

Aberdeen	v	Hibernian	0-2/1-1	2-0/3-0	-	2-2/4-0	0-2/1-0	2-0
Dundee Utd.	v	Partick	-	-	-	-	-	-
Dunfermline	v	Celtic	0-2/2-2	0-2/1-1	2-2/1-2	-	1-2/0-3	0-4
Hearts	v	Dundee	-	-	0-2/1-2	4-0/2-0	3-1/2-0	3-1/2-0
Motherwell	v	Livingston	-	-	-	-	-	0-0/1-2
Rangers	v	Kilmarnock	4-2/1-2	4-1/0-1	1-0/1-1	2-1/1-0	0-3/5-1	3-1/5-0

BELL'S SCOTTISH FIRST DIVISION

Arbroath	v	Alloa	0-2/1-2	2-3/3-0	0-2/1-2	2-2/2-0	-	-
Ayr	v	Clyde	2-4/3-1	-	-	-	2-1/2-0	2-1/0-1
Inv. CT	v	St Johnstone	-	-	-	-	-	-
Queen of Sth	v	Ross County	-	-	-	0-2/0-3	-	-
St Mirren	v	Falkirk	0-1/1-0	2-0/1-2	0-2/0-3	2-1/1-0	-	1-5/0-0

BELL'S SCOTTISH SECOND DIVISION

Berwick	v	Brechin	0-0/1-0	-	3-0/2-3	2-0/3-1	-	-
Dumbarton	v	Stenhsmuir	1-1/0-2	-	0-2/1-4	-	-	-
Forfar	v	Airdrie Utd.	-	-	-	-	-	-
Hamilton	v	Cowdenbeath	-	-	-	-	0-0/0-0	1-0/0-2
Stranraer	v	Raith	-	-	2-2/2-0	-	-	-

BELL'S SCOTTISH THIRD DIVISION

Albion	v	Stirling	-	-	-	-	-	1-3/2-0
East Fife	v	Peterhead	-	-	-	-	1-1/2-1	0-1/2-3
Elgin	v	Queen's Park	-	-	-	-	-	2-0/0-1
Morton	v	New Member	-	-	-	-	-	-
Montrose	v	E. Stirling	1-0/0-2	1-1/1-1	2-0/1-0	1-2/0-0	0-1/1-1	2-0/2-0

Sponsored by Stan James

TUESDAY 29TH OCTOBER 2002

NATIONWIDE LEAGUE DIVISION I

Brighton	v	Ipswich	-	-	-	-	-	-
Gillingham	v	Wolves	-	-	-	-	1-0	2-3
Grimsby	v	Burnley	-	4-1	-	-	1-0	3-1
Norwich	v	Nottm F.	-	1-0	-	1-0	0-0	1-0
Portsmouth	v	Preston	-	-	-	-	0-1	0-1
Reading	v	Bradford	0-0	0-3	-	-	-	-
Walsall	v	Crystal Pal.	-	-	-	2-2	-	2-2
Wimbledon	v	Rotherham	-	-	-	-	-	1-0

NATIONWIDE LEAGUE DIVISION II

Blackpool	v	Stockport	2-1	-	-	-	-	-
Brentford	v	Plymouth	3-2	3-1	3-1	-	-	-
Bristol C.	v	Huddersfield	-	-	1-2	-	-	1-1
Cheltenham	v	Port Vale	-	-	-	-	-	-
Colchester	v	Barnsley	-	-	-	-	-	-
Crewe	v	Luton	0-0	-	-	-	-	-
Mansfield	v	Cardiff	1-3	1-2	3-0	-	2-1	-
Notts Co.	v	Swindon	-	-	-	-	3-2	3-1
Oldham	v	Northampton	-	2-2	0-1	-	2-1	4-2
Tranmere	v	Peterboro	-	-	-	-	-	1-0
Wigan	v	QPR	-	-	-	-	-	1-2
Wycombe	v	Chesterfield	1-0	1-1	1-0	3-0	-	0-0

NATIONWIDE LEAGUE DIVISION III

Cambridge U.	v	Carlisle	1-3	-	1-0	-	-	-
Darlington	v	Scunthorpe	2-0	1-0	3-1	-	2-1	2-1
Hartlepool	v	Bristol R.	-	-	-	-	-	1-1
Leyton O.	v	Southend	-	-	0-3	2-1	0-2	2-1
Lincoln	v	Bury	-	-	-	-	-	-
Macclesfield	v	Oxford Utd	-	-	-	-	-	0-1
Rochdale	v	Exeter	2-0	3-0	1-1	0-2	3-0	2-0
Rushden & D	v	Boston	-	-	-	-	0-0	-
Shrewsbury	v	Hull	-	2-0	3-2	3-0	0-2	1-1
Swansea	v	Kidderminstr	-	-	-	-	-	2-1
Torquay	v	Bournemouth	-	-	-	-	-	-
York	v	Wrexham	1-0	1-0	1-1	-	-	-

WEDNESDAY 30TH OCTOBER 2002

NATIONWIDE LEAGUE DIVISION I

Derby	v	Sheff. Utd.	-	-	-	-	-	-
Leicester	v	Coventry	0-2	1-1	1-0	1-0	1-3	-

| Sheff. Weds. | v | Millwall | - | - | - | - | - | 1-1 |
| Stoke | v | Watford | - | - | - | - | - | - |

SATURDAY 2ND NOVEMBER 2002

FA BARCLAYCARD PREMIER DIVISION

Birmingham	v	Bolton	3-1	-	0-0	2-1	1-1	-
Blackburn	v	Aston Villa	0-2	5-0	2-1	-	-	3-0
Charlton	v	Sunderland	-	1-1	-	-	0-1	2-2
Fulham	v	Arsenal	-	-	-	-	-	1-3
Leeds	v	Everton	1-0	0-0	1-0	1-1	2-0	3-2
Liverpool	v	West Ham	0-0	5-0	2-2	1-0	3-0	2-1
Man. Utd.	v	Southampton	2-1	1-0	2-1	3-3	5-0	6-1
Newcastle	v	Middlesbro	3-1	-	1-1	2-1	1-2	3-0
Tottenham	v	Chelsea	1-2	1-6	2-2	0-1	0-3	2-3
WBA	v	Man. City	1-3	0-1	-	0-2	-	4-0

NATIONWIDE LEAGUE DIVISION I

Brighton	v	Bradford	-	-	-	-	-	-
Coventry	v	Rotherham	-	-	-	-	-	2-0
Grimsby	v	Gillingham	-	0-0	-	-	1-0	1-2
Ipswich	v	Crystal Pal.	3-1	-	3-0	1-0	-	-
Nottm F.	v	Sheff. Utd.	-	3-0	-	0-0	2-0	1-1
Portsmouth	v	Leicester	-	-	-	-	-	-
Preston	v	Burnley	1-1	2-3	4-1	0-0	2-1	2-3
Reading	v	Millwall	-	-	2-0	2-0	3-4	-
Sheff. Weds.	v	Derby	0-0	2-5	0-1	0-2	-	-
Walsall	v	Stoke	-	-	1-0	-	3-0	-
Watford	v	Wolves	-	-	0-2	-	3-2	1-1
Wimbledon	v	Norwich	-	-	-	-	0-0	0-1

NATIONWIDE LEAGUE DIVISION II

Brentford	v	Blackpool	1-1	3-1	-	2-0	-	2-0
Bristol C.	v	Notts Co.	4-0	-	-	2-2	4-0	3-2
Cardiff	v	Peterboro	-	0-0	1-3	-	-	0-2
Cheltenham	v	Huddersfield	-	-	-	-	-	-
Chesterfield	v	Barnsley	-	-	-	-	-	-
Mansfield	v	Colchester	1-1	1-1	-	-	-	-
Northampton	v	Luton	-	1-0	1-0	-	0-1	-
Oldham	v	Stockport	-	-	-	-	-	-
Port Vale	v	QPR	4-4	2-0	2-0	1-1	-	1-0
Tranmere	v	Plymouth	-	-	-	-	-	-
Wigan	v	Crewe	-	-	-	-	-	-
Wycombe	v	Swindon	-	-	-	-	0-0	1-1

Sponsored by Stan James

NATIONWIDE LEAGUE DIVISION III

Boston	v	Exeter	-	-		-	-	-
Bournemouth	v	Bristol R.	1-0	1-1	1-0	0-1	1-2	-
Cambridge U.	v	Swansea	2-1	4-1	2-1	-	3-3	-
Carlisle	v	Oxford Utd	-	-	-	-	-	2-1
Darlington	v	Lincoln	5-2	2-2	-	2-0	3-0	2-1
Hartlepool	v	York	-	-	-	2-1	1-0	3-0
Hull	v	Scunthorpe	0-2	2-1	2-3	-	2-1	0-1
Leyton O.	v	Bury	-	-	-	-	-	-
Macclesfield	v	Shrewsbury	-	2-1	-	4-2	2-1	2-1
Rochdale	v	Rushden & D	-	-	-	-	-	0-0
Southend	v	Wrexham	-	1-3	-	-	-	-
Torquay	v	Kidderminstr	-	-	-	-	1-1	1-4

BANK OF SCOTLAND SCOTTISH PREMIER DIVISION

Celtic	v	Aberdeen	1-0/3-0	2-0/3-1	2-0/3-2	7-0/5-1	6-0	2-0/1-0
Dundee	v	Rangers	-	-	0-4/1-1	2-3/1-7	1-1/0-1/0-3	0-0
Hibernian	v	Hearts	1-3/0-4	0-1/2-1	-	1-1/3-1	6-2/0-0	2-1/1-2
Kilmarnock	v	Dundee Utd.	0-2/2-3	1-3/1-0	2-0/2-0	1-1/1-0	1-0/0-0	2-0/2-2
Livingston	v	Dunfermline	-	-	-	0-1/1-0	-	0-0/4-1
Partick	v	Motherwell	-	-	-	-	-	-

BELL'S SCOTTISH FIRST DIVISION

Alloa	v	St Johnstone	-	-	-	-	-	-
Arbroath	v	Ayr	-	-	-	-	-	3-2/0-2
Clyde	v	Ross County	-	-	-	3-1/0-0	2-2/2-0	3-0/0-0
Inv. CT	v	St Mirren	-	-	-	1-1/5-0	-	1-2/4-2
Queen of Sth	v	Falkirk	-	-	-	-	-	-

BELL'S SCOTTISH SECOND DIVISION

Brechin	v	Stranraer	0-2/0-0	2-2/1-3	-	-	-	-
Cowdenbeath	v	Airdrie Utd.	-	-	-	-	-	-
Dumbarton	v	Berwick	1-0/2-2	1-4/0-2	0-0/1-1	2-1/0-2	-	-
Hamilton	v	Forfar	-	-	-	-	-	1-1/2-0
Stenhsmuir	v	Raith	-	-	-	-	-	-

BELL'S SCOTTISH THIRD DIVISION

East Fife	v	Albion	-	-	-	1-4/2-1	0-0/2-1	0-0/2-3
Elgin	v	Montrose	-	-	-	-	1-1/0-2	1-2/1-0
Morton	v	E. Stirling	-	-	-	-	-	-
New Member	v	Queen's Park	-	-	-	-	-	-
Stirling	v	Peterhead	-	-	-	-	-	2-1/0-2

SATURDAY 9TH NOVEMBER 2002

FA BARCLAYCARD PREMIER DIVISION

Arsenal	v	Newcastle	0-1	3-1	3-0	0-0	5-0	1-3
Aston Villa	v	Fulham	-	-	-	-	-	2-0
Bolton	v	WBA	1-0	-	2-1	1-1	0-1	-
Chelsea	v	Birmingham	-	-	-	-	-	-
Everton	v	Charlton	-	-	4-1	-	3-0	0-3
Man. City	v	Man. Utd.	-	-	-	-	0-1	-
Middlesbro	v	Liverpool	3-3	-	1-3	1-0	1-0	1-2
Southampton	v	Blackburn	2-0	3-0	3-3	-	-	1-2
Sunderland	v	Tottenham	0-4	-	-	2-1	2-3	1-2
West Ham	v	Leeds	0-2	3-0	1-5	0-0	0-2	0-0

NATIONWIDE LEAGUE DIVISION I

Bradford	v	Wimbledon	-	-	-	3-0	-	3-3
Burnley	v	Coventry	-	-	-	-	-	1-0
Crystal Pal.	v	Nottm F.	-	-	-	2-0	2-3	1-1
Derby	v	Portsmouth	-	-	-	-	-	-
Gillingham	v	Reading	-	-	2-1	2-2	-	-
Leicester	v	Walsall	-	-	-	-	-	-
Millwall	v	Preston	3-2	0-1	2-2	0-2	-	2-1
Norwich	v	Sheff. Weds.	-	-	-	-	1-0	2-0
Rotherham	v	Watford	0-0	-	-	-	-	1-1
Sheff. Utd.	v	Ipswich	1-3	0-1	1-2	2-2	-	-
Stoke	v	Grimsby	3-1	-	-	-	-	-
Wolves	v	Brighton	-	-	-	-	-	-

NATIONWIDE LEAGUE DIVISION II

Barnsley	v	Cardiff	-	-	-	-	-	-
Blackpool	v	Wigan	-	0-2	1-1	2-2	-	3-1
Colchester	v	Bristol C.	-	-	-	3-4	4-0	0-0
Crewe	v	Brentford	2-0	-	-	-	-	-
Huddersfield	v	Wycombe	-	-	-	-	-	2-1
Luton	v	Port Vale	-	-	-	-	1-1	-
Notts Co.	v	Mansfield	-	1-0	-	-	-	-
Peterboro	v	Chesterfield	1-1	-	-	-	-	1-1
Plymouth	v	Oldham	-	0-2	-	-	-	-
QPR	v	Northampton	-	-	-	-	-	0-1
Stockport	v	Cheltenham	-	-	-	-	-	-
Swindon	v	Tranmere	2-1	2-1	2-3	3-1	-	2-2

NATIONWIDE LEAGUE DIVISION III

Bristol R.	v	Southend	-	2-0	-	-	-	2-1
Bury	v	Torquay	-	-	-	-	-	-
Exeter	v	Hartlepool	2-0	1-1	2-1	1-2	1-1	0-2

Sponsored by Stan James

Kidderminstr	v	Carlisle	-	-	-	-	0-1	2-2
Lincoln	v	Hull	0-1	1-0	-	2-1	2-0	2-1
Oxford Utd	v	Rochdale	-	-	-	-	-	1-2
Rushden & D	v	Darlington	-	-	-	-	-	2-1
Scunthorpe	v	Boston	-	-	-	-	-	-
Shrewsbury	v	Cambridge U.	-	1-1	1-1	-	-	-
Swansea	v	Macclesfield	-	1-1	-	1-0	-	0-1
Wrexham	v	Bournemouth	2-0	2-1	0-1	1-0	2-2	2-1
York	v	Leyton O.	-	-	-	2-1	1-1	2-1

BANK OF SCOTLAND SCOTTISH PREMIER DIVISION

Dundee Utd.	v	Celtic	1-2/1-0	1-2/1-2	1-1/1-2	2-1/0-1	1-2/0-4	0-4
Hearts	v	Aberdeen	1-2/0-0	4-1/3-1	2-0/0-2	3-0/3-0	3-0	1-0/3-1
Livingston	v	Partick	-	-	1-0/1-1	-	-	-
Motherwell	v	Kilmarnock	1-0/2-0	0-1/1-1	0-0/1-2	0-4/2-0	1-2	2-2/2-0
Rangers	v	Hibernian	4-3/3-1	1-0/3-0	-	2-0/5-2	1-0/4-0	2-2/1-1

BELL'S SCOTTISH FIRST DIVISION

Ayr	v	Queen of Sth	1-0/2-2	-	-	-	-	-
Falkirk	v	Alloa	-	-	-	-	1-1/2-2	-
Ross County	v	Inv. CT	1-3/0-3	-	-	-	0-3/0-1	2-1/0-0
St Johnstone	v	Arbroath	-	-	-	-	-	-
St Mirren	v	Clyde	-	-	-	-	-	4-1/2-2

BELL'S SCOTTISH SECOND DIVISION

Airdrie Utd.	v	Dumbarton	-	-	-	-	-	-
Berwick	v	Hamilton	0-2/0-5	-	-	-	-	0-2/2-0
Forfar	v	Brechin	-	2-5/5-0	-	0-0/2-0	-	-
Raith	v	Cowdenbeath	-	-	-	-	-	-
Stranraer	v	Stenhsmuir	2-2/2-1	4-1/1-2	-	2-0/2-2	1-4/2-1	6-1/1-0

BELL'S SCOTTISH THIRD DIVISION

Albion	v	New Member	-	-	-	-	-	-
E. Stirling	v	Stirling	-	-	-	-	-	1-1/3-0
Montrose	v	East Fife	-	-	-	1-2/1-1	0-1/1-1	2-1/0-1
Peterhead	v	Elgin	-	-	-	-	1-0/1-1	1-1/1-0
Queen's Park	v	Morton	-	-	-	-	-	-

SUNDAY 10TH NOVEMBER 2002

BANK OF SCOTLAND SCOTTISH PREMIER DIVISION

Dundee	v	Dunfermline	-	-	1-0/3-1	-	3-0/0-1	2-2

SATURDAY 16TH NOVEMBER 2002

FA BARCLAYCARD PREMIER DIVISION

Arsenal	v	Tottenham	3-1	0-0	0-0	2-1	2-0	2-1

Sponsored by Stan James

Birmingham	v	Fulham	-	-	-	2-2	1-3	-

Match			C1	C2	C3	C4	C5	C6
Birmingham	v	Fulham	-	-	-	2-2	1-3	-
Blackburn	v	Everton	1-1	3-2	1-2	-	-	1-0
Chelsea	v	Middlesbro	1-0	-	2-0	1-1	2-1	2-2
Leeds	v	Bolton	-	2-0	-	-	-	0-0
Liverpool	v	Sunderland	0-0	-	-	1-1	1-1	1-0
Man. City	v	Charlton	2-1	2-2	-	1-1	1-4	-
Newcastle	v	Southampton	0-1	2-1	4-0	5-0	1-1	3-1
WBA	v	Aston Villa	-	-	-	-	-	-
West Ham	v	Man. Utd.	2-2	1-1	0-0	2-4	2-2	3-5

NATIONWIDE LEAGUE DIVISION I

Match			C1	C2	C3	C4	C5	C6
Brighton	v	Derby	-	-	-	-	-	-
Coventry	v	Wolves	-	-	-	-	-	0-1
Gillingham	v	Sheff. Weds.	-	-	-	-	2-0	2-1
Grimsby	v	Preston	-	3-1	-	-	1-2	2-2
Millwall	v	Leicester	-	-	-	-	-	-
Norwich	v	Crystal Pal.	1-1	-	0-1	0-1	0-0	2-1
Nottm F.	v	Bradford	-	2-2	-	-	-	1-0
Portsmouth	v	Stoke	1-0	2-0	-	-	-	-
Rotherham	v	Burnley	1-0	-	-	-	-	1-1
Sheff. Utd.	v	Reading	2-0	4-0	-	-	-	-
Watford	v	Ipswich	-	-	1-0	-	-	-
Wimbledon	v	Walsall	-	-	-	-	-	2-2

BANK OF SCOTLAND SCOTTISH PREMIER DIVISION

Match			C1	C2	C3	C4	C5	C6
Aberdeen	v	Rangers	0-3/2-2	1-1/1-0	1-1/2-4	1-5/1-1	1-2	0-3/0-1
Celtic	v	Partick	-	-	-	-	-	-
Dunfermline	v	Hearts	2-1/2-3	2-1/1-3	1-1/0-0	-	1-0	0-1/1-1
Hibernian	v	Dundee	-	-	-	5-2/1-2	5-1/3-0	1-2/2-2
Kilmarnock	v	Livingston	-	-	-	-	-	1-5/1-1
Motherwell	v	Dundee Utd.	1-3/1-1	1-0/1-0	1-0/2-0	2-2/1-3	2-1	0-0/2-0

BELL'S SCOTTISH FIRST DIVISION

Match			C1	C2	C3	C4	C5	C6
Alloa	v	Clyde	-	-	3-0/1-0	1-0/2-1	3-1/0-0	-
Falkirk	v	Ross County	-	-	-	-	2-3/1-1	4-2/1-4
Inv. CT	v	Queen of Sth	-	2-1/0-2	3-2/1-0	-	-	-
St Johnstone	v	Ayr	-	-	-	-	-	-
St Mirren	v	Arbroath	-	-	-	-	-	1-0/2-3

BELL'S SCOTTISH SECOND DIVISION

Match			C1	C2	C3	C4	C5	C6
Airdrie Utd.	v	Raith	-	1-0/1-0	0-1/2-2	1-4/0-2	1-1/3-0	2-2/1-1
Cowdenbeath	v	Brechin	-	-	0-1/0-2	6-1/1-1	2-1/2-1	-
Forfar	v	Dumbarton	-	-	-	5-0/4-3	-	-
Hamilton	v	Stenhsmuir	0-2/1-1	-	-	1-1/2-1	-	2-3/0-0
Stranraer	v	Berwick	1-1/1-1	-	-	-	2-2/1-1	0-2/2-2

Sponsored by Stan James

BELL'S SCOTTISH THIRD DIVISION

Albion	v	Morton	-	-	-	-	-	-
East Fife	v	Elgin	-	-	-	-	1-1/1-1	3-0/0-1
E. Stirling	v	Queen's Park	2-1/1-0	1-0/0-0	1-1/1-1	1-1/0-1	-	0-1/3-1
Montrose	v	Stirling	-	-	-	-	-	4-0/1-3
Peterhead	v	New Member	-	-	-	-	-	-

SATURDAY 23RD NOVEMBER 2002

FA BARCLAYCARD PREMIER DIVISION

Aston Villa	v	West Ham	0-0	2-0	0-0	2-2	2-2	2-1
Bolton	v	Chelsea	-	1-0	-	-	-	2-2
Charlton	v	Blackburn	-	-	0-0	1-2	-	0-2
Everton	v	WBA	-	-	-	-	-	-
Fulham	v	Liverpool	-	-	-	-	-	0-2
Man. Utd.	v	Newcastle	0-0	1-1	0-0	5-1	2-0	3-1
Middlesbro	v	Man. City	-	1-0	-	-	1-1	-
Southampton	v	Arsenal	0-2	1-3	0-0	0-1	3-2	0-2
Sunderland	v	Birmingham	-	1-1	2-1	-	-	-
Tottenham	v	Leeds	1-0	0-1	3-3	1-2	1-2	2-1

NATIONWIDE LEAGUE DIVISION I

Bradford	v	Sheff. Utd.	1-2	1-1	2-2	-	-	1-2
Burnley	v	Norwich	-	-	-	-	2-0	1-1
Crystal Pal.	v	Grimsby	3-0	-	3-1	3-0	0-1	5-0
Derby	v	Wimbledon	0-2	1-1	0-0	4-0	-	-
Ipswich	v	Coventry	-	-	-	-	2-0	-
Leicester	v	Rotherham	-	-	-	-	-	-
Preston	v	Brighton	-	-	-	-	-	-
Reading	v	Watford	-	-	-	-	-	-
Sheff. Weds.	v	Portsmouth	-	-	-	-	0-0	2-3
Stoke	v	Millwall	-	-	1-0	3-1	3-2	-
Walsall	v	Gillingham	1-0	1-0	2-1	-	-	1-1
Wolves	v	Nottm F.	-	2-1	-	3-0	2-0	1-0

NATIONWIDE LEAGUE DIVISION II

Brentford	v	Wigan	-	0-2	-	0-2	2-2	0-1
Cardiff	v	Chesterfield	-	-	-	2-1	3-3	2-1
Crewe	v	Blackpool	3-2	-	-	-	-	-
Huddersfield	v	Swindon	0-0	0-0	1-2	4-0	-	2-0
Luton	v	QPR	-	-	-	-	-	-
Mansfield	v	Bristol C.	-	-	-	-	-	-
Northampton	v	Port Vale	-	-	-	-	0-2	1-0
Notts Co.	v	Colchester	-	0-0	1-3	1-2	2-2	1-1
Oldham	v	Cheltenham	-	-	-	-	-	-

Sponsored by Stan James

Peterboro	v	Barnsley	-	-	-	-	-	-
Plymouth	v	Stockport	0-0	-	-	-	-	-
Wycombe	v	Tranmere	-	-	-	-	-	2-1

NATIONWIDE LEAGUE DIVISION III

Bristol R.	v	Wrexham	2-0	1-0	0-0	3-1	4-0	-
Carlisle	v	Bury	-	-	-	-	-	-
Exeter	v	Cambridge U.	0-1	1-0	0-3	-	-	-
Hull	v	Boston	-	-	-	-	-	-
Kidderminstr	v	Oxford Utd	-	-	-	-	-	0-0
Leyton O.	v	Hartlepool	2-0	2-1	1-1	2-1	3-1	2-0
Lincoln	v	Rushden & D	-	-	-	-	-	2-4
Macclesfield	v	Torquay	-	2-1	-	1-2	2-1	0-2
Rochdale	v	York	-	-	-	2-1	0-1	5-4
Scunthorpe	v	Swansea	1-0	1-0	1-2	-	-	2-2
Shrewsbury	v	Darlington	-	3-0	3-0	0-1	1-0	3-0
Southend	v	Bournemouth	-	5-3	-	-	-	-

BANK OF SCOTLAND SCOTTISH PREMIER DIVISION

Dundee	v	Dundee Utd.	-	-	2-2/1-3	0-2/3-0	3-0/2-3	1-1/0-1
Hibernian	v	Motherwell	2-0/1-1	1-1/1-0	-	2-2/2-2	2-0/1-1	1-1/4-0
Kilmarnock	v	Hearts	2-0/1-0	0-3/2-2	3-0/1-0	2-2/0-1	0-3/1-1	1-0/3-3
Livingston	v	Celtic	-	-	-	-	-	0-0/1-3
Partick	v	Aberdeen	-	-	-	-	-	-
Rangers	v	Dunfermline	3-1/4-0	7-0/1-1	1-1/1-0	-	4-1/2-0	4-0

BELL'S SCOTTISH FIRST DIVISION

Arbroath	v	Inv. CT	1-4/0-0	-	0-1/3-1	-	-	3-2/1-0
Ayr	v	Alloa	-	-	-	-	3-1/4-1	-
Clyde	v	Falkirk	-	-	-	-	3-1/0-3	1-1/2-3
Queen of Sth	v	St Mirren	-	-	-	-	-	-
Ross County	v	St Johnstone	-	-	-	-	-	-

BELL'S SCOTTISH SECOND DIVISION

Berwick	v	Forfar	-	-	-	2-2/2-0	1-1/1-0	1-1/0-2
Brechin	v	Airdrie Utd.	-	-	-	-	-	-
Dumbarton	v	Stranraer	1-1/2-2	-	-	-	-	-
Raith	v	Hamilton	-	3-1/2-1	0-2/1-1	-	-	-
Stenhsmuir	v	Cowdenbeath	-	-	1-2/4-1	-	-	0-3/0-1

BELL'S SCOTTISH THIRD DIVISION

Elgin	v	Albion	-	-	-	-	1-2/1-0	2-0/0-0
Morton	v	Montrose	-	-	-	-	-	-
New Member	v	E. Stirling	-	-	-	-	-	-
Queen's Park	v	Peterhead	-	-	-	-	-	0-1/2-0
Stirling	v	East Fife	2-1/4-1	-	3-2/0-1	-	-	2-1/0-1

Sponsored by Stan James

SATURDAY 30TH NOVEMBER 2002

FA BARCLAYCARD PREMIER DIVISION

Arsenal	v	Aston Villa	2-2	0-0	1-0	3-1	1-0	3-2
Birmingham	v	Tottenham	-	-	-	-	-	-
Blackburn	v	Fulham	-	-	-	2-0	1-2	3-0
Chelsea	v	Sunderland	6-2	-	-	4-0	2-4	4-0
Leeds	v	Charlton	-	-	4-1	-	3-1	0-0
Liverpool	v	Man. Utd.	1-3	1-3	2-2	2-3	2-0	3-1
Man. City	v	Bolton	1-2	-	-	2-0	-	-
Newcastle	v	Everton	4-1	1-0	1-3	1-1	0-1	6-2
WBA	v	Middlesbro	-	2-1	-	-	-	-
West Ham	v	Southampton	2-1	2-4	1-0	2-0	3-0	2-0

NATIONWIDE LEAGUE DIVISION I

Brighton	v	Reading	-	-	-	-	-	3-1
Coventry	v	Preston	-	-	-	-	-	2-2
Gillingham	v	Stoke	-	-	4-0	3-0	-	-
Grimsby	v	Leicester	-	-	-	-	-	-
Millwall	v	Bradford	-	-	-	-	-	3-1
Norwich	v	Derby	-	-	-	-	-	-
Nottm F.	v	Ipswich	-	2-1	-	0-1	-	-
Portsmouth	v	Walsall	-	-	-	5-1	-	1-1
Rotherham	v	Wolves	-	-	-	-	-	0-3
Sheff. Utd.	v	Crystal Pal.	3-0	-	1-1	3-1	1-0	1-3
Watford	v	Burnley	2-2	1-0	-	-	0-1	1-2
Wimbledon	v	Sheff. Weds.	4-2	1-1	2-1	0-2	4-1	1-1

NATIONWIDE LEAGUE DIVISION II

Barnsley	v	Oldham	2-0	-	-	-	-	-
Blackpool	v	Notts Co.	1-0	-	1-0	2-1	-	0-0
Bristol C.	v	Crewe	3-0	-	5-2	-	-	-
Cheltenham	v	Brentford	-	-	-	-	-	-
Chesterfield	v	Huddersfield	-	-	-	-	-	1-1
Colchester	v	Plymouth	-	-	-	-	-	-
Port Vale	v	Mansfield	-	-	-	-	-	-
QPR	v	Cardiff	-	-	-	-	-	2-1
Stockport	v	Wycombe	2-1	-	-	-	-	-
Swindon	v	Peterboro	-	-	-	-	2-1	0-0
Tranmere	v	Luton	-	-	-	-	-	-
Wigan	v	Northampton	2-1	1-1	1-0	-	2-1	3-0

NATIONWIDE LEAGUE DIVISION III

Boston	v	Leyton O.	-	-	-	-	-	-
Bournemouth	v	Scunthorpe	-	-	-	1-1	-	-
Bury	v	Exeter	-	-	-	-	-	-

Cambridge U.	v	Macclesfield	-	0-0	-	-	-	-
Darlington	v	Southend	-	-	2-1	1-0	1-1	2-2
Hartlepool	v	Kidderminstr	-	-	-	-	3-1	1-1
Oxford Utd	v	Lincoln	-	-	-	-	-	2-1
Rushden & D	v	Bristol R.	-	-	-	-	-	3-1
Swansea	v	Shrewsbury	-	0-1	1-1	1-1	-	3-3
Torquay	v	Rochdale	0-1	0-0	2-1	1-0	1-0	3-0
Wrexham	v	Hull	-	-	-	-	-	-
York	v	Carlisle	-	4-3	-	1-1	0-0	0-0

BANK OF SCOTLAND SCOTTISH PREMIER DIVISION

Celtic	v	Motherwell	1-0/5-0	0-2/4-1	2-0/1-0	0-1/4-0	1-0/1-0	2-0
Dundee Utd.	v	Aberdeen	1-0/4-0	5-0/0-0	1-0/3-0	3-1/1-1	3-5/1-1	1-1
Dunfermline	v	Hibernian	2-1/1-1	2-1/1-1	-	-	1-1/2-1	1-0
Hearts	v	Rangers	1-4/3-1	2-5/0-3	2-1/2-3	0-4/1-2	0-1/1-4	2-2/0-2
Livingston	v	Dundee	-	-	-	-	-	1-0
Partick	v	Kilmarnock	-	-	-	-	-	-

BELL'S SCOTTISH FIRST DIVISION

Alloa	v	Ross County	1-3/1-1	1-0/1-1	-	2-0/1-2	0-0/1-1	-
Arbroath	v	Queen of Sth	-	-	2-1/0-2	5-2/1-2	2-0/5-2	-
Inv. CT	v	Clyde	-	1-2/5-1	1-1/3-0	-	1-2/2-2	5-1/1-1
St Johnstone	v	Falkirk	0-0/3-1	-	-	-	-	-
St Mirren	v	Ayr	-	1-1/3-0	0-2/1-0	1-1/1-2	-	0-1/1-1

BELL'S SCOTTISH SECOND DIVISION

Berwick	v	Airdrie Utd.	-	-	-	-	-	-
Dumbarton	v	Cowdenbeath	-	1-2/2-3	5-0/6-1	1-1/2-0	2-4/3-0	-
Raith	v	Forfar	-	-	-	-	-	-
Stenhsmuir	v	Brechin	0-0/3-1	3-2/3-1	0-1/1-0	-	-	-
Stranraer	v	Hamilton	0-3/0-1	-	2-1/2-2	0-2/2-2	-	2-1/3-2

BELL'S SCOTTISH THIRD DIVISION

E. Stirling	v	Peterhead	-	-	-	-	1-3/1-0	2-3/1-0
Morton	v	Elgin	-	-	-	-	-	-
Montrose	v	Albion	2-1/0-4	1-2/1-3	1-2/2-3	2-1/1-2	0-2/0-1	1-2/2-0
New Member	v	East Fife	-	-	-	-	-	-
Queen's Park	v	Stirling	-	-	-	-	3-0/1-1	2-2/0-0

WEDNESDAY 4TH DECEMBER 2002

BANK OF SCOTLAND SCOTTISH PREMIER DIVISION

Aberdeen	v	Kilmarnock	3-0/2-1	0-0/0-0	0-1/2-1	2-2/5-1	1-2	2-0/1-1
Dundee	v	Partick	0-2/1-1	0-0/0-3	-	-	-	-
Dunfermline	v	Dundee Utd.	1-1/1-3	3-3/2-2	2-1/2-2	-	1-0/3-1	1-1
Hibernian	v	Celtic	0-4/1-3	2-1/0-1	-	0-2/2-1	0-0/2-5	1-4/1-1

Sponsored by Stan James

45

| Motherwell | v | Hearts | 0-2/0-1 | 1-4/2-4 | 3-2/0-4 | 2-1/0-2 | 2-0 | 2-0/1-2 |
| Rangers | v | Livingston | - | - | - | - | - | 0-0/3-0 |

SATURDAY 7TH DECEMBER 2002

FA BARCLAYCARD PREMIER DIVISION

Aston Villa	v	Newcastle	2-2	0-1	1-0	0-1	1-1	1-1
Bolton	v	Blackburn	-	2-1	-	3-1	1-4	1-1
Charlton	v	Liverpool	-	-	1-0	-	0-4	0-2
Everton	v	Chelsea	1-2	3-1	0-0	1-1	2-1	0-0
Fulham	v	Leeds	-	-	-	-	-	0-0
Man. Utd.	v	Arsenal	1-0	0-1	1-1	1-1	6-1	0-1
Middlesbro	v	West Ham	4-1	-	1-0	2-0	2-1	2-0
Southampton	v	Birmingham	-	-	-	-	-	-
Sunderland	v	Man. City	-	3-1	-	-	1-0	-
Tottenham	v	WBA	-	-	-	-	-	-

NATIONWIDE LEAGUE DIVISION I

Bradford	v	Gillingham	-	-	-	-	-	5-1
Burnley	v	Nottm F.	-	-	-	-	1-0	1-1
Crystal Pal.	v	Millwall	-	-	-	-	-	1-3
Derby	v	Watford	-	-	-	2-0	-	-
Ipswich	v	Rotherham	-	-	-	-	-	-
Leicester	v	Sheff. Utd.	-	-	-	-	-	-
Preston	v	Wimbledon	-	-	-	-	1-1	1-1
Reading	v	Portsmouth	0-0	0-1	-	-	-	-
Sheff. Weds.	v	Brighton	-	-	-	-	-	-
Stoke	v	Coventry	-	-	-	-	-	-
Walsall	v	Grimsby	-	0-0	-	1-0	-	4-0
Wolves	v	Norwich	3-2	5-0	2-2	1-0	4-0	0-0

BANK OF SCOTLAND SCOTTISH PREMIER DIVISION

Aberdeen	v	Motherwell	0-0/0-0	1-3/3-0	1-1/1-1	1-1/2-1	3-3	4-2/1-0
Dundee Utd.	v	Hibernian	0-1/0-0	1-1/1-1	-	3-1/0-0	0-1	3-1/1-2/2-1
Hearts	v	Livingston	-	-	-	-	-	1-3/2-3
Kilmarnock	v	Dundee	-	-	2-1/0-0	0-2/2-2	2-3	0-1/3-2
Partick	v	Dunfermline	-	-	-	-	-	-
Rangers	v	Celtic	2-0/3-1	1-0/2-0	0-0/2-2	4-2/4-0	5-1/0-3	0-2/1-1

BELL'S SCOTTISH FIRST DIVISION

Ayr	v	Inv. CT	-	-	-	1-0/1-3	3-3/1-1	3-0/1-0
Clyde	v	St Johnstone	-	-	-	-	-	-
Falkirk	v	Arbroath	-	-	-	-	-	3-2/1-3
Queen of Sth	v	Alloa	-	-	2-1/0-0	1-1/2-1	-	2-1/0-1
Ross County	v	St Mirren	-	-	-	-	-	0-1/4-1

Sponsored by Stan James

SATURDAY 14TH DECEMBER 2002

FA BARCLAYCARD PREMIER DIVISION

Aston Villa	v	WBA	-	-	-	-	-	-
Bolton	v	Leeds	-	2-3	-	-	-	0-3
Charlton	v	Man. City	1-1	2-1	-	0-1	4-0	-
Everton	v	Blackburn	0-2	1-0	0-0	-	-	1-2
Fulham	v	Birmingham	-	-	-	0-0	0-1	-
Man. Utd.	v	West Ham	2-0	2-1	4-1	7-1	3-1	0-1
Middlesbro	v	Chelsea	1-0	-	0-0	0-1	1-0	0-2
Southampton	v	Newcastle	2-2	2-1	2-1	4-2	2-0	3-1
Sunderland	v	Liverpool	1-2	-	-	0-2	1-1	0-1
Tottenham	v	Arsenal	0-0	1-1	1-3	2-1	1-1	1-1

NATIONWIDE LEAGUE DIVISION I

Bradford	v	Nottm F.	-	0-3	-	-	-	2-1
Burnley	v	Rotherham	3-3	-	-	-	-	3-0
Crystal Pal.	v	Norwich	2-0	-	5-1	1-0	1-1	3-2
Derby	v	Brighton	-	-	-	-	-	-
Ipswich	v	Watford	-	-	3-2	-	-	-
Leicester	v	Millwall	-	-	-	-	-	-
Preston	v	Grimsby	-	2-0	-	-	1-2	0-0
Reading	v	Sheff. Utd.	1-0	0-1	-	-	-	-
Sheff. Weds.	v	Gillingham	-	-	-	-	2-1	0-0
Stoke	v	Portsmouth	3-1	2-1	-	-	-	-
Walsall	v	Wimbledon	-	-	-	-	-	2-1
Wolves	v	Coventry	-	-	-	-	-	3-1

NATIONWIDE LEAGUE DIVISION II

Brentford	v	Chesterfield	1-0	0-0	-	1-1	-	0-0
Cardiff	v	Bristol C.	-	-	-	0-0	-	1-3
Crewe	v	Barnsley	-	-	3-1	0-1	2-2	2-0
Huddersfield	v	Stockport	-	1-0	3-0	0-2	0-0	-
Luton	v	Colchester	-	-	2-0	3-2	0-3	-
Mansfield	v	Blackpool	-	-	-	-	0-1	-
Northampton	v	Tranmere	-	-	-	-	-	4-1
Notts Co.	v	QPR	-	-	-	-	-	0-2
Oldham	v	Wigan	-	3-1	2-3	2-1	2-1	1-1
Peterboro	v	Cheltenham	-	-	-	1-0	-	-
Plymouth	v	Swindon	-	-	-	-	-	-
Wycombe	v	Port Vale	-	-	-	-	0-1	3-1

NATIONWIDE LEAGUE DIVISION III

Bristol R.	v	Oxford Utd	-	-	-	1-0	6-2	1-1
Carlisle	v	Wrexham	-	2-2	-	-	-	-
Exeter	v	Swansea	1-2	1-0	4-0	1-1	-	0-3

Sponsored by Stan James

Hull	v	Darlington	3-2	1-1	1-2	0-1	2-0	1-2
Kidderminstr	v	York	-	-	-	-	3-1	4-1
Leyton O.	v	Torquay	1-0	2-1	2-0	0-2	0-2	1-2
Lincoln	v	Cambridge U.	1-1	0-0	-	-	-	-
Macclesfield	v	Rushden & D	2-1	-	-	-	-	0-0
Rochdale	v	Hartlepool	1-3	2-1	0-1	2-0	2-1	0-0
Scunthorpe	v	Bury	-	-	-	0-2	-	-
Shrewsbury	v	Bournemouth	1-1	-	-	-	-	-
Southend	v	Boston	-	-	-	-	-	-

BANK OF SCOTLAND SCOTTISH PREMIER DIVISION

Dundee	v	Motherwell	-	-	1-0/1-0	0-1/4-1	1-2	3-1/2-0
Dunfermline	v	Aberdeen	2-3/3-0	1-1/3-3	1-1/1-2	-	0-0/3-2	1-0/0-0
Hearts	v	Partick	-	-	-	-	-	-
Kilmarnock	v	Celtic	1-3/2-0	0-0/1-2	2-0/0-0	0-1/1-1	0-1/1-0	0-1/0-2
Livingston	v	Hibernian	-	-	-	-	-	1-0/0-3
Rangers	v	Dundee Utd.	1-0/0-2	5-1/4-1	2-1/0-1	4-1/3-0	3-0/0-2	3-2

BELL'S SCOTTISH FIRST DIVISION

Alloa	v	St Mirren	-	-	-	-	-	-
Clyde	v	Arbroath	-	-	3-0/1-1	0-0/4-1	-	1-0/1-0
Falkirk	v	Inv. CT	-	-	-	0-2/2-2	2-2/2-1	1-2/0-0
Ross County	v	Ayr	-	-	-	-	1-1/0-1	3-2/1-1
St Johnstone	v	Queen of Sth	-	-	-	-	-	-

BELL'S SCOTTISH SECOND DIVISION

Airdrie Utd.	v	Stenhsmuir	-	-	-	-	-	-
Brechin	v	Raith	-	-	-	-	-	-
Cowdenbeath	v	Berwick	-	0-2/1-0	1-1/1-2	1-1/1-3	-	2-1/1-1
Forfar	v	Stranraer	-	3-1/2-1	-	-	0-0/2-3	1-1/3-2
Hamilton	v	Dumbarton	2-0/4-0	-	-	-	2-0/2-0	-

BELL'S SCOTTISH THIRD DIVISION

Albion	v	Queen's Park	1-1/2-1	0-0/1-2	2-1/1-0	2-4/0-3	-	2-1/2-0
East Fife	v	Morton	0-3/1-4	-	-	-	-	-
Elgin	v	E. Stirling	-	-	-	-	1-2/4-2	2-1/2-2
Peterhead	v	Montrose	-	-	-	-	2-0/1-1	4-0/3-1
Stirling	v	New Member	-	-	-	-	-	-

SATURDAY 21ST DECEMBER 2002

FA BARCLAYCARD PREMIER DIVISION

Arsenal	v	Middlesbro	2-0	-	1-1	5-1	0-3	2-1
Birmingham	v	Charlton	0-0	0-0	-	1-0	-	-
Blackburn	v	Man. Utd.	2-3	1-3	0-0	-	-	2-2
Chelsea	v	Aston Villa	1-1	0-1	2-1	1-0	1-0	1-3

Sponsored by Stan James

Leeds	v	Southampton	0-0	0-1	3-0	1-0	2-0	2-0
Liverpool	v	Everton	1-1	1-1	3-2	0-1	3-1	1-1
Man. City	v	Tottenham	-	-	-	-	0-1	-
Newcastle	v	Fulham	-	-	-	-	-	1-1
WBA	v	Sunderland	-	3-3	2-3	-	-	-
West Ham	v	Bolton	-	3-0	-	-	-	2-1

NATIONWIDE LEAGUE DIVISION I

Brighton	v	Leicester	-	-	-	-	-	-
Coventry	v	Derby	1-2	1-0	1-1	2-0	2-0	-
Gillingham	v	Burnley	1-0	2-0	2-1	2-2	0-0	2-2
Grimsby	v	Sheff. Weds.	-	-	-	-	0-1	0-0
Millwall	v	Wolves	-	-	-	-	-	1-0
Norwich	v	Walsall	-	-	-	1-1	-	1-1
Nottm F.	v	Reading	-	1-0	-	-	-	-
Portsmouth	v	Ipswich	0-1	0-1	0-0	1-1	-	-
Rotherham	v	Crystal Pal.	-	-	-	-	-	2-3
Sheff. Utd.	v	Preston	-	-	-	-	3-2	2-2
Watford	v	Bradford	-	-	1-0	1-0	-	0-0
Wimbledon	v	Stoke	-	-	-	-	-	-

NATIONWIDE LEAGUE DIVISION II

Barnsley	v	Mansfield	-	-	-	-	-	-
Blackpool	v	Peterboro	5-1	-	-	-	-	2-2
Bristol C.	v	Luton	5-0	3-0	-	0-0	3-1	-
Cheltenham	v	Wycombe	-	-	-	-	-	-
Chesterfield	v	Oldham	-	2-1	1-3	0-1	-	4-2
Colchester	v	Cardiff	1-1	2-1	-	0-3	-	0-1
Port Vale	v	Plymouth	-	-	-	-	-	-
QPR	v	Brentford	-	-	-	-	-	0-0
Stockport	v	Northampton	-	-	-	-	-	-
Swindon	v	Crewe	-	2-0	1-2	0-1	-	-
Tranmere	v	Notts Co.	-	-	-	-	-	4-2
Wigan	v	Huddersfield	-	-	-	-	-	1-0

NATIONWIDE LEAGUE DIVISION III

Boston	v	Shrewsbury	-	-	-	-	-	-
Bournemouth	v	Hull	-	-	-	-	-	-
Bury	v	Rochdale	-	-	-	-	-	-
Cambridge U.	v	Bristol R.	-	-	-	1-1	0-3	-
Darlington	v	Macclesfield	-	4-2	-	3-0	1-1	0-1
Hartlepool	v	Scunthorpe	0-1	0-1	1-2	-	1-0	3-2
Oxford Utd	v	Exeter	-	-	-	-	-	1-2
Rushden & D	v	Carlisle	-	-	-	-	-	3-1
Swansea	v	Leyton O.	1-0	1-1	1-1	0-0	-	0-1

Sponsored by Stan James

Torquay	v	Southend	-	-	2-0	0-1	1-1	2-1
Wrexham	v	Kidderminstr	-	-	-	-	-	-
York	v	Lincoln	-	-	2-1	2-0	0-0	2-0

BANK OF SCOTLAND SCOTTISH PREMIER DIVISION

Aberdeen	v	Livingston	-	-	-	-	-	0-3/3-0
Celtic	v	Dundee	-	-	6-1/5-0	6-2/2-2	1-0/2-1/0-2	3-1
Dundee Utd.	v	Hearts	1-0/1-0	0-0/0-1	0-0/1-3	0-2/0-1	0-4/1-1	0-2
Kilmarnock	v	Hibernian	4-2/1-1	2-1/1-1	-	0-2/1-0	0-1/1-1	0-0/1-0
Motherwell	v	Dunfermline	2-3/2-2	2-0/1-3	0-0/1-1	-	0-1/1-1	1-0
Partick	v	Rangers	-	-	-	-	-	-

BELL'S SCOTTISH FIRST DIVISION

Arbroath	v	Ross County	3-1/2-1	2-2/1-1	-	0-1/1-2	-	2-1/1-1
Ayr	v	Falkirk	-	1-2/1-3	4-2/1-2	1-1/3-3	5-2/6-0	2-2/0-0
Inv. CT	v	Alloa	1-0/3-1	-	3-2/1-1	-	2-1/2-0	-
Queen of Sth	v	Clyde	0-2/0-1	4-3/0-0	2-1/2-1	1-1/3-0	-	-
St Mirren	v	St Johnstone	0-3/2-1	-	-	-	0-1/1-0	-

BELL'S SCOTTISH SECOND DIVISION

Airdrie Utd.	v	Forfar	-	-	-	-	-	-
Brechin	v	Berwick	3-2/3-1	-	1-1/0-3	0-3/1-2	-	-
Cowdenbeath	v	Hamilton	-	-	-	-	2-0/1-1	2-1/2-1
Raith	v	Stranraer	-	-	2-0/3-2	-	-	-
Stenhsmuir	v	Dumbarton	0-1/1-4	-	0-3/0-2	-	-	-

BELL'S SCOTTISH THIRD DIVISION

E. Stirling	v	Montrose	1-3/4-2	4-1/1-2	3-1/2-1	2-0/1-0	1-2/0-1	0-1/2-1
New Member	v	Morton	-	-	-	-	-	-
Peterhead	v	East Fife	-	-	-	-	0-0/2-1	1-3/1-1
Queen's Park	v	Elgin	-	-	-	-	-	0-0/3-0
Stirling	v	Albion	-	-	-	-	-	2-2/0-3

THURSDAY 26TH DECEMBER 2002

FA BARCLAYCARD PREMIER DIVISION

Birmingham	v	Everton	-	-	-	-	-	-
Bolton	v	Newcastle	-	1-0	-	-	-	0-4
Chelsea	v	Southampton	1-0	4-2	1-0	1-1	1-0	2-4
Liverpool	v	Blackburn	0-0	0-0	2-0	-	-	4-3
Man. City	v	Aston Villa	-	-	-	-	1-3	-
Middlesbro	v	Man. Utd.	2-2	-	0-1	3-4	0-2	0-1
Sunderland	v	Leeds	0-1	-	-	1-2	0-2	2-0
Tottenham	v	Charlton	-	-	2-2	-	0-0	0-1
WBA	v	Arsenal	-	-	-	-	-	-
West Ham	v	Fulham	-	-	-	-	-	0-2

Sponsored by Stan James

NATIONWIDE LEAGUE DIVISION I

Bradford	v	Stoke	1-0	0-0	-	-	-	-
Burnley	v	Wolves	-	-	-	-	1-2	2-3
Coventry	v	Reading	-	-	-	-	-	-
Derby	v	Grimsby	-	-	-	-	-	-
Leicester	v	Ipswich	-	-	-	-	2-1	1-1
Millwall	v	Gillingham	0-2	1-0	3-3	2-2	-	1-2
Norwich	v	Brighton	-	-	-	-	-	-
Portsmouth	v	Crystal Pal.	2-2	-	1-1	3-1	2-4	4-2
Preston	v	Rotherham	0-0	-	-	-	-	2-1
Sheff. Weds.	v	Nottm F.	2-0	-	3-2	-	0-1	0-2
Walsall	v	Sheff. Utd.	-	-	-	2-1	-	1-2
Wimbledon	v	Watford	-	-	-	5-0	0-0	0-0

NATIONWIDE LEAGUE DIVISION II

Bristol C.	v	Plymouth	3-1	2-1	-	-	-	-
Cheltenham	v	Crewe	-	-	-	-	-	-
Colchester	v	Peterboro	-	1-0	-	-	2-2	2-1
Huddersfield	v	Tranmere	0-1	3-0	0-0	1-0	3-0	2-1
Luton	v	Cardiff	-	-	-	1-0	-	-
Mansfield	v	Stockport	-	-	-	-	-	-
Northampton	v	Chesterfield	-	0-0	1-0	-	-	0-2
Notts Co.	v	Barnsley	-	-	-	-	-	-
Oldham	v	Blackpool	-	0-1	3-0	1-1	-	2-1
Port Vale	v	Wigan	-	-	-	-	0-0	1-0
QPR	v	Wycombe	-	-	-	-	-	4-3
Swindon	v	Brentford	-	-	-	-	2-3	2-0

NATIONWIDE LEAGUE DIVISION III

Boston	v	York	-	-	-	-	-	-
Cambridge U.	v	Southend	-	-	3-0	-	-	-
Carlisle	v	Darlington	1-0	-	3-3	1-1	0-2	1-3
Hull	v	Hartlepool	1-0	2-1	4-0	0-3	0-0	1-1
Kidderminstr	v	Leyton O.	-	-	-	-	2-1	0-1
Macclesfield	v	Lincoln	-	1-0	0-0	1-1	2-0	0-1
Oxford Utd	v	Bournemouth	-	-	-	1-0	1-2	-
Rochdale	v	Wrexham	-	-	-	-	-	-
Scunthorpe	v	Rushden & D	-	-	-	-	-	1-1
Shrewsbury	v	Bury	1-1	-	-	-	-	-
Swansea	v	Bristol R.	-	-	-	-	0-0	2-1
Torquay	v	Exeter	2-0	1-2	1-0	1-0	2-1	0-2

BANK OF SCOTLAND SCOTTISH PREMIER DIVISION

Celtic	v	Hearts	2-2/2-0	1-0/0-0	1-1/3-0	4-0/2-3	6-1/1-0	2-0/2-0
Dundee	v	Aberdeen	-	-	0-2/1-2	1-3/0-2	2-2	1-4/2-3

Sponsored by Stan James

Dunfermline	v	Kilmarnock	2-1/3-1	1-1/3-2	0-3/0-6	-	1-0	0-2/2-0
Hibernian	v	Partick	-	-	-	-	-	-
Livingston	v	Dundee Utd.	-	-	-	-	-	2-0/1-1
Motherwell	v	Rangers	0-1/1-3	1-1/2-1	1-0/1-5	1-5	0-1/1-2	2-2

SATURDAY 28TH DECEMBER 2002

FA BARCLAYCARD PREMIER DIVISION

Arsenal	v	Liverpool	1-2	0-1	0-0	0-1	2-0	1-1
Aston Villa	v	Middlesbro	1-0	-	3-1	1-0	1-1	0-0
Blackburn	v	West Ham	2-1	3-0	3-0	-	-	7-1
Charlton	v	WBA	1-1	5-0	-	0-0	-	-
Everton	v	Bolton	-	3-2	-	-	-	3-1
Fulham	v	Man. City	-	-	3-0	0-0	-	-
Leeds	v	Chelsea	2-0	3-1	0-0	0-1	2-0	0-0
Man. Utd.	v	Birmingham	-	-	-	-	-	-
Newcastle	v	Tottenham	7-1	1-0	1-1	2-1	2-0	0-2
Southampton	v	Sunderland	3-0	-	-	1-2	0-1	2-0

NATIONWIDE LEAGUE DIVISION I

Brighton	v	Burnley	-	-	-	-	-	-
Crystal Pal.	v	Preston	-	-	-	-	0-2	2-0
Gillingham	v	Wimbledon	-	-	-	-	0-0	0-0
Grimsby	v	Norwich	1-4	-	0-1	2-1	2-0	0-2
Ipswich	v	Walsall	-	-	-	2-0	-	-
Nottm F.	v	Portsmouth	-	1-0	-	2-0	2-0	0-1
Reading	v	Derby	-	-	-	-	-	-
Rotherham	v	Millwall	0-0	-	-	-	3-2	0-0
Sheff. Utd.	v	Coventry	-	-	-	-	-	0-1
Stoke	v	Sheff. Weds.	-	-	-	-	-	-
Watford	v	Leicester	-	-	-	1-1	-	-
Wolves	v	Bradford	1-0	2-1	2-3	-	-	3-1

NATIONWIDE LEAGUE DIVISION II

Barnsley	v	Port Vale	1-0	-	0-2	3-1	-	-
Blackpool	v	Colchester	-	-	2-1	1-1	-	2-1
Brentford	v	Mansfield	-	-	3-0	-	-	-
Cardiff	v	Huddersfield	-	-	-	-	-	1-2
Chesterfield	v	Cheltenham	-	-	-	-	2-0	-
Crewe	v	Oldham	-	-	-	-	-	-
Peterboro	v	Northampton	-	-	-	1-0	1-2	2-0
Plymouth	v	Notts Co.	0-0	-	-	-	-	-
Stockport	v	Bristol C.	1-1	-	2-2	-	-	-
Tranmere	v	QPR	2-3	2-1	3-2	1-1	1-1	2-3
Wigan	v	Swindon	-	-	-	-	0-0	1-0

Wycombe	v	Luton	0-1	2-2	0-1	0-1	1-1	-

NATIONWIDE LEAGUE DIVISION III

Bournemouth	v	Rochdale	-	-	-	-	-	-
Bristol R.	v	Boston	-	-	-	-	-	-
Bury	v	Kidderminstr	-	-	-	-	-	-
Darlington	v	Torquay	2-3	1-2	0-2	1-1	2-0	1-3
Exeter	v	Macclesfield	-	1-3	-	0-3	0-0	0-0
Hartlepool	v	Cambridge U.	0-2	3-3	2-2	-	-	-
Leyton O.	v	Carlisle	2-1	-	2-1	0-1	1-0	0-0
Lincoln	v	Swansea	4-0	1-1	-	0-1	-	3-0
Rushden & D	v	Oxford Utd	-	-	-	-	-	2-1
Southend	v	Scunthorpe	-	-	0-1	-	1-0	2-0
Wrexham	v	Shrewsbury	2-1	-	-	-	-	-
York	v	Hull	-	-	-	1-1	0-0	2-1

BELL'S SCOTTISH FIRST DIVISION

Ayr	v	Arbroath	-	-	-	-	-	0-1/0-0
Falkirk	v	Queen of Sth	-	-	-	-	-	-
Ross County	v	Clyde	-	-	-	2-0/2-2	0-2/2-0	4-0/2-1
St Johnstone	v	Alloa	-	-	-	-	-	-
St Mirren	v	Inv. CT	-	-	-	3-2/2-0	-	1-1/0-0

BELL'S SCOTTISH SECOND DIVISION

Berwick	v	Stenhsmuir	0-6/1-0	-	1-2/2-1	-	4-1/1-0	1-1/2-1
Dumbarton	v	Raith	-	-	-	-	-	-
Forfar	v	Cowdenbeath	2-5/3-0	-	-	3-1/2-2	-	2-1/0-0
Hamilton	v	Brechin	5-1/4-0	-	-	-	4-1/1-0	-
Stranraer	v	Airdrie Utd.	-	-	1-2/1-2	-	-	-

BELL'S SCOTTISH THIRD DIVISION

Albion	v	E. Stirling	4-3/1-1	5-1/3-2	3-1/0-2	1-1/0-1	2-1/2-2	0-4/5-1
East Fife	v	Queen's Park	-	-	-	0-0/0-0	-	1-4/0-3
Elgin	v	Stirling	-	-	-	-	-	2-3/2-1
Morton	v	Peterhead	-	-	-	-	-	-
Montrose	v	New Member	-	-	-	-	-	-

SUNDAY 29TH DECEMBER 2002

BANK OF SCOTLAND SCOTTISH PREMIER DIVISION

Celtic	v	Dunfermline	5-1/4-2	1-2/5-1	5-0/5-0	-	3-1	3-1/5-0/5-0
Dundee	v	Hearts	-	-	1-0/2-0	1-0/0-0	1-1/0-0	1-1
Hibernian	v	Aberdeen	0-1/3-1	2-2/1-1	-	2-0/1-0	0-2	2-0/3-4
Kilmarnock	v	Rangers	1-4/1-1	0-3/1-1	1-3/0-5	1-1/0-2	2-4/1-2	2-2
Livingston	v	Motherwell	-	-	-	-	-	3-1
Partick	v	Dundee Utd.	-	-	-	-	-	-

Sponsored by Stan James

WEDNESDAY 1ST JANUARY 2003

FA BARCLAYCARD PREMIER DIVISION

Arsenal	v	Chelsea	3-3	2-0	1-0	2-1	1-1	2-1
Aston Villa	v	Bolton	-	1-3	-	-	-	3-2
Blackburn	v	Middlesbro	0-0	-	0-0	-	-	0-1
Charlton	v	West Ham	-	-	4-2	-	1-1	4-4
Everton	v	Man. City	-	-	-	-	3-1	-
Fulham	v	WBA	-	-	-	1-0	0-0	-
Leeds	v	Birmingham	-	-	-	-	-	-
Man. Utd.	v	Sunderland	5-0	-	-	4-0	3-0	4-1
Newcastle	v	Liverpool	1-1	1-2	1-4	2-2	2-1	0-2
Southampton	v	Tottenham	0-1	3-2	1-1	0-1	2-0	1-0

NATIONWIDE LEAGUE DIVISION II

Brighton	v	Wimbledon	-	-	-	-	-	-
Crystal Pal.	v	Coventry	-	0-3	-	-	-	1-3
Gillingham	v	Norwich	-	-	-	-	4-3	0-2
Grimsby	v	Bradford	1-1	-	2-0	-	-	0-1
Ipswich	v	Millwall	-	-	-	-	-	-
Nottm F.	v	Walsall	-	-	-	4-1	-	2-3
Reading	v	Leicester	-	-	-	-	-	-
Rotherham	v	Sheff. Weds.	-	-	-	-	-	1-1
Sheff. Utd.	v	Burnley	-	-	-	-	2-0	3-0
Stoke	v	Preston	-	-	0-1	2-1	-	-
Watford	v	Portsmouth	-	-	0-0	-	2-2	3-0
Wolves	v	Derby	-	-	-	-	-	-

NATIONWIDE LEAGUE DIVISION II

Barnsley	v	Northampton	-	-	-	-	-	-
Blackpool	v	Huddersfield	-	-	-	-	-	1-2
Brentford	v	Colchester	-	-	-	0-0	1-0	4-1
Cardiff	v	Swindon	-	-	-	-	-	3-0
Chesterfield	v	Luton	1-1	0-0	3-1	1-3	-	-
Crewe	v	Mansfield	-	-	-	-	-	-
Peterboro	v	QPR	-	-	-	-	-	4-1
Plymouth	v	Cheltenham	-	-	-	1-0	0-0	2-0
Stockport	v	Port Vale	-	3-0	4-2	1-0	-	-
Tranmere	v	Oldham	1-1	-	-	-	-	2-2
Wigan	v	Notts Co.	-	-	3-0	2-0	1-1	1-1
Wycombe	v	Bristol C.	2-0	1-2	-	1-2	1-2	2-1

NATIONWIDE LEAGUE DIVISION III

Bournemouth	v	Swansea	-	-	-	-	2-0	-
Bristol R.	v	Torquay	-	-	-	-	-	1-0
Bury	v	Hull	-	-	-	-	-	-

Sponsored by Stan James

Darlington	v	Rochdale	1-1	1-0	3-0	4-1	1-2	1-0
Exeter	v	Kidderminstr	-	-	-	-	2-1	2-1
Hartlepool	v	Carlisle	1-2	-	0-0	1-0	2-2	3-1
Leyton O.	v	Cambridge U.	1-1	0-2	2-0	-	-	-
Lincoln	v	Boston	-	-	-	-	-	-
Rushden & D	v	Shrewsbury	-	-	-	-	-	3-0
Southend	v	Oxford Utd	2-2	-	-	-	-	2-2
Wrexham	v	Macclesfield	-	-	2-1	-	-	-
York	v	Scunthorpe	-	-	-	-	2-0	0-2

BELL'S SCOTTISH FIRST DIVISION

Alloa	v	Falkirk	-	-	-	-	3-2/0-1	-
Arbroath	v	St Johnstone	-	-	-	-	-	-
Clyde	v	St Mirren	-	-	-	-	-	1-1/3-1
Inv. CT	v	Ross County	2-0/3-0	-	-	-	0-1/3-3	3-0/1-1
Queen of Sth	v	Ayr	1-2/1-3	-	-	-	-	-

BELL'S SCOTTISH SECOND DIVISION

Brechin	v	Forfar	-	2-0/1-1	-	0-2/1-0	-	-
Cowdenbeath	v	Raith	-	-	-	-	-	-
Dumbarton	v	Airdrie Utd.	-	-	-	-	-	-
Hamilton	v	Berwick	4-2/4-1	-	-	-	-	0-1/3-1
Stenhsmuir	v	Stranraer	0-1/4-0	3-0/0-1	-	1-1/1-1	1-2/2-2	0-0/0-0

BELL'S SCOTTISH THIRD DIVISION

East Fife	v	Montrose	-	-	-	0-0/2-0	3-1/1-0	1-2/2-0
Elgin	v	Peterhead	-	-	-	-	1-3/0-1	4-1/0-3
Morton	v	Queen's Park	-	-	-	-	-	-
New Member	v	Albion	-	-	-	-	-	-
Stirling	v	E. Stirling	-	-	-	-	-	1-1/1-0

THURSDAY 2ND JANUARY 2003

BANK OF SCOTLAND SCOTTISH PREMIER DIVISION

Aberdeen	v	Celtic	2-2/1-2	0-2/0-1	3-2/1-5	0-5/0-6	1-1/0-1	2-0/0-1
Dundee Utd.	v	Kilmarnock	0-0/2-0	1-2/1-1	0-2/0-0	0-0/2-2	0-1	0-2/0-2
Dunfermline	v	Livingston	-	-	-	3-0/4-1	-	1-2/1-0
Hearts	v	Hibernian	0-0/1-0	2-0/2-2	-	0-3/2-1	0-0/1-1	1-1
Motherwell	v	Partick	-	-	-	-	-	-
Rangers	v	Dundee	-	-	1-0/6-1	1-2/3-0	0-2	2-0/2-1

SATURDAY 4TH JANUARY 2003

NATIONWIDE LEAGUE DIVISION II

Bristol C.	v	Brentford	1-2	2-2	-	1-0	1-2	0-2
Cheltenham	v	Barnsley	-	-	-	-	-	-

Sponsored by Stan James

Colchester	v	Tranmere	-	-	-	-	-	2-1
Huddersfield	v	Plymouth	-	-	-	-	-	-
Luton	v	Blackpool	1-0	3-0	1-0	3-2	-	-
Mansfield	v	Wigan	0-1	-	-	-	-	-
Northampton	v	Wycombe	-	2-0	1-1	-	2-2	4-1
Notts Co.	v	Crewe	0-1	-	-	-	-	-
Oldham	v	Peterboro	-	-	-	-	1-4	2-0
Port Vale	v	Cardiff	-	-	-	-	-	0-2
QPR	v	Stockport	-	2-1	2-0	1-1	0-3	-
Swindon	v	Chesterfield	-	-	-	-	-	2-1

NATIONWIDE LEAGUE DIVISION III

Boston	v	Hartlepool	-	-	-	-	-	-
Cambridge U.	v	Bury	-	-	-	3-0	0-1	3-1
Carlisle	v	Southend	-	5-0	3-0	1-1	3-1	0-0
Hull	v	Bristol R.	-	-	-	-	-	0-0
Kidderminstr	v	Bournemouth	-	-	-	-	-	-
Macclesfield	v	Leyton O.	-	1-0	-	1-0	0-2	2-1
Oxford Utd	v	Wrexham	-	-	-	1-4	3-4	-
Rochdale	v	Lincoln	2-0	0-0	-	1-1	3-1	2-2
Scunthorpe	v	Exeter	4-1	2-1	2-0	-	0-2	3-4
Shrewsbury	v	York	2-0	-	-	0-1	2-0	3-2
Swansea	v	Darlington	1-1	4-0	2-0	0-0	-	2-0
Torquay	v	Rushden & D	-	-	-	-	-	1-1

BELL'S SCOTTISH FIRST DIVISION

Arbroath	v	St Mirren	-	-	-	-	-	0-2/0-3
Ayr	v	St Johnstone	-	-	-	-	-	-
Clyde	v	Alloa	-	-	2-1/0-1	0-1/0-0	0-0/1-1	-
Queen of Sth	v	Inv. CT	-	2-1/1-0	2-2/1-1	-	-	-
Ross County	v	Falkirk	-	-	-	-	0-2/4-1	1-2/4-2

SATURDAY 11TH JANUARY 2003

FA BARCLAYCARD PREMIER DIVISION

Birmingham	v	Arsenal	-	-	-	-	-	-
Bolton	v	Fulham	-	-	-	3-1	0-2	0-0
Chelsea	v	Charlton	-	-	2-1	-	0-1	0-1
Liverpool	v	Aston Villa	3-0	3-0	0-1	0-0	3-1	1-3
Man. City	v	Leeds	-	-	-	-	0-4	-
Middlesbro	v	Southampton	0-1	-	3-0	3-2	0-1	1-3
Sunderland	v	Blackburn	0-0	-	-	-	-	1-0
Tottenham	v	Everton	0-0	1-1	4-1	3-2	3-2	1-1
WBA	v	Man. Utd.	-	-	-	-	-	-
West Ham	v	Newcastle	0-0	0-1	2-0	2-1	1-0	3-0

Sponsored by Stan James

NATIONWIDE LEAGUE DIVISION I

Home		Away							
Bradford	v	Crystal Pal.	0-4	-	2-1	-	-		1-2
Burnley	v	Ipswich	-	-	-	-	-		-
Coventry	v	Brighton	-	-	-	-	-		-
Derby	v	Gillingham	-	-	-	-	-		-
Leicester	v	Stoke	-	-	-	-	-		-
Millwall	v	Watford	0-1	1-1	-	-	-		1-0
Norwich	v	Rotherham	-	-	-	-	-		0-0
Portsmouth	v	Sheff. Utd.	1-1	1-1	1-0	2-0	0-0		1-0
Preston	v	Nottm F.	-	-	-	-	1-1		2-1
Sheff. Weds.	v	Reading	-	-	-	-	-		-
Walsall	v	Wolves	-	-	-	1-1	-		0-3
Wimbledon	v	Grimsby	-	-	-	-	2-2		2-1

NATIONWIDE LEAGUE DIVISION II

Home		Away							
Bristol C.	v	Wigan	-	3-0	-	0-0	1-1		2-2
Cheltenham	v	Tranmere	-	-	-	-	-		-
Colchester	v	Crewe	-	-	-	-	-		-
Huddersfield	v	Peterboro	-	-	-	-	-		3-1
Luton	v	Plymouth	2-2	3-0	-	-	-		2-0
Mansfield	v	Wycombe	-	-	-	-	-		-
Northampton	v	Cardiff	4-0	-	-	-	-		1-2
Notts Co.	v	Stockport	1-2	-	-	-	-		-
Oldham	v	Brentford	-	1-1	-	3-0	3-0		3-2
Port Vale	v	Chesterfield	-	-	-	-	-		4-1
QPR	v	Barnsley	3-1	-	2-1	2-2	2-0		-
Swindon	v	Blackpool	-	-	-	-	-		1-0

NATIONWIDE LEAGUE DIVISION III

Home		Away							
Boston	v	Wrexham	-	-	-	-	-		-
Cambridge U.	v	Bournemouth	-	-	-	0-2	0-2		2-2
Carlisle	v	Lincoln	1-0	-	-	1-0	1-1		2-2
Hull	v	Exeter	2-0	3-2	2-1	4-0	2-1		2-0
Kidderminstr	v	Rushden & D	1-0	1-2	0-0	2-0	-		3-0
Macclesfield	v	Hartlepool	-	2-1	-	3-3	0-1		0-1
Oxford Utd	v	Darlington	-	-	-	-	-		1-2
Rochdale	v	Bristol R.	-	-	-	-	-		2-1
Scunthorpe	v	Leyton O.	1-2	1-0	2-0	-	1-1		4-1
Shrewsbury	v	Southend	-	-	3-1	2-1	0-1		2-0
Swansea	v	Bury	-	-	-	-	0-2		-
Torquay	v	York	-	-	-	0-0	2-2		0-3

BELL'S SCOTTISH FIRST DIVISION

Home		Away							
Alloa	v	Ayr	-	-	-	-	1-1/0-2		-
Falkirk	v	Clyde	-	-	-	-	3-2/1-1		1-1/1-6

Sponsored by Stan James

Inv. CT	v	Arbroath	2-0/4-1	-	2-1/2-0	-	-	5-1/3-2
St Johnstone	v	Ross County	-	-	-	-	-	-
St Mirren	v	Queen of Sth	-	-	-	-	-	-

BELL'S SCOTTISH SECOND DIVISION

Airdrie Utd.	v	Cowdenbeath	-	-	-	-	-	-
Berwick	v	Dumbarton	3-1/0-3	5-3/1-1	3-1/0-1	0-1/0-0	-	-
Forfar	v	Hamilton	-	-	-	-	-	3-0/1-4
Raith	v	Stenhsmuir	-	-	-	-	-	-
Stranraer	v	Brechin	0-1/0-1	4-0/0-2	-	-	-	-

BELL'S SCOTTISH THIRD DIVISION

Albion	v	East Fife	-	-	-	1-3/3-1	0-1/1-2	3-0/2-1
E. Stirling	v	Morton	-	-	-	-	-	-
Montrose	v	Elgin	-	-	-	-	0-0/2-1	0-2/1-0
Peterhead	v	Stirling	-	-	-	-	-	3-3/5-1
Queen's Park	v	New Member	-	-	-	-	-	-

SATURDAY 18TH JANUARY 2003

FA BARCLAYCARD PREMIER DIVISION

Arsenal	v	West Ham	2-0	4-0	1-0	2-1	3-0	2-0
Aston Villa	v	Tottenham	1-1	4-1	3-2	1-1	2-0	1-1
Blackburn	v	Birmingham	-	-	-	1-0	2-1	-
Charlton	v	Bolton	3-3	-	-	2-1	-	1-2
Everton	v	Sunderland	1-3	-	-	5-0	2-2	1-0
Fulham	v	Middlesbro	-	-	-	-	-	2-1
Leeds	v	WBA	-	-	-	-	-	-
Man. Utd.	v	Chelsea	1-2	2-2	1-1	3-2	3-3	0-3
Newcastle	v	Man. City	-	-	-	-	0-1	-
Southampton	v	Liverpool	0-1	1-1	1-2	1-1	3-3	2-0

NATIONWIDE LEAGUE DIVISION I

Brighton	v	Portsmouth	-	-	-	-	-	-
Crystal Pal.	v	Burnley	-	-	-	-	0-1	1-2
Gillingham	v	Leicester	-	-	-	-	-	-
Grimsby	v	Millwall	-	0-1	-	-	-	2-2
Ipswich	v	Preston	-	-	-	-	-	-
Nottm F.	v	Coventry	0-1	-	1-0	-	-	2-1
Reading	v	Walsall	-	-	0-1	-	2-2	-
Rotherham	v	Bradford	-	-	-	-	-	1-1
Sheff. Utd.	v	Sheff. Weds.	-	-	-	-	1-1	0-0
Stoke	v	Derby	-	-	-	-	-	-
Watford	v	Norwich	-	-	1-1	-	4-1	2-1
Wolves	v	Wimbledon	-	-	-	-	0-1	1-0

NATIONWIDE LEAGUE DIVISION II

Barnsley	v	Luton	-	-	-	-	-	-
Blackpool	v	Northampton	-	1-1	2-1	-	-	1-2
Brentford	v	Notts Co.	2-0	-	-	0-2	3-1	2-1
Cardiff	v	Cheltenham	-	-	-	-	3-1	
Chesterfield	v	Mansfield	-	-	-	-	4-0	-
Crewe	v	Huddersfield	-	2-5	1-2	1-1	1-0	-
Peterboro	v	Port Vale	-	-	-	-	2-0	3-0
Plymouth	v	QPR	-	-	-	-	-	-
Stockport	v	Swindon	-	4-2	2-1	3-0	-	-
Tranmere	v	Bristol C.	-	-	1-1	-	-	1-0
Wigan	v	Colchester	1-0	-	1-1	0-1	3-1	2-3
Wycombe	v	Oldham	-	2-1	3-0	0-0	2-1	2-1

NATIONWIDE LEAGUE DIVISION III

Bournemouth	v	Macclesfield	-	-	1-0	-	-	-
Bristol R.	v	Scunthorpe	-	-	-	1-1	-	1-1
Bury	v	Boston	-	-	-	-	-	-
Darlington	v	Kidderminstr	-	-	-	-	1-2	2-0
Exeter	v	Carlisle	2-1	-	2-0	1-1	1-0	1-0
Hartlepool	v	Oxford Utd	-	-	-	-	-	0-1
Leyton O.	v	Hull	1-1	2-1	1-2	0-0	2-2	0-0
Lincoln	v	Shrewsbury	-	1-0	-	1-2	2-2	1-2
Rushden & D	v	Cambridge U.	-	-	-	-	-	-
Southend	v	Rochdale	-	-	1-1	3-3	3-0	0-0
Wrexham	v	Torquay	-	-	-	-	-	-
York	v	Swansea	-	-	-	1-0	-	0-2

BELL'S SCOTTISH FIRST DIVISION

Alloa	v	Queen of Sth	-	-	2-1/3-5	3-1/6-1	-	2-0/4-1
Arbroath	v	Falkirk	-	-	-	-	-	1-0/0-1
Inv. CT	v	Ayr	-	-	-	1-1/1-1	7-3/1-0	3-1/1-1
St Johnstone	v	Clyde	-	-	-	-	-	-
St Mirren	v	Ross County	-	-	-	-	-	1-0/1-1

BELL'S SCOTTISH SECOND DIVISION

Berwick	v	Stranraer	1-2/2-0	-	-	-	1-1/0-2	2-2/4-1
Brechin	v	Cowdenbeath	-	-	2-1/1-1	2-0/1-2	0-0/2-0	-
Dumbarton	v	Forfar	-	-	-	3-3/0-0	-	-
Raith	v	Airdrie Utd.	-	1-1/1-1	1-3/0-1	1-1/2-0	1-1/5-0	2-2/2-1
Stenhsmuir	v	Hamilton	0-1/3-1	-	-	0-0/0-1	-	2-0/0-3

BELL'S SCOTTISH THIRD DIVISION

Elgin	v	East Fife	-	-	-	-	1-3/1-3	1-1/2-0
Morton	v	Albion	-	-	-	-	-	-
New Member	v	Peterhead	-	-	-	-	-	-

Sponsored by Stan James

| Queen's Park | v | E. Stirling | 3-3/3-0 | 0-1/0-2 | 0-4/2-1 | 2-1/0-1 | - | 2-3/1-0 |
| Stirling | v | Montrose | - | - | - | - | - | 1-1/0-1 |

SATURDAY 25TH JANUARY 2003

NATIONWIDE LEAGUE DIVISION II

Bristol C.	v	Stockport	1-1	-	1-1	-	-	-
Cheltenham	v	Chesterfield	-	-	-	-	0-1	-
Colchester	v	Blackpool	-	-	2-2	1-1	-	1-1
Huddersfield	v	Cardiff	-	-	-	-	-	2-2
Luton	v	Wycombe	0-0	0-0	3-1	1-1	1-2	-
Mansfield	v	Brentford	-	-	3-1	-	-	-
Northampton	v	Peterboro	-	-	-	0-1	0-0	2-1
Notts Co.	v	Plymouth	2-1	-	-	-	-	-
Oldham	v	Crewe	-	-	-	-	-	-
Port Vale	v	Barnsley	1-3	-	1-0	2-2	-	-
QPR	v	Tranmere	2-0	0-0	0-0	2-1	2-0	1-2
Swindon	v	Wigan	-	-	-	-	2-2	1-1

NATIONWIDE LEAGUE DIVISION III

Boston	v	Bristol R.	-	-	-	-	-	-
Cambridge U.	v	Hartlepool	1-0	2-0	1-2	-	-	-
Carlisle	v	Leyton O.	1-0	-	1-1	2-1	1-0	6-1
Hull	v	York	-	-	-	1-1	0-0	4-0
Kidderminstr	v	Bury	-	-	-	-	-	-
Macclesfield	v	Exeter	-	2-2	-	1-0	0-2	1-2
Oxford Utd	v	Rushden & D	-	-	-	-	-	3-2
Rochdale	v	Bournemouth	-	-	-	-	-	-
Scunthorpe	v	Southend	-	-	1-1	-	1-1	2-0
Shrewsbury	v	Wrexham	0-1	-	-	-	-	-
Swansea	v	Lincoln	1-2	0-0	-	2-1	-	0-0
Torquay	v	Darlington	1-1	2-1	2-2	1-0	2-1	2-1

TUESDAY 28TH JANUARY 2003

FA BARCLAYCARD PREMIER DIVISION

Birmingham	v	Man. Utd.	-	-	-	-	-	-
Bolton	v	Everton	-	0-0	-	-	-	2-2
Middlesbro	v	Aston Villa	3-2	-	0-0	0-4	1-1	2-1
Sunderland	v	Southampton	0-1	-	-	2-0	2-2	1-1
WBA	v	Charlton	1-2	1-0	-	2-0	-	-

BANK OF SCOTLAND SCOTTISH PREMIER DIVISION

| Partick | v | Livingston | - | - | 1-3/1-1 | - | - | - |

WEDNESDAY 29TH JANUARY 2003

FA BARCLAYCARD PREMIER DIVISION

Chelsea	v	Leeds	0-0	0-0	1-0	0-2	1-1	2-0
Liverpool	v	Arsenal	2-0	4-0	0-0	2-0	4-0	1-2
Man. City	v	Fulham	-	-	3-0	4-0	-	-
Tottenham	v	Newcastle	1-2	2-0	2-0	3-1	4-2	1-3
West Ham	v	Blackburn	2-1	2-1	2-0	-	-	2-0

BANK OF SCOTLAND SCOTTISH PREMIER DIVISION

Aberdeen	v	Hearts	4-0/0-0	1-4/2-2	2-0/2-5	3-1/1-2	1-1/1-0	3-2/2-3
Celtic	v	Dundee Utd.	1-0/3-0	4-0/1-1	2-1/2-1	4-1/2-0	2-1	5-1/1-0
Dunfermline	v	Dundee	-	-	2-0/2-0	-	1-0	1-0/2-0
Hibernian	v	Rangers	2-1/1-2	3-4/1-2	-	0-1/2-2	1-0/0-0	0-3
Kilmarnock	v	Motherwell	2-4/1-0	2-1/4-1	0-0/0-1	0-1/0-2	3-2/1-2	2-0/1-4

SATURDAY 1ST FEBRUARY 2003

FA BARCLAYCARD PREMIER DIVISION

Arsenal	v	Fulham	-	-	-	-	-	4-1
Aston Villa	v	Blackburn	1-0	0-4	1-3	-	-	2-0
Bolton	v	Birmingham	2-1	-	3-1	3-3	2-2	-
Chelsea	v	Tottenham	3-1	2-0	2-0	1-0	3-0	4-0
Everton	v	Leeds	0-0	2-0	0-0	4-4	2-2	0-0
Man. City	v	WBA	3-2	1-0	-	2-1	-	0-0
Middlesbro	v	Newcastle	0-1	-	2-2	2-2	1-3	1-4
Southampton	v	Man. Utd.	6-3	1-0	0-3	1-3	2-1	1-3
Sunderland	v	Charlton	-	0-0	-	-	3-2	2-2
West Ham	v	Liverpool	1-2	2-1	2-1	1-0	1-1	1-1

NATIONWIDE LEAGUE DIVISION I

Bradford	v	Ipswich	2-1	2-1	0-0	-	0-2	-
Burnley	v	Reading	-	-	1-1	3-0	-	-
Coventry	v	Watford	-	-	-	4-0	-	0-2
Derby	v	Rotherham	-	-	-	-	-	-
Leicester	v	Crystal Pal.	-	1-1	-	-	-	-
Millwall	v	Sheff. Utd.	-	-	-	-	-	2-0
Norwich	v	Stoke	2-0	0-0	-	-	-	-
Portsmouth	v	Grimsby	1-0	-	0-1	1-2	1-1	4-2
Preston	v	Gillingham	1-0	1-3	1-1	0-2	0-0	0-2
Sheff. Weds.	v	Wolves	-	-	-	-	0-1	2-2
Walsall	v	Brighton	-	-	-	-	-	-
Wimbledon	v	Nottm F.	1-0	-	1-3	-	2-1	1-0

NATIONWIDE LEAGUE DIVISION II

Barnsley	v	Swindon	1-1	-	1-3	1-0	-	-

Sponsored by Stan James

Blackpool	v	Bristol C.	1-0	2-2	-	1-2	-	5-1
Brentford	v	Huddersfield	-	-	-	-	-	3-0
Cardiff	v	Oldham	-	-	-	1-1	-	3-1
Chesterfield	v	QPR	-	-	-	-	-	2-3
Crewe	v	Northampton	-	-	-	-	-	-
Peterboro	v	Luton	0-1	-	-	-	1-1	-
Plymouth	v	Mansfield	-	-	3-0	2-1	2-0	1-0
Stockport	v	Colchester	-	-	-	-	-	-
Tranmere	v	Port Vale	2-0	1-2	1-1	2-1	-	3-1
Wigan	v	Cheltenham	-	-	-	-	-	-
Wycombe	v	Notts Co.	1-0	-	1-1	2-0	3-1	3-0

NATIONWIDE LEAGUE DIVISION III

Bournemouth	v	Boston	-	-	-	-
Bristol R.	v	Carlisle	-	3-1	-	-	-	0-0
Bury	v	Oxford Utd	-	1-0	1-0	1-2	3-1	-
Darlington	v	Cambridge U.	2-0	1-1	0-0	-	-	-
Exeter	v	Shrewsbury	-	2-2	0-1	1-2	1-0	2-2
Hartlepool	v	Torquay	1-1	3-0	4-1	2-0	3-1	4-1
Leyton O.	v	Rochdale	2-1	2-0	3-0	0-0	1-1	4-2
Lincoln	v	Kidderminstr	-	-	-	-	3-3	0-1
Rushden & D	v	Swansea	-	-	-	-	-	4-0
Southend	v	Hull	-	-	0-1	1-2	1-1	2-0
Wrexham	v	Scunthorpe	-	-	-	3-1	-	-
York	v	Macclesfield	-	-	0-2	0-2	1-3	1-0

BANK OF SCOTLAND SCOTTISH PREMIER DIVISION

Dundee	v	Hibernian	-	-	-	3-4/1-0	1-2/0-2	2-1/1-0
Hearts	v	Dunfermline	2-0/1-1	3-1/2-0	2-1/2-0	-	2-0/7-1	1-1/2-0
Livingston	v	Kilmarnock	-	-	-	-	-	0-1
Partick	v	Celtic	-	-	-	-	-	-

BELL'S SCOTTISH FIRST DIVISION

Ayr	v	St Mirren	-	0-2/2-2	1-1/2-2	0-3/1-2	-	4-2/4-1
Clyde	v	Inv. CT	-	4-3/1-6	4-1/1-1	-	1-1/2-2	1-1/1-0
Falkirk	v	St Johnstone	2-0/1-4	-	-	-	-	-
Queen of Sth	v	Arbroath	-	-	0-0/3-0	2-3/1-0	1-1/1-0	-
Ross County	v	Alloa	1-2/3-1	2-4/0-2	-	1-0/3-4	1-0/2-3	-

BELL'S SCOTTISH SECOND DIVISION

Airdrie Utd.	v	Brechin	-	-	-	-	-	-
Cowdenbeath	v	Stenhsmuir	-	-	0-2/0-2	-	-	1-1/2-4
Forfar	v	Berwick	-	-	-	1-1/2-0	3-5/0-1	2-1/0-0
Hamilton	v	Raith	-	2-0/1-4	3-2/1-2	-	-	-
Stranraer	v	Dumbarton	2-0/1-0	-	-	-	-	-

Sponsored by Stan James

BELL'S SCOTTISH THIRD DIVISION

Albion	v	Elgin	-	-	-	-	1-1/0-1	4-4/2-2
East Fife	v	Stirling	2-2/1-3	-	2-3/1-0	-	-	1-1/1-1
E. Stirling	v	New Member	-	-	-	-	-	-
Montrose	v	Morton	-	-	-	-	-	-
Peterhead	v	Queen's Park	-	-	-	-	-	2-1/1-2

SUNDAY 2ND FEBRUARY 2003

BANK OF SCOTLAND SCOTTISH PREMIER DIVISION

Dundee Utd.	v	Motherwell	1-1/2-0	4-0/1-0	2-2/0-3	0-2/1-2	1-1/2-0/1-0	1-1/1-0
Rangers	v	Aberdeen	2-2/4-0	3-3/2-0	2-1/3-1	3-0/5-0	3-1/1-0	2-0/2-0

SATURDAY 8TH FEBRUARY 2003

FA BARCLAYCARD PREMIER DIVISION

Birmingham	v	Chelsea	-	-	-	-	-	-
Blackburn	v	Southampton	2-1	1-0	0-2	-	-	2-0
Charlton	v	Everton	-	-	1-2	-	1-0	1-2
Fulham	v	Aston Villa	-	-	-	-	-	0-0
Leeds	v	West Ham	1-0	3-1	4-0	1-0	0-1	3-0
Liverpool	v	Middlesbro	5-1	-	3-1	0-0	0-0	2-0
Man. Utd.	v	Man. City	-	-	-	-	1-1	-
Newcastle	v	Arsenal	1-2	0-1	1-1	4-2	0-0	0-2
Tottenham	v	Sunderland	2-0	-	-	3-1	2-1	2-1
WBA	v	Bolton	2-2	-	2-3	4-4	0-2	-

NATIONWIDE LEAGUE DIVISION I

Brighton	v	Wolves	-	-	-	-	-	-
Coventry	v	Burnley	-	-	-	-	-	0-2
Grimsby	v	Stoke	1-1	-	-	-	-	-
Ipswich	v	Sheff. Utd.	3-1	2-2	4-1	1-1	-	-
Nottm F.	v	Crystal Pal.	-	-	-	2-0	0-3	4-2
Portsmouth	v	Derby	-	-	-	-	-	-
Preston	v	Millwall	2-1	2-1	0-1	3-2	-	1-0
Reading	v	Gillingham	-	-	0-0	2-2	-	-
Sheff. Weds.	v	Norwich	-	-	-	-	3-2	0-5
Walsall	v	Leicester	-	-	-	-	-	-
Watford	v	Rotherham	2-0	-	-	-	-	3-2
Wimbledon	v	Bradford	-	-	-	3-2	-	1-2

NATIONWIDE LEAGUE DIVISION II

Brentford	v	Crewe	0-2	-	-	-	-	-
Bristol C.	v	Colchester	-	-	-	1-1	1-1	3-1
Cardiff	v	Barnsley	-	-	-	-	-	-

Sponsored by Stan James

Cheltenham	v	Stockport	-	-	-	-	-
Chesterfield	v	Peterboro	2-1	-	-	-	0-1
Mansfield	v	Notts Co.	-	0-2	-	-	-
Northampton	v	QPR	-	-	-	-	2-2
Oldham	v	Plymouth	-	2-0	-	-	-
Port Vale	v	Luton	-	-	-	3-0	-
Tranmere	v	Swindon	2-1	3-0	0-0	3-1	0-0
Wigan	v	Blackpool		3-0	3-0	5-1	0-1
Wycombe	v	Huddersfield	-	-	-	-	2-4

NATIONWIDE LEAGUE DIVISION III

Boston	v	Scunthorpe	-	-	-	-	-
Bournemouth	v	Wrexham	2-1	0-1	0-0	1-0	1-2	3-0
Cambridge U.	v	Shrewsbury	-	4-3	0-0	-	-	-
Carlisle	v	Kidderminstr	-	-	-	2-0	1-0
Darlington	v	Rushden & D	-	-	-	-	0-0
Hartlepool	v	Exeter	1-1	1-1	4-3	2-1	2-0	2-0
Hull	v	Lincoln	2-1	0-2	-	1-1	1-1	1-1
Leyton O.	v	York	-	-	-	0-0	1-1	1-2
Macclesfield	v	Swansea	-	3-0	-	1-2	-	1-3
Rochdale	v	Oxford Utd	-	-	-	-	1-1
Southend	v	Bristol R.	-	1-1	-	-	2-1
Torquay	v	Bury	-	-	-	-	-

BANK OF SCOTLAND SCOTTISH PREMIER DIVISION

Aberdeen	v	Partick	-	-	-	-	-
Celtic	v	Livingston	-	-	-	-	3-2/5-1
Dundee Utd.	v	Dundee	-	-	0-1/0-2	2-1/1-0	0-2	2-2/1-0
Dunfermline	v	Rangers	2-5/0-3	0-0/2-3	0-2/0-3	-	0-0	1-4/2-4/1-1
Hearts	v	Kilmarnock	3-2/2-0	5-3/1-1	2-1/2-2	2-2/0-0	0-2/3-0	2-0
Motherwell	v	Hibernian	1-1/2-1	1-1/6-2	-	2-2/2-0	1-3	1-3/4-0

BELL'S SCOTTISH FIRST DIVISION

Arbroath	v	Clyde	-	-	0-0/0-3	2-1/1-1	-	2-1/2-0
Ayr	v	Ross County	-	-	-	-	1-0/0-2	2-0/0-0
Inv. CT	v	Falkirk	-	-	-	2-3/0-3	2-3/1-1	1-2/3-2
Queen of Sth	v	St Johnstone	-	-	-	-	-	-
St Mirren	v	Alloa	-	-	-	-	-	-

BELL'S SCOTTISH SECOND DIVISION

Berwick	v	Cowdenbeath	-	2-1/0-2	3-1/2-1	0-2/0-0	-	2-5/1-0
Dumbarton	v	Hamilton	1-3/0-3	-	-	-	2-3/1-2	-
Raith	v	Brechin	-	-	-	-	-	-
Stenhsmuir	v	Airdrie Utd.	-	-	-	-	-	-
Stranraer	v	Forfar	-	2-2/4-0	-	-	2-0/3-1	2-0/0-3

Sponsored by Stan James

BELL'S SCOTTISH THIRD DIVISION

E. Stirling	v	Elgin	-	-	-	-	0-2/1-0	2-1/0-3
Morton	v	East Fife	0-0/2-0	-	-	-	-	-
Montrose	v	Peterhead	-	-	-	-	0-2/2-2	0-3/2-1
New Member	v	Stirling	-	-	-	-	-	-
Queen's Park	v	Albion	1-1/0-0	5-1/2-4	0-0/0-0	2-0/0-1	-	1-2/0-3

SATURDAY 15TH FEBRUARY 2003

NATIONWIDE LEAGUE DIVISION I

Bradford	v	Brighton	-	-	-	-	-	-
Burnley	v	Preston	1-2	1-1	0-1	0-3	3-0	2-1
Crystal Pal.	v	Ipswich	0-0	-	3-2	2-2	-	-
Derby	v	Sheff. Weds.	2-2	3-0	1-0	3-3	-	-
Gillingham	v	Grimsby	-	0-2	-	-	1-0	2-1
Leicester	v	Portsmouth	-	-	-	-	-	-
Millwall	v	Reading	-	-	1-1	5-0	2-0	-
Norwich	v	Wimbledon	-	-	-	-	1-2	2-1
Rotherham	v	Coventry	-	-	-	-	-	0-0
Sheff. Utd.	v	Nottm F.	-	1-0	-	2-1	1-3	0-0
Stoke	v	Walsall	-	-	2-0	-	0-0	-
Wolves	v	Watford	-	-	0-0	-	2-2	1-0

NATIONWIDE LEAGUE DIVISION II

Barnsley	v	Chesterfield	-	-	-	-	-	-
Blackpool	v	Brentford	1-0	1-2	-	0-1	-	1-3
Colchester	v	Mansfield	2-1	2-0	-	-	-	-
Crewe	v	Wigan	-	-	-	-	-	-
Huddersfield	v	Cheltenham	-	-	-	-	-	-
Luton	v	Northampton	-	2-2	1-0	-	0-2	-
Notts Co.	v	Bristol C.	2-0	-	-	4-4	2-1	2-0
Peterboro	v	Cardiff	-	2-0	2-1	-	-	1-1
Plymouth	v	Tranmere	-	-	-	-	-	-
QPR	v	Port Vale	1-2	0-1	3-2	3-2	-	4-1
Stockport	v	Oldham	-	-	-	-	-	-
Swindon	v	Wycombe	-	-	-	-	1-1	1-1

NATIONWIDE LEAGUE DIVISION III

Bristol R.	v	Bournemouth	3-2	5-3	1-0	2-2	1-1	-
Bury	v	Leyton O.	-	-	-	-	-	-
Exeter	v	Boston	-	-	-	-	-	-
Kidderminstr	v	Torquay	-	-	-	-	2-0	1-0
Lincoln	v	Darlington	2-0	3-1	-	1-0	2-2	1-1
Oxford Utd	v	Carlisle	-	-	-	-	-	1-1
Rushden & D	v	Rochdale	-	-	-	-	-	1-1

Sponsored by Stan James

Scunthorpe	v	Hull	2-2	2-0	3-2	-	0-1	2-1
Shrewsbury	v	Macclesfield	-	4-3	-	0-1	2-2	1-1
Swansea	v	Cambridge U.	3-1	1-1	2-0	-	1-1	-
Wrexham	v	Southend	-	3-1	-	-	-	-
York	v	Hartlepool	-	-	-	2-1	1-1	1-0

BANK OF SCOTLAND SCOTTISH PREMIER DIVISION

Aberdeen	v	Dundee Utd.	3-3/1-1	1-1/1-0	0-3/0-4	1-2/3-1	4-1/1-2	2-1/4-0
Dundee	v	Livingston	-	-	-	-	-	1-0/2-0
Hibernian	v	Dunfermline	0-0/1-0	5-2/1-0	-	-	3-0	5-1/1-1
Kilmarnock	v	Partick	-	-	-	-	-	-
Motherwell	v	Celtic	2-1/0-1	2-3/1-1	1-2/1-7	3-2/1-1	3-3	1-2/0-4
Rangers	v	Hearts	3-0/0-0	3-1/2-2	3-0/0-0	1-0/1-0	1-0/2-0	3-1/2-0

BELL'S SCOTTISH FIRST DIVISION

Alloa	v	Arbroath	1-1/0-2	3-0/3-1	1-1/1-2	0-0/2-1	-	-
Clyde	v	Ayr	2-3/1-1	-	-	-	0-1/2-2	2-2/2-2
Falkirk	v	St Mirren	1-1/1-1	3-1/2-2	1-1/1-0	3-1/2-0	-	3-2/0-0
Ross County	v	Queen of Sth	-	-	-	1-1/2-0	-	
St Johnstone	v	Inv. CT	-	-	-	-	-	-

BELL'S SCOTTISH SECOND DIVISION

Airdrie Utd.	v	Berwick	-	-	-	-	-	-
Brechin	v	Stenhsmuir	0-0/1-1	1-1/4-3	1-0/0-2	-	-	-
Cowdenbeath	v	Dumbarton	-	0-2/2-0	0-2/2-1	0-2/1-2	1-1/2-2	-
Forfar	v	Raith	-	-	-	-	-	-
Hamilton	v	Stranraer	4-0/2-1	-	1-2/1-0	2-1/2-0	-	0-1/2-0

BELL'S SCOTTISH THIRD DIVISION

Albion	v	Montrose	1-2/2-1	3-2/4-2	4-1/0-0	1-3/0-2	3-2/2-1	0-0/0-0
East Fife	v	New Member	-	-	-	-	-	-
Elgin	v	Morton	-	-	-	-	-	-
Peterhead	v	E. Stirling	-	-	-	-	2-4/1-2	3-2/2-1
Stirling	v	Queen's Park	-	-	-	-	0-1/0-2	0-0/3-2

SATURDAY 22ND FEBRUARY 2003

FA BARCLAYCARD PREMIER DIVISION

Birmingham	v	Liverpool	-	-	-	-	-	-
Bolton	v	Man. Utd.	-	0-0	-	-	-	0-4
Charlton	v	Aston Villa	-	-	0-1	-	3-3	1-2
Chelsea	v	Blackburn	1-1	0-1	1-1	-	-	0-0
Everton	v	Southampton	7-1	0-2	1-0	4-1	1-1	2-0
Leeds	v	Newcastle	0-1	4-1	0-1	3-2	1-3	3-4
Man. City	v	Arsenal	-	-	-	-	0-4	-
Sunderland	v	Middlesbro	2-2	1-2	-	1-1	1-0	0-1

Sponsored by Stan James

| Tottenham | v | Fulham | - | - | - | - | - | 4-0 |
| WBA | v | West Ham | - | - | - | - | - | - |

NATIONWIDE LEAGUE DIVISION I

Brighton	v	Millwall	-	-	-	-	-	-
Burnley	v	Derby	-	-	-	-	-	-
Coventry	v	Bradford	-	-	-	4-0	0-0	4-0
Crystal Pal.	v	Sheff. Weds.	-	1-0	-	-	4-1	4-1
Ipswich	v	Grimsby	1-1	-	0-1	2-0	-	-
Leicester	v	Wimbledon	1-0	0-1	1-1	2-1	-	-
Nottm F.	v	Stoke	-	1-0	-	-	-	-
Portsmouth	v	Gillingham	-	-	-	-	0-0	2-1
Preston	v	Wolves	-	-	-	-	2-0	1-2
Reading	v	Rotherham	-	-	-	-	2-0	-
Sheff. Utd.	v	Norwich	2-3	2-2	2-1	0-0	1-1	2-1
Walsall	v	Watford	1-1	0-0	-	-	-	0-3

NATIONWIDE LEAGUE DIVISION II

Barnsley	v	Huddersfield	3-1	-	7-1	4-2	3-1	-
Cardiff	v	Plymouth	-	-	1-0	-	4-1	-
Cheltenham	v	Colchester	-	-	-	-	-	-
Chesterfield	v	Crewe	1-0	-	-	-	-	-
Luton	v	Brentford	1-0	2-0	-	1-2	3-1	-
Northampton	v	Bristol C.	-	2-1	-	-	2-0	0-3
Oldham	v	Notts Co.	-	-	1-3	1-2	0-1	4-1
Peterboro	v	Stockport	0-2	-	-	-	-	-
Port Vale	v	Swindon	1-0	0-1	0-1	2-0	3-0	0-2
QPR	v	Mansfield	-	-	-	-	-	-
Tranmere	v	Blackpool	-	-	-	-	-	4-0
Wycombe	v	Wigan	-	1-2	2-1	0-2	1-2	1-0

NATIONWIDE LEAGUE DIVISION III

Boston	v	Kidderminstr	-	-	-	-	-	-
Bournemouth	v	Exeter	-	-	-	-	-	-
Bristol R.	v	Macclesfield	-	-	0-0	-	-	0-2
Hartlepool	v	Swansea	1-1	4-2	1-2	0-1	-	7-1
Hull	v	Cambridge U.	1-3	1-0	0-3	-	-	-
Leyton O.	v	Shrewsbury	-	2-3	6-1	1-2	2-0	2-4
Rochdale	v	Carlisle	2-2	-	1-1	3-2	6-0	1-1
Scunthorpe	v	Lincoln	2-0	0-1	-	-	2-1	1-1
Southend	v	Rushden & D	-	-	-	-	-	4-2
Torquay	v	Oxford Utd	-	-	-	-	-	3-3
Wrexham	v	Darlington	-	-	-	-	-	-
York	v	Bury	0-2	-	-	-	-	-

Sponsored by Stan James

BELL'S SCOTTISH SECOND DIVISION

Berwick	v	Raith	-	-	-	-	-	-
Dumbarton	v	Brechin	1-1/1-2	-	1-2/2-0	1-3/2-1	0-2/1-0	1-2/2-1
Forfar	v	Stenhsmuir	-	1-1/0-1	-		2-2/7-0	1-2/2-0
Hamilton	v	Airdrie Utd.	-	0-0/0-2	1-1/0-2	-	-	-
Stranraer	v	Cowdenbeath	-	-	-	-	-	3-0/2-1

BELL'S SCOTTISH THIRD DIVISION

Albion	v	Peterhead	-	-	-	-	0-0/0-1	1-0/2-1
East Fife	v	E. Stirling	-	-	-	1-0/3-1	3-1/4-1	0-4/1-0
Elgin	v	New Member	-	-	-	-	-	-
Morton	v	Stirling	3-2/1-1	1-3/1-0	-	-	-	-
Montrose	v	Queen's Park	3-2/1-1	1-3/4-3	1-0/3-0	2-1/0-2	-	3-1/3-1

SATURDAY 1ST MARCH 2003

FA BARCLAYCARD PREMIER DIVISION

Arsenal	v	Charlton	-	-	0-0	-	5-3	2-4
Aston Villa	v	Birmingham	-	-	-	-	-	-
Blackburn	v	Man. City	-	-	-	1-4	-	-
Fulham	v	Sunderland	-	-	-	-	-	2-0
Liverpool	v	Bolton	-	2-1	-	-	-	1-1
Man. Utd.	v	Leeds	1-0	3-0	3-2	2-0	3-0	1-1
Middlesbro	v	Everton	4-2	-	2-2	2-1	1-2	1-0
Newcastle	v	Chelsea	3-1	3-1	0-1	0-1	0-0	1-2
Southampton	v	WBA	-	-	-	-	-	-
West Ham	v	Tottenham	4-3	2-1	2-1	1-0	0-0	0-1

NATIONWIDE LEAGUE DIVISION I

Bradford	v	Walsall	-	-	-	-	-	2-0
Derby	v	Leicester	2-0	0-4	2-0	3-0	2-0	2-3
Gillingham	v	Brighton	-	-	-	-	-	-
Grimsby	v	Coventry	-	-	-	-	-	0-1
Millwall	v	Portsmouth	-	-	-	-	-	1-0
Norwich	v	Ipswich	3-1	2-1	0-0	0-0	-	-
Rotherham	v	Sheff. Utd.	-	-	-	-	-	1-1
Sheff. Weds.	v	Preston	-	-	-	-	1-3	1-2
Stoke	v	Burnley	-	-	1-4	2-2	-	-
Watford	v	Nottm F.	-	-	-	-	3-0	1-2
Wimbledon	v	Reading	-	-	-	-	-	-
Wolves	v	Crystal Pal.	0-3	-	0-0	2-1	1-3	0-1

NATIONWIDE LEAGUE DIVISION II

Blackpool	v	Wycombe	0-0	2-4	0-0	1-2	-	2-2

Brentford	v	Tranmere	-		-	-	-	4-0
Bristol C.	v	Cheltenham	-	-	-	-	-	-
Colchester	v	Port Vale	-	-	-	-	0-1	2-0
Crewe	v	Peterboro	1-1	-	-	-	-	-
Huddersfield	v	Northampton	-	-	-	-	-	2-0
Mansfield	v	Oldham	-	-	-	-	-	-
Notts Co.	v	Luton	1-2	-	1-2	0-0	1-3	-
Plymouth	v	Barnsley	-	-	-	-	-	-
Stockport	v	Cardiff	-	-	-	-	-	-
Swindon	v	QPR	1-1	3-1	3-1	0-1	-	0-1
Wigan	v	Chesterfield	-	2-1	3-1	3-0	-	1-1

NATIONWIDE LEAGUE DIVISION III

Bury	v	Bournemouth	2-1	-	-	2-2	2-5	2-1
Cambridge U.	v	Torquay	2-1	1-1	2-0	-	-	-
Carlisle	v	Hull	0-0	-	0-0	0-4	0-0	0-0
Darlington	v	Hartlepool	1-2	1-1	2-0	1-1	1-1	1-1
Exeter	v	Bristol R.	-	-	-	-	-	1-0
Kidderminstr	v	Scunthorpe	-	-	-	-	0-0	1-0
Lincoln	v	Leyton O.	1-1	1-0	-	0-0	2-3	2-0
Macclesfield	v	Southend	-	-	-	1-2	1-0	0-0
Oxford Utd	v	Boston	-	-	-	-	-	-
Rushden & D	v	York	-	-	-	-	-	3-0
Shrewsbury	v	Rochdale	-	1-0	3-2	2-4	0-4	1-0
Swansea	v	Wrexham	-	-	-	-	0-1	-

BANK OF SCOTLAND SCOTTISH PREMIER DIVISION

Celtic	v	Hibernian	5-0/4-1	5-0/0-0	-	4-0/1-1	3-0/1-1	3-0
Dundee Utd.	v	Dunfermline	1-1/2-1	0-0/2-2	1-1/1-1	-	3-2/1-0	3-2/0-2
Hearts	v	Motherwell	1-1/4-1	2-0/1-1	3-0/0-2	1-1/0-0	3-0/3-0	3-1
Kilmarnock	v	Aberdeen	3-0/1-1	1-0/2-1	4-0/4-2	2-0/1-0	1-0/0-0	3-1
Livingston	v	Rangers	-	-	-	-	-	0-2/2-1
Partick	v	Dundee	0-0/2-2	0-3/1-2	-	-	-	-

BELL'S SCOTTISH FIRST DIVISION

Alloa	v	St Johnstone	-	-	-	-	-	-
Arbroath	v	Ayr	-	-	-	-	-	3-2/0-2
Clyde	v	Ross County	-	-	-	3-1/0-0	2-2/2-0	3-0/0-0
Inv. CT	v	St Mirren	-	-	-	1-1/5-0	-	1-2/4-2
Queen of Sth	v	Falkirk	-	-	-	-	-	-

BELL'S SCOTTISH SECOND DIVISION

Airdrie Utd.	v	Stranraer	-	-	3-2/2-0	-	-	-
Brechin	v	Hamilton	0-2/0-1	-	-	-	0-0/3-4	-
Cowdenbeath	v	Forfar	1-3/1-2	-	-	0-3/4-1	-	3-2/1-2

Sponsored by Stan James

Raith	v	Dumbarton	-	-	-	-	-	-
Stenhsmuir	v	Berwick	1-1/1-1	-	1-2/1-1	-	2-0/0-2	3-0/1-3

BELL'S SCOTTISH THIRD DIVISION

E. Stirling	v	Albion	0-1/1-4	1-0/2-0	0-1/4-1	4-3/3-1	1-1/1-0	1-2/1-2
New Member	v	Montrose	-	-	-	-	-	-
Peterhead	v	Morton	-	-	-	-	-	-
Queen's Park	v	East Fife	-	-	-	0-1/1-0	-	1-2/2-0
Stirling	v	Elgin	-	-	-	-	-	0-1/3-1

TUESDAY 4TH MARCH 2003

NATIONWIDE LEAGUE DIVISION I

Bradford	v	Leicester	-	-	-	3-1	0-0	-
Gillingham	v	Nottm F.	-	-	-	-	1-3	3-1
Grimsby	v	Sheff. Utd.	2-4	-	1-2	2-2	0-1	1-0
Millwall	v	Burnley	2-1	1-0	1-2	1-1	-	0-2
Norwich	v	Reading	1-1	0-0	-	-	-	-
Rotherham	v	Walsall	1-2	-	-	-	2-3	2-0
Watford	v	Preston	1-0	3-1	-	-	2-3	1-1
Wimbledon	v	Portsmouth	-	-	-	-	1-1	3-3
Wolves	v	Ipswich	0-0	1-1	1-0	2-1	-	-

NATIONWIDE LEAGUE DIVISION II

Blackpool	v	Barnsley	-	-	-	-	-	-
Brentford	v	Cardiff	-	-	1-0	2-1	-	2-1
Bristol C.	v	Oldham	-	1-0	-	1-1	2-2	3-0
Colchester	v	Northampton	0-0	-	1-0	-	0-2	3-1
Crewe	v	Wycombe	3-0	-	-	-	-	-
Huddersfield	v	QPR	1-2	1-1	2-0	1-0	2-1	1-0
Mansfield	v	Luton	-	-	-	-	-	4-1
Notts Co.	v	Port Vale	-	-	-	-	0-1	1-3
Plymouth	v	Peterboro	1-1	-	0-2	2-1	-	-
Stockport	v	Chesterfield	1-0	-	-	-	-	-
Wigan	v	Tranmere	-	-	-	-	-	1-2

NATIONWIDE LEAGUE DIVISION III

Bury	v	Bristol R.	2-1	-	-	0-0	1-0	-
Cambridge U.	v	Rochdale	2-2	1-1	1-1	-	-	-
Carlisle	v	Scunthorpe	3-2	-	0-1	-	1-2	3-0
Darlington	v	York	-	-	-	2-2	1-1	3-1
Exeter	v	Wrexham	-	-	-	-	-	-
Kidderminstr	v	Southend	-	-	-	-	2-1	2-0
Lincoln	v	Hartlepool	2-1	1-1	-	1-2	0-2	2-0
Macclesfield	v	Hull	-	2-0	-	0-2	0-0	0-0

Sponsored by Stan James

Oxford Utd	v	Leyton O.	-	-	-	-	-	1-1
Rushden & D	v	Bournemouth	-	-	-	-	-	-
Shrewsbury	v	Torquay	-	1-2	1-2	1-2	1-1	0-1
Swansea	v	Boston	-	-	-	-	-	-

WEDNESDAY 5TH MARCH 2003

NATIONWIDE LEAGUE DIVISION I

Derby	v	Crystal Pal.	-	0-0	-	-	-	-
Sheff. Weds.	v	Coventry	0-0	0-0	1-2	0-0	-	2-1
Stoke	v	Brighton	-	-	-	-	-	3-1

NATIONWIDE LEAGUE DIVISION II

Swindon	v	Cheltenham	-	-	-	-	-	

SATURDAY 8TH MARCH 2003

NATIONWIDE LEAGUE DIVISION I

Brighton	v	Rotherham	-	1-2	4-1	1-1	-	-
Burnley	v	Bradford	-	-	-	-	-	1-1
Coventry	v	Wimbledon	1-1	0-0	2-1	2-0	-	3-1
Crystal Pal.	v	Watford	-	-	2-2	-	1-0	0-2
Ipswich	v	Stoke	1-1	2-3	-	-	-	-
Leicester	v	Sheff. Weds.	1-0	1-1	0-2	3-0	-	-
Nottm F.	v	Grimsby	-	-	-	2-1	3-1	0-0
Portsmouth	v	Norwich	0-1	1-1	1-2	2-1	2-0	1-2
Preston	v	Derby	-	-	-	-	-	-
Reading	v	Wolves	2-1	0-0	-	-	-	-
Sheff. Utd.	v	Gillingham	-	-	-	-	1-2	0-0
Walsall	v	Millwall	2-1	2-0	3-0	-	0-0	0-0

NATIONWIDE LEAGUE DIVISION II

Barnsley	v	Stockport	-	-	1-1	2-1	0-2	2-2
Cardiff	v	Notts Co.	-	1-1	-	2-1	-	2-1
Cheltenham	v	Mansfield	-	-	-	1-0	2-2	2-3
Chesterfield	v	Plymouth	1-2	2-1	-	-	2-1	-
Luton	v	Huddersfield	-	-	-	-	-	-
Northampton	v	Swindon	-	-	-	-	0-1	1-1
Oldham	v	Colchester	-	-	1-0	1-2	1-1	4-1
Peterboro	v	Wigan	-	-	-	-	2-0	0-2
Port Vale	v	Blackpool	-	-	-	-	-	1-1
QPR	v	Bristol C.	-	-	1-1	-	-	0-0
Tranmere	v	Crewe	-	0-3	3-0	2-0	1-3	-
Wycombe	v	Brentford	0-1	0-0	-	2-0	0-0	5-3

Sponsored by Stan James

NATIONWIDE LEAGUE DIVISION III

Boston	v	Carlisle	-	-	-	-	-
Bournemouth	v	Darlington	-	-	-	-	-
Bristol R.	v	Shrewsbury	2-0	-	-	-	0-0
Hartlepool	v	Bury	-	-	-	-	-
Hull	v	Oxford Utd	-	-	-	-	3-0
Leyton O.	v	Exeter	1-1	1-0	2-0	4-1	2-1	1-1
Rochdale	v	Kidderminstr	-	-	-	0-0	2-0
Scunthorpe	v	Macclesfield	-	1-0	-	2-2	1-1
Southend	v	Lincoln	-	-	2-2	1-0	1-1
Torquay	v	Swansea	2-0	2-0	1-1	1-0	-	1-2
Wrexham	v	Rushden & D	-	-	-	-	-
York	v	Cambridge U.	-	-	-	-	-

BANK OF SCOTLAND SCOTTISH PREMIER DIVISION

Celtic	v	Rangers	0-1/0-1	1-1/2-0	5-1/0-3	1-1/0-1	6-2/1-0	2-1/1-1
Dundee	v	Kilmarnock	-	-	1-1/2-1	0-0/1-2	0-0/2-2/2-1	1-2/2-0
Dunfermline	v	Partick	-	-	-	-	-
Hibernian	v	Dundee Utd.	1-1/2-0	1-3/1-2	-	3-2/1-0	3-0/1-0	0-1
Livingston	v	Hearts	-	-	-	-	2-1/2-0
Motherwell	v	Aberdeen	2-2/2-2	1-2/1-2	2-2/1-1	5-6/1-0	1-1/0-1/0-2	3-2

BELL'S SCOTTISH FIRST DIVISION

Ayr	v	Queen of Sth	1-0/2-2	-	-	-	-
Falkirk	v	Alloa	-	-	-	1-1/2-2	-
Ross County	v	Inv. CT	1-3/0-3	-	-	0-3/0-1	2-1/0-0
St Johnstone	v	Arbroath	-	-	-	-	-
St Mirren	v	Clyde	-	-	-	-	4-1/2-2

BELL'S SCOTTISH SECOND DIVISION

Airdrie Utd.	v	Dumbarton	-	-	-	-	-
Berwick	v	Hamilton	0-2/0-5	-	-	-	0-2/2-0
Forfar	v	Brechin	-	2-5/5-0	-	0-0/2-0	-
Raith	v	Cowdenbeath	-	-	-	-	-
Stranraer	v	Stenhsmuir	2-2/2-1	4-1/1-2	-	2-0/2-2	1-4/2-1	6-1/1-0

BELL'S SCOTTISH THIRD DIVISION

Albion	v	New Member	-	-	-	-	-
E. Stirling	v	Stirling	-	-	-	-	1-1/3-0
Montrose	v	East Fife	-	-	1-2/1-1	0-1/1-1	2-1/0-1
Peterhead	v	Elgin	-	-	-	1-0/1-1	1-1/1-0
Queen's Park	v	Morton	-	-	-	-	-

Sponsored by Stan James

SATURDAY 15TH MARCH 2003

FA BARCLAYCARD PREMIER DIVISION

Aston Villa	v	Man. Utd.	0-0	0-2	1-1	0-1	0-1	1-1
Blackburn	v	Arsenal	0-2	1-4	1-2	-	-	2-3
Charlton	v	Newcastle	-	-	2-2	-	2-0	1-1
Everton	v	West Ham	2-1	2-1	6-0	1-0	1-1	5-0
Fulham	v	Southampton	-	-	-	-	-	2-1
Leeds	v	Middlesbro	1-1	-	2-0	2-0	1-1	1-0
Man. City	v	Birmingham	1-0	0-1	-	1-0	-	3-0
Sunderland	v	Bolton	-	-	3-1	-	-	1-0
Tottenham	v	Liverpool	0-2	3-3	2-1	1-0	2-1	1-0
WBA	v	Chelsea	-	-	-	-	-	-

NATIONWIDE LEAGUE DIVISION I

Brighton	v	Nottm F.	-	-	-	-	-	-
Derby	v	Bradford	-	-	-	0-1	2-0	-
Gillingham	v	Rotherham	3-1	-	-	-	-	2-1
Grimsby	v	Watford	-	0-1	2-1	-	2-1	0-3
Leicester	v	Preston	-	-	-	-	-	-
Norwich	v	Coventry	-	-	-	-	-	2-0
Portsmouth	v	Wolves	0-2	3-2	1-0	2-3	3-1	2-3
Reading	v	Crystal Pal.	1-6	-	-	-	-	-
Sheff. Weds.	v	Ipswich	-	-	-	-	-	-
Stoke	v	Sheff. Utd.	0-4	2-2	-	-	-	-
Walsall	v	Burnley	1-3	0-0	3-1	-	-	1-0
Wimbledon	v	Millwall	-	-	-	-	-	2-2

NATIONWIDE LEAGUE DIVISION II

Blackpool	v	Plymouth	2-2	0-0	-	-	1-0	-
Brentford	v	Stockport	2-2	-	-	-	-	-
Bristol C.	v	Peterboro	2-0	-	-	-	2-1	1-0
Cheltenham	v	Northampton	-	-	-	2-1	-	-
Colchester	v	Huddersfield	-	-	-	-	-	3-3
Crewe	v	Port Vale	-	0-1	0-0	2-1	-	-
Mansfield	v	Swindon	-	-	-	-	-	-
Notts Co.	v	Chesterfield	0-0	-	2-0	1-0	-	1-1
Oldham	v	QPR	0-2	-	-	-	-	1-0
Tranmere	v	Cardiff	-	-	-	-	-	0-1
Wigan	v	Luton	-	1-1	1-3	1-0	2-1	-
Wycombe	v	Barnsley	-	-	-	-	-	-

NATIONWIDE LEAGUE DIVISION III

Cambridge U.	v	Kidderminstr	-	-	-	-	-	-
Darlington	v	Exeter	0-1	3-2	4-0	1-0	1-1	4-0
Hartlepool	v	Southend	-	-	2-4	1-2	1-0	5-1

Sponsored by Stan James

Leyton O.	v	Bristol R.	-	-	-	-	-	3-1
Lincoln	v	Wrexham	-	-	1-0	-	-	-
Macclesfield	v	Bury	-	-	-	-	-	-
Rochdale	v	Boston	-	-	-	-	-	-
Rushden & D	v	Hull	-	-	-	-	-	3-3
Shrewsbury	v	Oxford Utd	-	-	-	-	-	1-0
Swansea	v	Carlisle	0-1	-	1-1	1-0	-	0-0
Torquay	v	Scunthorpe	1-2	2-4	1-0	-	0-2	0-0
York	v	Bournemouth	1-2	0-1	0-1	-	-	-

BANK OF SCOTLAND SCOTTISH PREMIER DIVISION

Aberdeen	v	Dundee	-	-	2-2/1-2	0-2/0-1	0-2/0-2	0-0
Dundee Utd.	v	Livingston	-	-	-	-	-	0-0
Hearts	v	Celtic	2-2/1-2	1-2/1-1	2-1/2-4	1-2/1-0	2-4/0-3	0-1/1-4
Kilmarnock	v	Dunfermline	2-2/2-1	2-1/3-0	0-0/0-0	-	2-1/2-1	0-0
Partick	v	Hibernian	-	-	-	-	-	-
Rangers	v	Motherwell	5-0/0-2	2-2/1-0	2-1/2-1	4-1/6-2	2-0	3-0/3-0

BELL'S SCOTTISH FIRST DIVISION

Arbroath	v	Inv. CT	1-4/0-0	-	0-1/3-1	-	-	3-2/1-0
Ayr	v	Alloa	-	-	-	-	3-1/4-1	-
Clyde	v	Falkirk	-	-	-	-	3-1/0-3	1-1/2-3
Queen of Sth	v	St Mirren	-	-	-	-	-	-
Ross County	v	St Johnstone	-	-	-	-	-	-

BELL'S SCOTTISH SECOND DIVISION

Brechin	v	Stranraer	0-2/0-0	2-2/1-3	-	-	-	-
Cowdenbeath	v	Airdrie Utd.	-	-	-	-	-	-
Dumbarton	v	Berwick	1-0/2-2	1-4/0-2	0-0/1-1	2-1/0-2	-	-
Hamilton	v	Forfar	-	-	-	-	-	1-1/2-0
Stenhsmuir	v	Raith	-	-	-	-	-	-

BELL'S SCOTTISH THIRD DIVISION

East Fife	v	Albion	-	-	-	1-4/2-1	0-0/2-1	0-0/2-3
Elgin	v	Montrose	-	-	-	-	1-1/0-2	1-2/1-0
Morton	v	E. Stirling	-	-	-	-	-	-
New Member	v	Queen's Park	-	-	-	-	-	-
Stirling	v	Peterhead	-	-	-	-	-	2-1/0-2

TUESDAY 18TH MARCH 2003

NATIONWIDE LEAGUE DIVISION I

Bradford	v	Sheff. Weds.	-	-	-	1-1	-	0-2
Burnley	v	Leicester	-	-	-	-	-	-
Crystal Pal.	v	Wimbledon	-	0-3	-	-	3-1	4-0
Ipswich	v	Reading	5-2	1-0	-	-	-	-

Sponsored by Stan James

Millwall	v	Norwich	-	-	-	-	-	4-0
Preston	v	Walsall	2-0	0-0	1-0	-	-	1-1
Rotherham	v	Grimsby	-	-	-	-	-	1-1
Sheff. Utd.	v	Brighton	-	-	-	-	-	-
Watford	v	Gillingham	0-0	0-2	-	-	0-0	2-3
Wolves	v	Stoke	2-0	1-1	-	-	-	-

NATIONWIDE LEAGUE DIVISION II

Barnsley	v	Tranmere	3-0	-	1-1	3-0	1-1	-
Cardiff	v	Blackpool	-	-	-	1-1	1-1	2-2
Chesterfield	v	Colchester	-	-	3-1	0-1	-	3-6
Huddersfield	v	Mansfield	-	-	-	-	-	-
Luton	v	Oldham	-	1-1	2-0	1-1	0-0	-
Northampton	v	Notts Co.	-	-	1-1	-	1-0	0-2
Peterboro	v	Wycombe	6-3	-	-	-	3-2	2-1
Plymouth	v	Crewe	1-0	-	-	-	-	-
Port Vale	v	Brentford	-	-	-	-	1-1	2-1
QPR	v	Cheltenham	-	-	-	-	-	-
Stockport	v	Wigan	-	-	-	-	-	-

NATIONWIDE LEAGUE DIVISION III

Bournemouth	v	Leyton O.	-	-	-	-	-	-
Bristol R.	v	York	1-1	1-2	2-0	-	-	2-2
Bury	v	Rushden & D	-	-	-	-	-	-
Carlisle	v	Macclesfield	-	-	-	0-1	1-0	3-2
Exeter	v	Lincoln	3-3	1-2	-	3-0	0-0	1-1
Hull	v	Torquay	2-0	3-3	1-0	0-0	1-2	1-0
Kidderminstr	v	Shrewsbury	-	-	-	-	3-1	1-0
Oxford Utd	v	Cambridge U.	-	-	-	1-0	1-1	-
Scunthorpe	v	Rochdale	2-2	2-0	0-1	-	0-0	2-1
Southend	v	Swansea	-	-	2-0	2-1	-	4-2
Wrexham	v	Hartlepool	-	-	-	-	-	-

WEDNESDAY 19TH MARCH 2003

NATIONWIDE LEAGUE DIVISION I

Coventry	v	Portsmouth	-	-	-	-	-	2-0
Nottm F.	v	Derby	1-1	-	2-2	-	-	-

NATIONWIDE LEAGUE DIVISION II

Swindon	v	Bristol C.	-	-	3-2	-	1-1	1-2

NATIONWIDE LEAGUE DIVISION III

Boston	v	Darlington	-	-	-	-	-	-

Sponsored by Stan James

SATURDAY 22ND MARCH 2003

FA BARCLAYCARD PREMIER DIVISION

Arsenal	v	Everton	3-1	4-0	1-0	4-1	4-1	4-3
Birmingham	v	WBA	2-3	1-0	4-0	1-1	2-1	0-1
Bolton	v	Tottenham	-	1-1	-	-	-	1-1
Chelsea	v	Man. City	-	-	-	-	2-1	-
Liverpool	v	Leeds	4-0	3-1	1-3	3-1	1-2	1-1
Man. Utd.	v	Fulham	-	-	-	-	-	3-2
Middlesbro	v	Charlton	-	2-1	2-0	-	0-0	0-0
Newcastle	v	Blackburn	2-1	1-1	1-1	-	-	2-1
Southampton	v	Aston Villa	0-1	1-2	1-4	2-0	2-0	1-3
West Ham	v	Sunderland	2-0	-	-	1-1	0-2	3-0

NATIONWIDE LEAGUE DIVISION I

Bradford	v	Reading	0-0	4-1	-	-	-	-
Burnley	v	Grimsby	-	2-1	-	-	1-1	1-0
Coventry	v	Leicester	0-0	0-2	1-1	0-1	1-0	-
Crystal Pal.	v	Walsall	-	-	-	3-2	-	2-0
Ipswich	v	Brighton	-	-	-	-	-	-
Millwall	v	Sheff. Weds.	-	-	-	-	-	1-2
Nottm F.	v	Norwich	-	4-1	-	1-1	0-0	2-0
Preston	v	Portsmouth	-	-	-	-	1-0	2-0
Rotherham	v	Wimbledon	-	-	-	-	-	3-2
Sheff. Utd.	v	Derby	-	-	-	-	-	-
Watford	v	Stoke	-	-	-	-	-	-
Wolves	v	Gillingham	-	-	-	-	1-1	2-0

NATIONWIDE LEAGUE DIVISION II

Barnsley	v	Colchester	-	-	-	-	-	-
Cardiff	v	Mansfield	1-2	4-1	4-2	-	2-0	-
Chesterfield	v	Wycombe	4-2	1-0	2-0	1-2	-	0-1
Huddersfield	v	Bristol C.	-	-	2-2	-	-	1-0
Luton	v	Crewe	6-0	-	-	-	-	-
Northampton	v	Oldham	-	0-0	1-1	-	2-1	0-1
Peterboro	v	Tranmere	-	-	-	-	-	5-0
Plymouth	v	Brentford	1-4	0-0	3-0	-	-	-
Port Vale	v	Cheltenham	-	-	-	-	-	-
QPR	v	Wigan	-	-	-	-	-	1-1
Stockport	v	Blackpool	1-0	-	-	-	-	-
Swindon	v	Notts Co.	-	-	-	-	1-2	1-0

NATIONWIDE LEAGUE DIVISION III

Boston	v	Rushden & D	-	-	-	-	1-1	-
Bournemouth	v	Torquay	-	-	-	-	-	-
Bristol R.	v	Hartlepool	-	-	-	-	-	0-1

Sponsored by Stan James

Bury	v	Lincoln	-	-	-	-	-	-
Carlisle	v	Cambridge U.	3-0	-	1-1	-	-	-
Exeter	v	Rochdale	0-0	3-0	2-1	2-0	0-1	1-1
Hull	v	Shrewsbury	-	1-4	1-1	0-0	1-0	3-0
Kidderminstr	v	Swansea	-	-	-	-	-	0-2
Oxford Utd	v	Macclesfield	-	-	-	-	-	0-2
Scunthorpe	v	Darlington	3-2	1-0	0-1	-	1-1	7-1
Southend	v	Leyton O.	-	-	2-2	1-1	0-1	1-2
Wrexham	v	York	0-0	1-2	1-1	-	-	-

BELL'S SCOTTISH SECOND DIVISION

Berwick	v	Forfar	-	-	-	2-2/2-0	1-1/1-0	1-1/0-2
Brechin	v	Airdrie Utd.	-	-	-	-	-	-
Dumbarton	v	Stranraer	1-1/2-2	-	-	-	-	-
Raith	v	Hamilton	-	3-1/2-1	0-2/1-1	-	-	-
Stenhsmuir	v	Cowdenbeath	-	-	1-2/4-1	-	-	0-3/0-1

BELL'S SCOTTISH THIRD DIVISION

Elgin	v	Albion	-	-	-	-	1-2/1-0	2-0/0-0
Morton	v	Montrose	-	-	-	-	-	-
New Member	v	E. Stirling	-	-	-	-	-	-
Queen's Park	v	Peterhead	-	-	-	-	-	0-1/2-0
Stirling	v	East Fife	2-1/4-1	-	3-2/0-1	-	-	2-1/0-1

SATURDAY 29TH MARCH 2003

NATIONWIDE LEAGUE DIVISION I

Brighton	v	Crystal Pal.	-	-	-	-	-	-
Derby	v	Millwall	-	-	-	-	-	-
Gillingham	v	Ipswich	-	-	-	-	-	-
Grimsby	v	Wolves	1-3	-	0-0	1-0	0-2	1-1
Leicester	v	Nottm F.	2-2	-	3-1	-	-	-
Norwich	v	Bradford	2-0	2-3	2-2	-	-	1-4
Portsmouth	v	Burnley	-	-	-	-	2-0	1-1
Reading	v	Preston	-	-	2-1	2-2	-	-
Sheff. Weds.	v	Watford	-	-	-	2-2	2-3	2-1
Stoke	v	Rotherham	-	-	-	-	1-1	-
Walsall	v	Coventry	-	-	-	-	-	0-1
Wimbledon	v	Sheff. Utd.	-	-	-	-	0-0	1-1

NATIONWIDE LEAGUE DIVISION II

Blackpool	v	QPR	-	-	-	-	-	2-2
Brentford	v	Northampton	-	0-0	-	-	1-1	3-0
Bristol C.	v	Barnsley	-	-	1-1	-	-	-
Cheltenham	v	Luton	-	-	-	-	-	1-1
Colchester	v	Swindon	-	-	-	-	0-1	1-3

Sponsored by Stan James

Crewe	v	Stockport	1-0	0-1	0-2	3-2	1-2	0-0
Mansfield	v	Peterboro	-	2-0	1-0	3-1	-	-
Notts Co.	v	Huddersfield	-	-	-	-	-	2-1
Oldham	v	Port Vale	3-0	-	-	-	4-1	2-0
Tranmere	v	Chesterfield	-	-	-	-	-	0-0
Wigan	v	Plymouth	-	1-1	-	-	-	-
Wycombe	v	Cardiff	-	-	-	3-1	-	0-1

NATIONWIDE LEAGUE DIVISION III

Cambridge U.	v	Scunthorpe	0-2	2-2	0-0	1-3	-	-
Darlington	v	Bury	-	-	-	-	-	-
Hartlepool	v	Bournemouth	-	-	-	-	-	-
Leyton O.	v	Wrexham	-	-	-	-	-	-
Lincoln	v	Bristol R.	-	-	1-0	-	-	0-1
Macclesfield	v	Kidderminstr	0-1	-	-	-	1-0	0-1
Rochdale	v	Hull	1-2	2-1	3-0	0-2	1-0	3-2
Rushden & D	v	Exeter	-	-	-	-	-	2-1
Shrewsbury	v	Carlisle	-	-	1-1	4-1	0-1	1-0
Swansea	v	Oxford Utd	-	-	-	-	1-2	0-0
Torquay	v	Boston	-	-	-	-	-	-
York	v	Southend	-	1-1	-	2-2	1-0	2-1

SATURDAY 5TH APRIL 2003

FA BARCLAYCARD PREMIER DIVISION

Aston Villa	v	Arsenal	2-2	1-0	3-2	1-1	0-0	1-2
Bolton	v	Man. City	1-0	-	-	0-1	-	-
Charlton	v	Leeds	-	-	1-1	-	1-2	0-2
Everton	v	Newcastle	2-0	0-0	1-0	0-2	1-1	1-3
Fulham	v	Blackburn	-	-	-	2-2	2-1	2-0
Man. Utd.	v	Liverpool	1-0	1-1	2-0	1-1	0-1	0-1
Middlesbro	v	WBA	-	1-0	-	-	-	-
Southampton	v	West Ham	2-0	3-0	1-0	2-1	2-3	2-0
Sunderland	v	Chelsea	3-0	-	-	4-1	1-0	0-0
Tottenham	v	Birmingham	-	-	-	-	-	-

NATIONWIDE LEAGUE DIVISION I

Bradford	v	Millwall	-	-	-	-	-	1-2
Burnley	v	Watford	4-1	2-0	-	-	2-0	1-0
Crystal Pal.	v	Sheff. Utd.	0-1	-	1-0	1-1	0-1	0-1
Derby	v	Norwich	-	-	-	-	-	-
Ipswich	v	Nottm F.	-	0-1	-	3-1	-	-
Leicester	v	Grimsby	-	-	-	-	-	-
Preston	v	Coventry	-	-	-	-	-	4-0
Reading	v	Brighton	-	-	-	-	-	0-0

Match			C1	C2	C3	C4	C5	C6
Sheff. Weds.	v	Wimbledon	3-1	1-1	1-2	5-1	0-5	1-2
Stoke	v	Gillingham	-	-	0-0	1-1	-	-
Walsall	v	Portsmouth	-	-	-	1-0	-	0-0
Wolves	v	Rotherham	-	-	-	-	-	2-1

NATIONWIDE LEAGUE DIVISION II

Match			C1	C2	C3	C4	C5	C6
Brentford	v	Cheltenham	-	-	-	-	-	-
Cardiff	v	QPR	-	-	-	-	-	1-1
Crewe	v	Bristol C.	1-2	-	1-0	-	-	-
Huddersfield	v	Chesterfield	-	-	-	-	-	0-0
Luton	v	Tranmere	-	-	-	-	-	-
Mansfield	v	Port Vale	-	-	-	-	-	-
Northampton	v	Wigan	0-1	1-0	3-3	-	1-0	0-2
Notts Co.	v	Blackpool	1-1	-	0-1	2-1	-	1-0
Oldham	v	Barnsley	0-1	-	-	-	-	-
Peterboro	v	Swindon	-	-	-	-	4-0	1-1
Plymouth	v	Colchester	-	-	-	-	-	-
Wycombe	v	Stockport	0-2	-	-	-	-	-

NATIONWIDE LEAGUE DIVISION III

Match			C1	C2	C3	C4	C5	C6
Bristol R.	v	Rushden & D	-	-	-	-	-	0-3
Carlisle	v	York	-	1-2	-	0-1	1-1	2-1
Exeter	v	Bury	-	-	-	-	-	-
Hull	v	Wrexham	-	-	-	-	-	-
Kidderminstr	v	Hartlepool	-	-	-	-	0-1	3-2
Leyton O.	v	Boston	-	-	-	-	-	-
Lincoln	v	Oxford Utd	-	-	-	-	-	1-0
Macclesfield	v	Cambridge U.	-	3-1	-	-	-	-
Rochdale	v	Torquay	2-1	0-1	0-2	1-1	2-1	2-0
Scunthorpe	v	Bournemouth	-	-	-	3-1	-	-
Shrewsbury	v	Swansea	-	0-1	1-0	1-1	-	3-0
Southend	v	Darlington	-	-	2-1	1-2	0-2	1-0

BANK OF SCOTLAND SCOTTISH PREMIER DIVISION

Match			C1	C2	C3	C4	C5	C6
Dundee	v	Celtic	-	-	1-1/0-3	1-2/0-3	1-2	0-4/0-3
Dunfermline	v	Motherwell	1-1/3-1	0-2/2-1	1-1/1-2	-	1-2/1-2	5-2/3-1
Hearts	v	Dundee Utd.	1-0/1-2	2-1/2-0	0-1/4-1	3-0/1-2	3-1	1-2/1-2
Kilmarnock	v	Hibernian	4-2/1-1	2-1/1-1	-	0-2/1-0	0-1/1-1	0-0/1-0
Livingston	v	Aberdeen	-	-	-	-	-	2-2/0-0
Rangers	v	Partick	-	-	-	-	-	-

BELL'S SCOTTISH FIRST DIVISION

Match			C1	C2	C3	C4	C5	C6
Alloa	v	Clyde	-	-	3-0/1-0	1-0/2-1	3-1/0-0	-
Falkirk	v	Ross County	-	-	-	-	2-3/1-1	4-2/1-4
Inv. CT	v	Queen of Sth	-	2-1/0-2	3-2/1-0	-	-	-

Sponsored by Stan James

| St Johnstone | v | Ayr | - | - | - | - | - | - |
| St Mirren | v | Arbroath | - | - | - | - | - | 1-0/2-3 |

BELL'S SCOTTISH SECOND DIVISION

Airdrie Utd.	v	Raith	-	1-0/1-0	0-1/2-2	1-4/0-2	1-1/3-0	2-2/1-1
Cowdenbeath	v	Brechin	-	-	0-1/0-2	6-1/1-1	2-1/2-1	-
Forfar	v	Dumbarton	-	-	-	5-0/4-3	-	-
Hamilton	v	Stenhsmuir	0-2/1-1	-	-	1-1/2-1	-	2-3/0-0
Stranraer	v	Berwick	1-1/1-1	-	-	-	2-2/1-1	0-2/2-2

BELL'S SCOTTISH THIRD DIVISION

Albion	v	Morton	-	-	-	-	-	-
East Fife	v	Elgin	-	-	-	-	1-1/1-1	3-0/0-1
E. Stirling	v	Queen's Park	2-1/1-0	1-0/0-0	1-1/1-1	1-1/0-1	-	0-1/3-1
Montrose	v	Stirling	-	-	-	-	-	4-0/1-3
Peterhead	v	New Member	-	-	-	-	-	-

SATURDAY 12TH APRIL 2003

FA BARCLAYCARD PREMIER DIVISION

Arsenal	v	Southampton	3-1	3-0	1-1	3-1	1-0	1-1
Birmingham	v	Sunderland	-	0-1	0-0	-	-	-
Blackburn	v	Charlton	-	-	1-0	1-1	-	4-1
Chelsea	v	Bolton	-	2-0	-	-	-	5-1
Leeds	v	Tottenham	0-0	1-0	2-0	1-0	4-3	2-1
Liverpool	v	Fulham	-	-	-	-	-	0-0
Man. City	v	Middlesbro	-	2-0	-	-	1-1	-
Newcastle	v	Man. Utd.	5-0	0-1	1-2	3-0	1-1	4-3
WBA	v	Everton	-	-	-	-	-	-
West Ham	v	Aston Villa	0-2	2-1	0-0	1-1	1-1	1-1

NATIONWIDE LEAGUE DIVISION I

Brighton	v	Preston	-	-	-	-	-	-
Coventry	v	Ipswich	-	-	-	-	0-1	-
Gillingham	v	Walsall	2-0	2-1	0-1	-	-	2-0
Grimsby	v	Crystal Pal.	2-1	-	2-0	1-0	2-2	5-2
Millwall	v	Stoke	-	-	2-0	1-0	2-0	-
Norwich	v	Burnley	-	-	-	-	2-3	2-1
Nottm F.	v	Wolves	-	3-0	-	1-1	0-0	2-2
Portsmouth	v	Sheff. Weds.	-	-	-	-	2-1	0-0
Rotherham	v	Leicester	-	-	-	-	-	-
Sheff. Utd.	v	Bradford	3-0	2-1	2-2	-	-	2-2
Watford	v	Reading	-	-	-	-	-	-
Wimbledon	v	Derby	1-1	0-0	2-1	2-2	-	-

Sponsored by Stan James

NATIONWIDE LEAGUE DIVISION II

Barnsley	v	Peterboro	-	-	-	-	-	-
Blackpool	v	Crewe	1-2	-	-	-	-	-
Bristol C.	v	Mansfield	-	-	-	-	-	-
Cheltenham	v	Oldham	-	-	-	-	-	-
Chesterfield	v	Cardiff	-	-	-	1-1	2-2	0-2
Colchester	v	Notts Co.	-	2-0	2-1	0-3	2-0	0-1
Port Vale	v	Northampton	-	-	-	-	2-2	0-1
QPR	v	Luton	-	-	-	-	-	-
Stockport	v	Plymouth	3-1	-	-	-	-	-
Swindon	v	Huddersfield	6-0	1-1	3-0	2-0	-	0-1
Tranmere	v	Wycombe	-	-	-	-	-	1-1
Wigan	v	Brentford	-	4-0	-	1-0	1-3	1-1

NATIONWIDE LEAGUE DIVISION III

Boston	v	Hull	-	-	-	-	-	-
Bournemouth	v	Southend	-	2-1	-	-	-	-
Bury	v	Carlisle	-	-	-	-	-	-
Cambridge U.	v	Exeter	3-2	2-1	1-1	-	-	-
Darlington	v	Shrewsbury	-	3-1	1-0	2-2	3-0	3-3
Hartlepool	v	Leyton O.	3-1	2-2	1-0	1-0	2-1	3-1
Oxford Utd	v	Kidderminstr	-	-	-	-	-	1-1
Rushden & D	v	Lincoln	-	-	-	-	-	0-0
Swansea	v	Scunthorpe	1-1	2-0	1-2	-	-	2-2
Torquay	v	Macclesfield	-	2-0	-	3-2	2-0	1-2
Wrexham	v	Bristol R.	1-0	1-0	1-0	2-1	1-0	-
York	v	Rochdale	-	-	-	0-3	0-2	0-0

BANK OF SCOTLAND SCOTTISH PREMIER DIVISION

Aberdeen	v	Dunfermline	3-0/0-2	1-2/2-0	2-1/3-1	-	0-0/1-0	3-2/1-0
Celtic	v	Kilmarnock	6-0/0-0	4-0/4-0	1-1/1-0	5-1/4-2	2-1/6-0	1-0
Dundee Utd.	v	Rangers	1-0/0-1	2-1/1-2	0-0/1-2	0-4/0-2	1-1	1-6/0-1
Hibernian	v	Livingston	-	-	-	-	-	0-3
Motherwell	v	Dundee	-	-	2-1/1-2	0-2/0-3	0-2/0-3	4-2/2-1
Partick	v	Hearts	-	-	-	-	-	-

BELL'S SCOTTISH FIRST DIVISION

Alloa	v	Ross County	1-3/1-1	1-0/1-1	-	2-0/1-2	0-0/1-1	-
Arbroath	v	Queen of Sth	-	-	2-1/0-2	5-2/1-2	2-0/5-2	-
Inv. CT	v	Clyde	-	1-2/5-1	1-1/3-0	-	1-2/2-2	5-1/1-1
St Johnstone	v	Falkirk	0-0/3-1	-	-	-	-	-
St Mirren	v	Ayr	-	1-1/3-0	0-2/1-0	1-1/1-2	-	0-1/1-1

BELL'S SCOTTISH SECOND DIVISION

Berwick	v	Airdrie Utd.	-	-	-	-	-	-
Dumbarton	v	Cowdenbeath	-	1-2/2-3	5-0/6-1	1-1/2-0	2-4/3-0	-

Sponsored by Stan James

Raith	v	Forfar	-	-	-	-	-
Stenhsmuir	v	Brechin	0-0/3-1	3-2/3-1	0-1/1-0	-	-
Stranraer	v	Hamilton	0-3/0-1	-	2-1/2-2	0-2/2-2	-	2-1/3-2

BELL'S SCOTTISH THIRD DIVISION

E. Stirling	v	Peterhead	-	-	-	1-3/1-0	2-3/1-0
Morton	v	Elgin	-	-	-	-	-
Montrose	v	Albion	2-1/0-4	1-2/1-3	1-2/2-3	2-1/1-2	0-2/0-1	1-2/2-0
New Member	v	East Fife	-	-	-	-	-
Queen's Park	v	Stirling	-	-	-	3-0/1-1	2-2/0-0

SATURDAY 19TH APRIL 2003

FA BARCLAYCARD PREMIER DIVISION

Aston Villa	v	Chelsea	0-2	0-2	0-3	0-0	1-1	1-1
Bolton	v	West Ham	-	1-1	-	-	-	1-0
Charlton	v	Birmingham	2-1	1-1	-	1-0	-	-
Everton	v	Liverpool	1-1	2-0	0-0	0-0	2-3	1-3
Fulham	v	Newcastle	-	-	-	-	-	3-1
Man. Utd.	v	Blackburn	2-2	4-0	3-2	-	-	2-1
Middlesbro	v	Arsenal	0-2	-	1-6	2-1	0-1	0-4
Southampton	v	Leeds	0-2	0-2	3-0	0-3	1-0	0-1
Sunderland	v	WBA	-	2-0	3-0	-	-	-
Tottenham	v	Man. City	-	-	-	-	0-0	-

NATIONWIDE LEAGUE DIVISION I

Bradford	v	Watford	-	-	2-0	3-2	-	4-3
Burnley	v	Gillingham	5-1	0-0	0-5	0-3	1-1	2-0
Crystal Pal.	v	Rotherham	-	-	-	-	-	2-0
Derby	v	Coventry	2-1	3-1	0-0	0-0	1-0	-
Ipswich	v	Portsmouth	1-1	2-0	3-0	0-1	-	-
Leicester	v	Brighton	-	-	-	-	-	-
Preston	v	Sheff. Utd.	-	-	-	-	3-0	3-0
Reading	v	Nottm F.	-	3-3	-	-	-	-
Sheff. Weds.	v	Grimsby	-	-	-	-	1-0	0-0
Stoke	v	Wimbledon	-	-	-	-	-	-
Walsall	v	Norwich	-	-	-	2-2	-	2-0
Wolves	v	Millwall	-	-	-	-	-	1-0

NATIONWIDE LEAGUE DIVISION II

Brentford	v	QPR	-	-	-	-	-	0-0
Cardiff	v	Colchester	1-2	0-2	-	3-2	-	1-1
Crewe	v	Swindon	-	2-0	0-2	2-1	-	-
Huddersfield	v	Wigan	-	-	-	-	-	0-0
Luton	v	Bristol C.	2-2	0-0	-	1-2	0-3	-
Mansfield	v	Barnsley	-	-	-	-	-	-
Northampton	v	Stockport	-	-	-	-	-	-
Notts Co.	v	Tranmere	-	-	-	-	-	3-0

Sponsored by Stan James

Oldham	v	Chesterfield	-	2-0	2-0	1-2	-	1-1
Peterboro	v	Blackpool	0-0	-	-	-	-	3-2
Plymouth	v	Port Vale	-	-	-	-	-	-
Wycombe	v	Cheltenham	-	-	-	-	-	-

NATIONWIDE LEAGUE DIVISION III

Bristol R.	v	Cambridge U.	-	-	-	1-0	2-1	-
Carlisle	v	Rushden & D	-	-	-	-	-	3-0
Exeter	v	Oxford Utd	-	-	-	-	-	3-2
Hull	v	Bournemouth	-	-	-	-	-	-
Kidderminstr	v	Wrexham	-	-	-	-	-	-
Leyton O.	v	Swansea	1-0	2-2	1-1	0-1	-	2-2
Lincoln	v	York	-	-	1-2	4-2	2-1	1-3
Macclesfield	v	Darlington	-	2-1	-	2-1	1-1	1-1
Rochdale	v	Bury	-	-	-	-	-	-
Scunthorpe	v	Hartlepool	2-1	1-1	1-0	-	3-0	1-0
Shrewsbury	v	Boston	-	-	-	-	-	-
Southend	v	Torquay	-	-	0-0	0-2	1-1	1-1

BELL'S SCOTTISH FIRST DIVISION

Ayr	v	Inv. CT	-	-	-	1-0/1-3	3-3/1-1	3-0/1-0
Clyde	v	St Johnstone	-	-	-	-	-	-
Falkirk	v	Arbroath	-	-	-	-	-	3-2/1-3
Queen of Sth	v	Alloa	-	-	2-1/0-0	1-1/2-1	-	2-1/0-1
Ross County	v	St Mirren	-	-	-	-	-	0-1/4-1

BELL'S SCOTTISH SECOND DIVISION

Airdrie Utd.	v	Stenhsmuir	-	-	-	-	-	-
Brechin	v	Raith	-	-	-	-	-	-
Cowdenbeath	v	Berwick	-	0-2/1-0	1-1/1-2	1-1/1-3	-	2-1/1-1
Forfar	v	Stranraer	-	3-1/2-1	-	-	0-0/2-3	1-1/3-2
Hamilton	v	Dumbarton	2-0/4-0	-	-	-	2-0/2-0	-

BELL'S SCOTTISH THIRD DIVISION

Albion	v	Queen's Park	1-1/2-1	0-0/1-2	2-1/1-0	2-4/0-3	-	2-1/2-0
East Fife	v	Morton	0-3/1-4	-	-	-	-	-
Elgin	v	E. Stirling	-	-	-	-	1-2/4-2	2-1/2-2
Peterhead	v	Montrose	-	-	-	-	2-0/1-1	4-0/3-1
Stirling	v	New Member	-	-	-	-	-	-

MONDAY 21ST APRIL 2003

FA BARCLAYCARD PREMIER DIVISION

Arsenal	v	Man. Utd.	1-2	3-2	3-0	1-2	1-0	3-1
Birmingham	v	Southampton	-	-	-	-	-	-
Blackburn	v	Bolton	-	3-1	-	3-1	1-1	1-1
Chelsea	v	Everton	2-2	2-0	3-1	1-1	2-1	3-0
Leeds	v	Fulham	-	-	-	-	-	0-1
Liverpool	v	Charlton	-	-	3-3	-	3-0	2-0

Sponsored by Stan James

Man. City	v	Sunderland	-	0-1	-	-	4-2	-
Newcastle	v	Aston Villa	4-3	1-0	2-1	0-1	3-0	3-0
WBA	v	Tottenham	-	-	-	-	-	-
West Ham	v	Middlesbro	0-0	-	4-0	0-1	1-0	1-0

NATIONWIDE LEAGUE DIVISION I

Brighton	v	Sheff. Weds.	-	-	-	-	-	
Coventry	v	Stoke	-	-	-	-	-	-
Gillingham	v	Bradford	-	-	-	-		0-4
Grimsby	v	Walsall	-	3-0	-	1-0	-	2-2
Millwall	v	Crystal Pal.	-	-	-	-		3-0
Norwich	v	Wolves	1-0	0-2	0-0	1-0	1-0	2-0
Nottm F.	v	Burnley	-	-	-	-	5-0	1-0
Portsmouth	v	Reading	1-0	0-2	-	-	-	-
Rotherham	v	Ipswich	-	-	-	-	-	-
Sheff. Utd.	v	Leicester	-	-	-	-	-	-
Watford	v	Derby	-	-	-	0-0	-	-
Wimbledon	v	Preston	-	-	-	-	3-1	2-0

NATIONWIDE LEAGUE DIVISION II

Barnsley	v	Crewe	-	-	2-2	0-2	3-0	2-0
Blackpool	v	Mansfield	-	-	-	-	2-2	-
Bristol C.	v	Cardiff	-	-	-	0-0	-	1-1
Cheltenham	v	Peterboro	-	-	-	2-1	-	-
Chesterfield	v	Brentford	0-2	0-0	-	1-0	-	0-1
Colchester	v	Luton	-	-	2-2	3-0	3-1	-
Port Vale	v	Wycombe	-	-	-	-	0-1	1-1
QPR	v	Notts Co.	-	-	-	-	-	3-2
Stockport	v	Huddersfield	-	3-0	1-1	1-1	0-0	-
Swindon	v	Plymouth	-	-	-	-	-	-
Tranmere	v	Northampton	-	-	-	-	-	2-0
Wigan	v	Oldham	-	1-0	2-0	0-1	3-1	1-0

NATIONWIDE LEAGUE DIVISION III

Boston	v	Southend	-	-	-	-	-	-
Bournemouth	v	Shrewsbury	0-0	-	-	-	-	-
Bury	v	Scunthorpe	-	-	-	3-0	-	-
Cambridge U.	v	Lincoln	1-3	1-1	-	-	-	-
Darlington	v	Hull	1-0	4-3	0-1	0-0	0-2	0-1
Hartlepool	v	Rochdale	1-2	2-0	0-1	3-2	1-1	1-1
Oxford Utd	v	Bristol R.	-	-	-	0-5	0-1	0-0
Rushden & D	v	Macclesfield	1-1	-	-	-	-	2-0
Swansea	v	Exeter	3-1	2-1	2-0	3-0	-	4-2
Torquay	v	Leyton O.	0-0	1-1	1-1	0-0	1-2	1-1
Wrexham	v	Carlisle	-	2-2	-	-	-	-
York	v	Kidderminstr	-	-	-	-	1-0	0-1

Sponsored by Stan James

SATURDAY 26TH APRIL 2003

FA BARCLAYCARD PREMIER DIVISION

Birmingham	v	Middlesbro	-	1-1	-	-	-	-
Bolton	v	Arsenal	-	0-1	-	-	-	0-2
Charlton	v	Southampton	-	-	5-0	-	1-1	1-1
Chelsea	v	Fulham	-	-	-	-	-	3-2
Everton	v	Aston Villa	0-1	1-4	0-0	0-0	0-1	3-2
Leeds	v	Blackburn	0-0	4-0	1-0	-	-	3-1
Man. City	v	West Ham	-	-	-	-	1-0	-
Sunderland	v	Newcastle	1-2	-	-	2-2	1-1	0-1
Tottenham	v	Man. Utd.	1-2	0-2	2-2	3-1	3-1	3-5
WBA	v	Liverpool	-	-	-	-	-	

NATIONWIDE LEAGUE DIVISION I

Brighton	v	Watford	-	-	-	-	-	-
Burnley	v	Sheff. Weds.	-	-	-	-	1-0	1-2
Coventry	v	Gillingham	-	-	-	-	-	1-2
Crystal Pal.	v	Stoke	2-0	-	-	-	-	-
Ipswich	v	Wimbledon	-	-	-	-	-	-
Leicester	v	Norwich	-	-	-	-	-	-
Nottm F.	v	Millwall	-	-	-	-	-	1-2
Portsmouth	v	Rotherham	-	-	-	-	-	0-0
Preston	v	Bradford	-	-	-	-	-	1-1
Reading	v	Grimsby	1-1	-	-	-	-	-
Sheff. Utd.	v	Wolves	2-3	1-0	1-1	3-0	1-0	2-2
Walsall	v	Derby	-	-	-	-	-	

NATIONWIDE LEAGUE DIVISION II

Barnsley	v	Brentford	-	-	-	-	-	-
Cardiff	v	Wigan	0-2	-	-	0-0	-	2-2
Cheltenham	v	Blackpool	-	-	-	-	0-1	-
Chesterfield	v	Bristol C.	1-1	1-0	-	0-2	-	2-1
Luton	v	Stockport	1-1	-	-	-	-	-
Northampton	v	Plymouth	-	2-1	-	1-1	-	-
Oldham	v	Swindon	5-1	-	-	-	1-0	2-0
Peterboro	v	Notts Co.	1-3	1-0	-	-	1-0	0-1
Port Vale	v	Huddersfield	0-0	4-1	2-0	1-2	-	1-1
QPR	v	Crewe	-	3-2	0-1	1-0	1-0	-
Tranmere	v	Mansfield	-	-	-	-	-	-
Wycombe	v	Colchester	-	-	2-2	3-0	1-1	0-0

NATIONWIDE LEAGUE DIVISION III

Boston	v	Macclesfield	-	-	-	-	-	-
Bournemouth	v	Lincoln	-	-	2-0	-	-	-
Bristol R.	v	Darlington	-	-	-	-	-	1-0
Hartlepool	v	Shrewsbury	-	2-1	1-1	1-0	1-3	2-2
Hull	v	Kidderminstr	-	-	-	-	0-0	2-1

Sponsored by Stan James

Leyton O.	v	Rushden & D	-	-	-	-	-	2-1
Rochdale	v	Swansea	2-3	3-0	0-3	0-0	-	2-0
Scunthorpe	v	Oxford Utd	-	-	-	1-0	-	1-0
Southend	v	Bury	-	-	-	-	-	-
Torquay	v	Carlisle	1-2	-	2-2	4-1	4-2	2-1
Wrexham	v	Cambridge U.	-	-	-	1-1	2-2	5-0
York	v	Exeter	-	-	-	0-0	0-3	2-3

BELL'S SCOTTISH FIRST DIVISION

Alloa	v	Inv. CT	0-2/1-0	-	1-1/1-4	-	1-4/1-1	-
Clyde	v	Queen of Sth	0-2/2-1	0-0/3-1	2-0/2-1	3-0/3-1	-	-
Falkirk	v	Ayr	-	2-1/4-0	1-0/3-0	2-1/1-0	3-0/1-2	1-2/0-2
Ross County	v	Arbroath	2-0/1-0	0-0/1-0	-	2-0/1-1	-	0-2/0-1
St Johnstone	v	St Mirren	4-0/1-0	-	-	-	2-0/2-2	

BELL'S SCOTTISH SECOND DIVISION

Berwick	v	Brechin	0-0/1-0	-	3-0/2-3	2-0/3-1	-	
Dumbarton	v	Stenhsmuir	1-1/0-2	-	0-2/1-4	-	-	
Forfar	v	Airdrie Utd.	-	-	-	-	-	
Hamilton	v	Cowdenbeath	-	-	-	-	0-0/0-0	1-0/0-2
Stranraer	v	Raith	-	-	2-2/2-0	-	-	

BELL'S SCOTTISH THIRD DIVISION

Albion	v	Stirling	-	-	-	-	-	1-3/2-0
East Fife	v	Peterhead	-	-	-	-	1-1/2-1	0-1/2-3
Elgin	v	Queen's Park	-	-	-	-	-	2-0/0-1
Morton	v	New Member	-	-	-	-	-	-
Montrose	v	E. Stirling	1-0/0-2	1-1/1-1	2-0/1-0	1-2/0-0	0-1/1-1	2-0/2-0

SATURDAY 3RD MAY 2003

FA BARCLAYCARD PREMIER DIVISION

Arsenal	v	Leeds	3-0	2-1	3-1	2-0	2-1	1-2
Aston Villa	v	Sunderland	1-0	-	-	1-1	0-0	0-0
Blackburn	v	WBA	-	-	-	2-1	1-0	-
Fulham	v	Everton	-	-	-	-	-	2-0
Liverpool	v	Man. City	-	-	-	-	3-2	-
Man. Utd.	v	Charlton	-	-	4-1	-	2-1	0-0
Middlesbro	v	Tottenham	0-3	-	0-0	2-1	1-1	1-1
Newcastle	v	Birmingham	-	-	-	-	-	-
Southampton	v	Bolton	-	0-1	-	-	-	0-0
West Ham	v	Chelsea	3-2	2-1	1-1	0-0	0-2	2-1

NATIONWIDE LEAGUE DIVISION II

Blackpool	v	Chesterfield	0-1	2-1	1-1	2-2	1-3	1-0
Brentford	v	Peterboro	0-1	-	3-0	-	1-0	2-1
Bristol C.	v	Port Vale	-	-	2-0	-	1-1	1-1
Colchester	v	QPR	-	-	-	-	-	3-1
Crewe	v	Cardiff	-	-	-	-	-	-

Sponsored by Stan James

Huddersfield	v	Oldham	3-2	-	-	-	-	0-0
Mansfield	v	Northampton	1-0	-	-	0-0	-	-
Notts Co.	v	Cheltenham	-	-	-	-	-	-
Plymouth	v	Wycombe	0-0	4-2	-	-	-	-
Stockport	v	Tranmere	-	3-1	0-0	2-1	1-1	-
Swindon	v	Luton	-	-	-	-	1-3	-
Wigan	v	Barnsley	-	-	-	-	-	-

NATIONWIDE LEAGUE DIVISION III

Bury	v	Wrexham	0-0	-	-	0-2	1-4	2-2
Cambridge U.	v	Boston	-	-	-	-	-	-
Carlisle	v	Bournemouth	-	0-1	-	-	-	-
Darlington	v	Leyton O.	1-1	1-0	1-1	3-1	1-1	3-0
Exeter	v	Southend	-	-	2-1	0-1	2-2	2-1
Kidderminstr	v	Bristol R.	-	-	-	-	-	2-0
Lincoln	v	Torquay	1-2	1-1	-	2-1	1-2	0-0
Macclesfield	v	Rochdale	-	1-0	-	1-2	0-0	0-1
Oxford Utd	v	York	-	-	-	-	-	2-2
Rushden & D	v	Hartlepool	-	-	-	-	-	2-1
Shrewsbury	v	Scunthorpe	-	0-2	2-1	-	0-2	2-2
Swansea	v	Hull	0-0	2-0	2-0	0-0	-	1-0

BELL'S SCOTTISH FIRST DIVISION

Arbroath	v	Alloa	0-2/1-2	2-3/3-0	0-2/1-2	2-2/2-0	-	-
Ayr	v	Clyde	2-4/3-1	-	-	-	2-1/2-0	2-1/0-1
Inv. CT	v	St Johnstone	-	-	-	-	-	-
Queen of Sth	v	Ross County	-	-	-	0-2/0-3	-	-
St Mirren	v	Falkirk	0-1/1-0	2-0/1-2	0-2/0-3	2-1/1-0	-	1-5/0-0

BELL'S SCOTTISH SECOND DIVISION

Airdrie Utd.	v	Hamilton	-	0-0/3-2	3-2/1-0	-	-	-
Brechin	v	Dumbarton	2-1/0-3	-	0-0/3-3	0-2/1-2	3-1/1-0	3-2/0-1
Cowdenbeath	v	Stranraer	-	-	-	-	-	2-2/1-1
Raith	v	Berwick	-	-	-	-	-	-
Stenhsmuir	v	Forfar	-	1-4/2-2	-	-	2-0/0-1	1-1/0-0

BELL'S SCOTTISH THIRD DIVISION

E. Stirling	v	East Fife	-	-	-	0-2/1-0	2-5/1-0	2-1/1-2
New Member	v	Elgin	-	-	-	-	-	-
Peterhead	v	Albion	-	-	-	-	1-2/1-1	0-0/0-2
Queen's Park	v	Montrose	0-2/0-1	1-1/0-2	3-0/1-2	2-1/1-1	-	2-2/0-1
Stirling	v	Morton	1-3/4-3	1-3/2-2	-	-	-	-

SUNDAY 4TH MAY 2003

NATIONWIDE LEAGUE DIVISION I

Bradford	v	Portsmouth	3-1	1-3	2-1	-	-	3-1
Derby	v	Ipswich	-	-	-	-	1-1	1-3
Gillingham	v	Crystal Pal.	-	-	-	-	4-1	3-0

Sponsored by Stan James

			1	2	3	4	5	6
Grimsby	v	Brighton	-	-	-	-		-
Millwall	v	Coventry	-	-	-	-		3-2
Norwich	v	Preston	-	-	-	-	1-2	3-0
Rotherham	v	Nottm F.	-	-	-	-		1-2
Sheff. Weds.	v	Walsall	-	-	-	-		2-1
Stoke	v	Reading	1-1	1-2	0-4	2-1	0-0	2-0
Watford	v	Sheff. Utd.	-	-	1-1	-	4-1	0-3
Wimbledon	v	Burnley	-	-	-	-	0-2	0-0
Wolves	v	Leicester	-	-	-	-	-	-

SATURDAY 10TH MAY 2003

BELL'S SCOTTISH FIRST DIVISION

			1	2	3	4	5	6
Alloa	v	St Mirren	-		-	-	-	-
Clyde	v	Arbroath	-	-	3-0/1-1	0-0/4-1	-	1-0/1-0
Falkirk	v	Inv. CT	-	-	-	0-2/2-2	2-2/2-1	1-2/0-0
Ross County	v	Ayr	-	-	-	-	1-1/0-1	3-2/1-1
St Johnstone	v	Queen of Sth	-	-	-	-	-	-

BELL'S SCOTTISH SECOND DIVISION

			1	2	3	4	5	6
Berwick	v	Stenhsmuir	0-6/1-0	-	1-2/2-1	-	4-1/1-0	1-1/2-1
Dumbarton	v	Raith	-	-	-	-	-	-
Forfar	v	Cowdenbeath	2-5/3-0	-	-	3-1/2-2	-	2-1/0-0
Hamilton	v	Brechin	5-1/4-0	-	-	-	4-1/1-0	-
Stranraer	v	Airdrie Utd.	-	-	1-2/1-2	-	-	-

BELL'S SCOTTISH THIRD DIVISION

			1	2	3	4	5	6
Albion	v	E. Stirling	4-3/1-1	5-1/3-2	3-1/0-2	1-1/0-1	2-1/2-2	0-4/5-1
East Fife	v	Queen's Park	-	-	-	0-0/0-0	-	1-4/0-3
Elgin	v	Stirling	-	-	-	-	-	2-3/2-1
Morton	v	Peterhead	-	-	-	-	-	-
Montrose	v	New Member	-	-	-	-	-	-

SUNDAY 11TH MAY 2003

FA BARCLAYCARD PREMIER DIVISION

			1	2	3	4	5	6
Birmingham	v	West Ham	-	-	-	-	-	-
Bolton	v	Middlesbro	-	-	-	-	-	1-0
Charlton	v	Fulham	-	-	-	1-0	-	1-1
Chelsea	v	Liverpool	1-0	4-1	2-1	2-0	3-0	4-0
Everton	v	Man. Utd.	0-2	0-2	1-4	1-1	1-3	0-2
Leeds	v	Aston Villa	0-0	1-1	0-0	1-2	1-2	1-1
Man. City	v	Southampton	-	-	-	-	0-1	-
Sunderland	v	Arsenal	1-0	-	-	0-0	1-0	1-1
Tottenham	v	Blackburn	2-1	0-0	2-1	-	-	1-0
WBA	v	Newcastle	-	-	-	-	-	-

Sponsored by Stan James

FA Barclaycard Premiership

Champions: Arsenal
Runners-up: Liverpool

Relegated: Ipswich
Derby
Leicester

Nationwide First Division

Champions: Man City
Runners-up: West Brom

Play-off champions:
Birmingham

Relegated: Crewe
Barnsley
Stockport

Nationwide Second Division

Champions: Brighton
Runners-up: Reading

Play-off champions:
Stoke

Relegated: Bournemouth
Bury
Wrexham
Cambridge Utd

Nationwide Third Division

Champions: Plymouth
Runners-up: Luton
Third: Mansfield
Play-off champions:
Cheltenham
Relegated from league:
Halifax

Bank of Scotland Premier League

Champions: Celtic
Runners-up: Rangers
Relegated: St Johnstone

Bell's Scottish First Division

Champions: Partick
Runners-up: Airdrie

Relegated: Raith

Bell's Scottish Second Division

Champions: Queen Of South
Runners-up Alloa

Relegated: Morton

Sponsored by Stan James

Bell's Scottish Third Division

Champions: Brechin
Runners-up: Dumbarton

Nationwide Conference

Champions: Boston Utd
Runners-up: Dagenham & Red
Bottom of table: Dover

Dr Martens Premier

Champions: Kettering
Runners-up: Tamworth
Bottom of table: Salisbury

Unibond Premier

Champions: Burton
Runners-up: Vauxhall M.
Bottom of table: Bamber Br.

Ryman Premier

Champions: Gravesend
Runners-up: Canvey Island
Bottom of table: Croydon

AXA FA Cup

Champions: Arsenal
Runners-up: Chelsea

Worthington Cup

Champions: Blackburn
Runners-up: Tottenham

LDV Vans Trophy

Champions: Blackpool
Runners-up: Cambridge Utd

Scotttish FA Cup

Champions: Rangers
Runners-up: Celtic

CIS Insurance Cup

Champions: Rangers
Runners-up: Ayr Utd

LIVE ON SKY SPORTS

August			kick-off
Sun 19	Man Utd	Fulham	16:00
Sun18	Arsenal	Birmingham	16.05
Sun18	Aston Villa	Liverpool	14.00
Aug 19	Newcastle	West Ham Utd	20.00
Aug 23	Chelsea	Manchester Utd	20.00
Aug 24	Man City	Newcastle	12.15
	WBA	Leeds Utd	17.30
Aug 27	Arsenal	WBA	20.00
Aug 28	Fulham	West Ham	20.00
September			
Sun 1	Bolton	Aston Villa	14.00
	Chelsea	Arsenal	16.05
Mon 2	Liverpool	Newcastle	20.00
Tue 3	Man Utd	Middlesbrough	20.00
Tue 10	Arsenal	Manchester City	20.00
Wed 11	Newcastle	Leeds Utd	20.00
Sat14	Leeds	Manchester Utd	12.00
Sun 15	Man City	Blackburn	14.00
	Birmingham	Aston Villa	16.00
Mon 16	Tottenham	West Ham	20.00
Sun 22	Newcastle	Sunderland	16.00
	Aston Villa	Everton	14.00
Mon 23	Fulham	Chelsea	20.00
Sat 28	Leeds	Arsenal	12.00
	Birmingham	Newcastle	17.30
Mon 30	WBA	Blackburn	20.00
October			
Sun 6	Arsenal	Sunderland	14.00
	Liverpool	Chelsea	16.05
Mon 7	Man Utd	Everton	20.00
Sat 19	Leeds Utd	Liverpool	12 00
Sun 20	Charlton	Middlesbrough	16.05
Mon 21	Aston Villa	Southampton	20.00
Sun 27	Southampton	Fulham	14.00
	West Ham	Everton	16.00
Mon 28	Bolton	Sunderland	20.00

Sponsored by Stan James

November			kick-off
Sun 3	Tottenham	Chelsea	14.00
	Charlton	Sunderland	16.05
Mon 4	Newcastle	Middlesbrough	20.00
Sat 9	Man City	Man Utd	12.15
Sun 10	Sunderland	Tottenham	16.05
Sun 17	West Ham	Manchester Utd	16.05
Sat 23	Man Utd	Newcastle	12.15
Sun 24	Charlton	Blackburn	16.05
December			
Sun1	Liverpool	Manchester Utd	12.15
Mon 2	West Ham	Southampton	20.00
Sat 7	Man Utd	Arsenal	12.15
Sun 8	Tottenham	West Brom	16.05
Sun 15	Sunderland	Liverpool	16.05
Mon 16	Bolton	Leeds	20.00
Sun 22	Liverpool	Everton	16.05
Mon 23	Man City	Tottenham	20.00
Thu 26	Middlesbrough	Man Utd	16.00
Sun 29	Arsenal	Liverpool	16.05

A GAME OF TWO HALVES: Expert post match analysis

Sponsored by Stan James

ARSENAL

Nickname: The Gunners
Colours: Red and White
Ground: Highbury

Capacity: 38,500
Tel: 020 7704 4000 Web: www.arsenal.co.uk

THE stats astonish. The only time in 48 League/Cup games they failed to score was when the reserves lost a Worthington tie – the only domestic away game they lost.

The Gunners won 17 of their last 18 with clean sheets in 11 of the last 15. Still, after their 1998 double, they spent just £1.6 million and then won nothing. Now, to replace Adams, they have spent £5.5m on Pascal Cygan, the Lille centre-back who impressed Wenger in the Champions League.

Problems? With £125m needed for the new stadium, there's little cash to splash. Ljungberg and Pires, who contributed the most assists (15), will miss the start. How demoralised will Vieira, Wiltord and Henry remain after the French World Cup disaster, and Seaman after his cat flap?

Longest run without loss: 28
Longest run without win: 3

Figaro's forecast: 3rd

Your forecast:

2001/02 Premiership Stats			
	Apps	Gls	YC	RC
T Adams	10 (0)	0		
D Seaman	17 (0)	0	0	0
L Dixon	3 (10)	0	0	0
A Cole	29 (0)	2	6	0
P Vieira	35 (1)	2	10	1
M Keown	21 (1)	0	4	1
T Adams	10 (0)	0	1	0
R Pires	27 (1)	9	6	0
F Ljungberg	24 (1)	12	4	0
F Jeffers	2 (4)	2	1	0
D Bergkamp	22 (11)	9	2	0
S Wiltord	23 (10)	10	0	0
Lauren	27 (0)	2	8	0
S Taylor	9 (1)	0	1	0
T Henry	31 (2)	24	4	0
R Parlour	25 (2)	0	5	2
G van Bronckhorst	13 (8)	1	4	1
Edu	8 (6)	1	3	0
G Grimandi	11 (15)	0	2	0
M Upson	10 (4)	0	2	0
O Luzhny	15 (3)	0	3	1
S Campbell	29 (2)	2	2	0
R Wright	12 (0)	0	0	0
Kanu	9 (13)	3	2	0
I Stepanovs	6 (0)	0	1	0

Key Stat: The only club with more players than Arsenal's 11 at the World Cup Finals was Inter Milan with 13.

Sponsored by Stan James

ASTON VILLA

Nickname: The Villans
Colours: Claret and Blue
Ground: Villa Park

Capacity: 43,000
Tel: 0121 327 2299   www.astonvilla-fc.co.uk

THEY hit No. 1 in October but only stayed a week, winning just one of their next 13. Graham Taylor did nothing to arrest the slow descent to mid-table and Boateng will be missed.

On the positive side, Alpay's stock has risen in the World Cup and Peter Crouch has made the transition to the top flight smoothly while Hendrie and Barry continued to progress. Vassell's early success with England took the edge off his club shows, but with new boy Marcus Allback (signed for just £2.5m from Heerenveen), top scorer Angel (if he stays), Balaban, Merson and Dublin, Taylor will not be short of striking options.

Look for injections of pace down the left wing from Michael Boulding, signed from Grimsby where he was top scorer last season. Stefan Postma (£1.5m from De Graafschap) is new as well.

Longest run without loss: 8
Longest run without win: 4

Figaro's forecast:	9th
Your forecast:	

2001/02 Premiership Stats				
	Apps	Gls	YC	RC
P Schmeichel	29 (0)	1	0	0
M Delaney	30 (0)	0	4	0
A Wright	23 (0)	0	1	0
O Mellberg	32 (0)	0	3	0
O Alpay	14 (0)	0	3	0
G Boateng	37 (0)	1	5	0
I Taylor	7 (9)	3	2	0
J Angel	26 (3)	12	3	0
D Dublin	9 (12)	4	2	0
P Merson	18 (3)	2	0	0
S Staunton	30 (3)	0	2	0
P Enckelman	9 (0)	0	0	0
G Barry	16 (4)	0	0	0
P Crouch	7 (0)	2	0	0
L Hendrie	25 (4)	2	3	0
S Stone	14 (8)	1	2	0
B Balaban	0 (8)	0	0	0
M Hadji	17 (6)	2	3	0
T Hitzlsperger	11 (1)	1	1	0
D Vassell	30 (6)	12	3	0
H Kachloul	17 (5)	2	3	0
JlloydSamuel	17 (6)	0	2	0
D Ginola	0 (5)	0	0	1

Key Stat: For over six months, two was the most they scored in a game.

BIRMINGHAM CITY

Nickname: The Blues
Colours: Blue
Ground: St Andrews

Capacity: 30,016
Tel: 0121 772 0101   www.bcfc.com

THE main quality Steve Bruce has given this team is guts. After they drew their home leg of the play-off semi-final and had to go into the Lions' New Den, the Blues boss pinned this notice up: "The moment you start thinking what you are going to do if you lose – you've lost." Millwall were then beaten and Blues promoted after being 14th in mid-November.

Newcomers Aliou Cisse (who shut out Henry in the World Cup) and Robbie Savage have no common language, only a common interest: Savage got the most cautions in the Premiership last season (14) while the Senegal captain committed the most fouls per game in the World Cup. So an increase in the foul count is on the er... cards as they meet Owen and Van Nistelrooy rather than Stockport's finest. Kenny Cunningham's come from Wimbledon for £3.5m too.

Longest run without loss: 13
Longest run without win: 6

Figaro's forecast: 17th

Your forecast:

2001/02 Nationwide Stats	Apps	Gls	YC	RC
I Bennett	18 (0)	0	0	0
N Eaden	24 (5)	1	0	0
M Grainger	39 (1)	4	9	1
D Sonner	10 (5)	1	2	2
D Purse	35 (1)	3	11	1
D Holdsworth	4 (1)	0	1	0
J McCarthy	3 (1)	0	0	0
S John	15 (0)	7	1	0
G Horsfield	32 (7)	11	7	0
B Hughes	27 (4)	7	4	0
S Lazaridis	22 (10)	0	0	0
M Hughes	3 (0)	0	0	0
G Hyde	1 (3)	0	1	0
C Woodhouse	18 (10)	0	5	1
J Gill	14 (0)	0	2	0
T Mooney	29 (4)	13	2	0
M Johnson	30 (2)	1	3	0
N Vaesen	22 (1)	0	1	0
A Johnson	9 (13)	3	2	0
T Williams	4 (0)	0	0	0
T Luntala	9 (6)	0	0	0
D Johnson	5 (3)	1	2	0
P Furlong	2 (9)	1	3	0
O Tebily	7 (0)	0	0	0
J Hutchinson	0 (3)	0	0	0
A Bak	2 (2)	0	1	0
C Ferrari	0 (4)	0	0	0
D Carter	12 (1)	1	0	0
S Vickers	13 (1)	1	0	0
J Kenna	21 (0)	0	0	0
P Devlin	11 (2)	1	2	0
M O'Connor	24 (0)	0	4	0
Marcelo	17 (4)	12	3	0
D Burrows	9 (3)	0	2	0
A Kelly	6 (0)	0	0	0
O Bragstad	3 (0)	0	0	0
C Fleming	6 (0)	0	1	0

Key Stat: Both West Brom and Man City did the double over them.

Sponsored by Stan James

BLACKBURN ROVERS

Nickname: Rovers
Colours: Blue and White
Ground: Ewood Park

Capacity: 31,367
Tel: 01254 698888   www.rovers.co.uk

ARTE ET LABORE

A top ten finish and the Worthington Cup with its UEFA Cup place kept those "Souey for the chop?" headlines well out of sight. The boss and Henning Berg have now both signed new contracts.

Effective World Cup shows from Damien Duff, Hakan Unsal and Brad Friedel have followed, while Jansen got within a sniff of the England squad. Starlet David Dunn turned heads and defenders last season too.

Rovers even raised a smile when Andrew Cole announced his retirement from internationals long after he'd stopped being picked. Blackburn must punish the minnows. "Nil points" from Derby and Sunderland was criminal.

With Bjornebye out till Christmas, defenders Andy Todd from Charlton (750k) and 21-y-o Marc Sebastian Peltzer from Kaiserslautern (370k) have been drafted in.

Longest run without loss: 8
Longest run without win: 4

Figaro's forecast: 8th

Your forecast:

2001/02 Premiership Stats				
	Apps	Gls	YC	RC
B Friedel	36 (0)	0	0	0
J Curtis	10 (0)	0	0	0
H Berg	34 (0)	1	2	0
Tugay	32 (1)	3	8	0
S Bjornebye	23 (0)	0	3	0
C Short	21 (1)	0	4	3
G Flitcroft	26 (3)	1	7	0
D Dunn	26 (3)	7	4	0
A Cole	15 (0)	9	2	1
M Jansen	34 (1)	10	2	0
D Duff	31 (1)	7	3	0
M Hughes	4 (17)	1	3	0
N-E Johansson	14 (6)	0	0	0
C Hignett	4 (16)	4	3	0
A Mahon	10 (3)	1	0	0
Yordi	5 (3)	2	0	0
K Gillespie	21 (11)	3	3	0
E Ostenstad	2 (2)	0	0	0
C Grabbi	10 (4)	1	1	0
H Unsal	7 (1)	0	2	0
A Kelly	2 (0)	0	0	0
M Taylor	12 (7)	0	0	0
L Neill	31 (0)	1	8	0
N Blake	0 (3)	1	0	0
M Bent	1 (8)	0	2	0
J McAteer	1 (3)	0	0	0
D Johnson	6 (1)	1	1	0

Key Stat: They took points off each of the top four sides last season.

BOLTON WANDERERS

Nickname: The Trotters
Colours: Blue and White
Ground: Reebok Stadium

Capacity: 27,400
Tel: 01204 673673   www.boltonwfc.co.uk

NEUTRALS warmed to the Wanderers. After thrashing Leicester 5-0 then beating Liverpool to go top, they drew at Elland Rd and Highbury, and won at Old Trafford. Ricketts played for England.

Of course it couldn't last. The decline was remorseless and contained the odd thrashing but signing Youri Djorkaeff proved a masterstroke – and he has now agreed a further two years.

Newcomers? Turkish midfielder Akin Bulent from Galatasaray, Nigerian star Jay-Jay Okocha (PSG) and 22-y-o striker Delroy Facey (Huddersfield). Paul Balsom, the coach who has helped Sweden with match analysis and physical preparation for four years, will be working with Wanderers too. The threat of prison hangs over Danish midfield pitbull Stig Tofting for a scuffle at Copenhagen's "Cafe Ketchup".

Longest run without loss: 5
Longest run without win: 11

Figaro's forecast: 16th

Your forecast:

2001/02 Premiership Stats				
	Apps	Gls	YC	RC
S Banks	1 (0)	0	0	0
B N'Gotty	24 (2)	1	0	0
M Whitlow	28 (1)	0	9	0
G Bergsson	30 (0)	1	2	0
C Hendry	3 (0)	0	2	0
P Warhurst	25 (0)	0	7	1
B Hansen	10 (7)	1	0	0
P Frandsen	25 (4)	3	4	0
H Pedersen	5 (6)	0	0	0
D Holdsworth	9 (2)2	2	4	1
R Gardner	29 (2)	3	3	1
D Holden	0 (0)	0	0	0
Y Djorkaeff	12 (0)	4	0	0
G Farrelly	11 (7)	0	1	0
K Nolan	34 (1)	8	5	0
F Bobic	14 (2)	4	2	0
M Ricketts	26 (11)	12	4	0
D Norris	0 (0)	0	0	0
N Southall	10 (8)	1	1	0
R Wallace	14 (5)	3	2	0
J Jaaskelainen	34 (0)	0	2	2
M Espartero	0 (3)	0	0	0
A Barness	19 (6)	0	1	0
S Charlton	35 (1)	0	3	0
L Richardson	0 (1)	0	0	0
J Johnson	4 (6)	0	2	0
S Tofting	6 (0)	0	1	0
K Poole	3 (0)	0	0	0
J Smith	0 (1)	0	0	0
K Konstantinidis	3 (0)	0	1	1
I Marshall	0 (2)	0	0	0
D Diawara	4 (5)	0	1	1

Key Stat: Only the relegated sides conceded more goals last year.

CHARLTON ATHLETIC

Nickname: The Addicks
Colours: Red and White
Ground: The Valley

Capacity: 20,043
Tel: 0208 333 4000   www.charlton-athletic.co.uk

A tough year is in prospect especially if manager Alan Curbishley gets itchy feet.

Their worst winless run came at the death, though by then Paul Konchesky, Scott Parker and Luke Young may have had one eye on their U-21 England stint in Switzerland – where they did not distinguish themselves.

That the Addicks conceded more than two only five times was down to the heroics of our own Dean Kiely in goal, not any defensive organisation in front of him. The goals dried up in the New Year as they scored more than one in only two of their final 17 league games.

They do have a new £4.3m ground and kit sponsorship deal but by mid-July the only new faces were Gary Rowett, signed for £2.5m from Leicester, and Man Utd reserve Paul Rachubka.

Longest run without loss: 5
Longest run without win: 8

| Figaro's forecast: | 19th |
| Your forecast: | |

2001/02 Premiership Stats				
	Apps	Gls	YC	RC
D Kiely	38 (0)	0	2	0
R Kishishev	0 (3)	0	0	0
C Powell	35 (1)	1	3	0
G Stuart	31 (0)	3	3	1
R Rufus	10 (0)	1	1	0
A Todd	3 (2)	0	2	0
C Bart-Williams	10 (6)	1	2	0
M Kinsella	14 (3)	0	2	0
J Euell	31 (5)	11	3	0
J Robinson	16 (12)	1	4	0
S Brown	11 (3)	2	3	1
S Parker	36 (2)	1	8	1
P Konchesky	22 (12)	1	3	0
L Young	34 (0)	0	5	0
C Jensen	16 (2)	1	0	0
J Johansson	21 (9)	5	1	0
G Peacock	1 (4)	0	0	0
J Fortune	14 (4)	0	2	0
M Svensson	6 (6)	0	1	0
J Costa	22 (2)	0	9	0
K Lisbie	10 (12)	5	2	0
C MacDonald	0 (2)	1	0	0
M Fish	25 (0)	0	3	0
S Bartlett	10 (4)	2	2	0
J Salako	2 (1)	0	0	0

Key Stat: Charlton have scored only three in their last seven games.

Sponsored by Stan James

CHELSEA

Nickname: The Blues
Colours: Royal Blue and White
Ground: Stamford Bridge

Capacity: 41,000
Tel: 020 7385 5545   www.chelseafc.co.uk

UNBACKABLE – expect less of the same at Stagnant Bridge.

By early July, Hasselbaink was being hawked around Europe for £20m to reduce and service the debts. Jimmy Floyd (23 goals in 35 games last year) would be a huge loss, especially now he has found his best partner to date in Eidur Gudjohnsen.

Like several major Spanish and Italian teams, they are rich on paper, but have no money. Ranieiri was told to forget signing Conceicao and Geremi from Real Madrid during the World Cup.

On the plus side John Terry had an outstanding season while Lampard bedded in well and Gallas is a find. Spanish U-21 midfielder Enrique de Lucas has come from Espanol on a free but Sam Dalla Bona and Slavisa Jokanovic have gone. Striker Forsell could be out for up to two months after a knee op.

Longest run without loss: 9
Longest run without win: 3

Figaro's forecast: 7th

Your forecast:

2001/02 Premiership Stats				
	Apps	Gls	YC	RC
E De Goey	6 (0)	0	0	0
C Babayaro	18 (0)	0	6	0
M Desailly	24 (0)	1	5	0
F Lampard	34 (3)	5	1	1
J Hasselbaink	35 (0)	23	4	0
S Jokanovic	12 (8)	0	4	1
B Zenden	13 (9)	3	1	0
M Stanic	18 (9)	1	8	0
W Gallas	27 (3)	1	4	0
G Le Saux	26 (1)	1	6	0
M Melchiot	35 (2)	2	4	0
E Petit	26 (1)	1	3	0
A Ferrer	2 (2)	0	0	0
J Morris	2 (3)	0	1	0
E Gudjohnsen	26 (6)	14	2	0
C Cudicini	27 (1)	0	1	0
G Zola	19 (16)	3	1	0
J Terry	32 (1)	1	4	0
R Huth	0 (1)	0	0	0
J Gronkjaer	11 (2)	0	4	0
M Bosnich	5 (0)	0	0	0
M Forssell	2 (2)	0 4	0	0
J Kitamirike	0 (0)	0	0	0
S Dalla Bona	16 (8)	4	7	0
J Keenan	0 (1)	0	0	0
C Cole	2 (1)	1	0	0

Key Stat: Chelsea Village plc are allegedly £97 million in debt.

Sponsored by Stan James

EVERTON

Nickname: The Toffees
Colours: Blue and White
Ground: Goodison Park

Capacity: 40,200
Tel: 0151 330 2200   www.evertonfc.com

HOW appropriate that an Everton flag was on display during the World Cup Final: this club have been flagging for years.

The Toffees are celebrating their 100th successive season in the top flight, but they so nearly came unstuck last time and still lack the resources to make a quantum leap this year.

I have great respect for David Moyes, the Premiership's youngest manager, because of his achievements at Preston, but you have to suspect that part of his appeal to the Everton board was that he came cheap. I am not convinced he "turned them round" either: his arrival coincided with a set of cushier fixtures.

Nigerian World Cup defender Joseph Yobo has been imported from Marseille for £5m, Alex Nyarko has gone to PSG on loan. A top ten finish would be a result.

Longest run without loss: 5
Longest run without win: 5

Figaro's forecast: 15th

Your forecast:

2001/02 Premiership Stats				
	Apps	Gls	YC	RC
P Gerrard	13 (0)	0	0	0
S Watson	24 (1)	4	1	0
A Pistone	25 (0)	1	6	0
A Stubbs	29 (1)	2	5	0
D Weir	36 (0)	4	6	1
D Unsworth	28 (4)	3	5	0
N Alexandersson	28 (3)	2	1	0
T Radzinski	23 (4)	6	1	0
K Campbell	21 (2)	4	1	0
D Ferguson	17 (5)	6	6	1
M Pembridge	10 (4)	1	0	0
J Blomqvist	10 (5)	1	2	0
S Simonsen	25 (0)	0	1	0
I Tal	1 (5)	0	0	0
G Naysmith	23 (1)	0	2	0
T Gravesen	22 (3)	2	7	1
S Gemmill	31 (1)	1	4	0
J-M Moore	3 (13)	2	2	0
A Cleland	0 (3)	0	0	0
T Linderoth	4 (4)	0	0	0
D Ginola	2 (3)	0	0	0
L Carsley	8 (0)	1	0	0
P Clarke	5 (2)	0	2	0
T Hibbert	7 (3)	0	1	0
K McLeod	0 (0)	0	0	0
N Chadwick	2 (7)	3	0	0
A Xavier	11 (1)	0	0	0
P Gascoigne	8 (10)	1	2	0
D Cadamarteri	2 (1)	0	0	0

Key Stat: They conceded 16 in their last 5 aways.

FULHAM

Nickname: The Cottagers
Colours: White
Ground: Loftus Road

Capacity: 19,150
Tel: 020 7384 4700   www.fulhamfc.co.uk

FORGET their easy passage to an FA Cup semi, it will have irked Chairman Mo that co-promoted Bolton enjoyed the more spectacular results while Blackburn had the more spectacular season. Hence "Director of Football" Franco Baresi is now perched on Jean Tigana's shoulder.

Argentinian striker Facundo Sava (23 goals in 34 games last year) has come from Gimnasia for £2m and goal scoring midfielder Victor Sikora from Vitesse Arnheim for £3.5m. The most exciting new boy is Japanese World Cup midfield dynamo Junichi Inamoto. Keeper Martin Herrera has come from Alaves as cover for Van der Saar. Defender Chris Coleman is back and Steve Finnan impressed for Ireland in the World Cup, while Zak Knight and Sean Davis did well in the England U-21 campaign in Switzerland. They might kick on.

Longest run without loss: 6
Longest run without win: 6

Figaro's forecast: 11th
Your forecast:

2001/02 Premiership Stats				
	Apps	Gls	YC	RC
E Van der Sar	37 (0)	0	1	0
S Finnan	38 (0)	0	3	0
R Brevett	34 (1)	0	6	0
A Melville	35 (0)	0	3	0
J Harley	5 (5)	0	0	0
L Clark	5 (4)	0	0	0
S Marlet	21 (5)	6	1	0
J Collins	29 (4)	0	0	0
M Taylor	1 (0)	0	0	0
S Malbranque	33 (4)	8	3	0
B Hayles	27 (7)	8	7	0
Z Knight	8 (2)	0	0	0
S Legwinski	30 (3)	3	7	0
B Goldbaek	8 (5)	1	1	0
L Saha	28 (8)	8	4	0
L Boa Morte	15 (8)	1	6	2
S Davis	25 (5)	0	4	0
A Goma	32 (1)	0	7	0
A Ouaddou	4 (4)	0	0	0
K Betsy	0 (1)	0	0	0
E Lewis	1 (0)	0	0	0
C Willock	0 (2)	0	0	0
A Stolcers	0 (5)	0	0	0
K Symons	2 (2)	0	1	0

Key Stat: They failed to score in five of their last nine.

Sponsored by Stan James

LEEDS UNITED

Nickname: United
Colours: White
Ground: Elland Road

Capacity: 40,000
Tel: 01132 266000   www.lufc.co.uk

FOR Venables to be running a team controlled by shareholders is ironic given his crafty cockney run-ins with the DTI, but he's a better coach and tactician than his predecessor and has more savvy dealing with the media.

After off-field distractions you don't want the distraction of a book about the distractions. O'Leary left behind Ferdinand, Kewell, Viduka, Fowler, Smith, Woodgate, Keane and debts of around £80 million. His transfer deficit was over £67m. With Duberry, Dacourt and Ferdinand gone, Ian Harte having a poor World Cup and Bowyer, even after Liverpool, still not certain to stay, they may overtake Newcastle but not the top three.

Still Bridges and Radebe are back. United took four points off Arsenal and won six more Premier points than any other team in 2001. A Cup maybe? About time too.

Longest run without loss: 12
Longest run without win: 8

Figaro's forecast: 4th
Your forecast:

2001/02 Premiership Stats				
	Apps	Gls	YC	RC
N Martyn	38 (0)	0	1	0
G Kelly	19 (1)	0	2	0
I Harte	34 (2)	5	1	0
O Dacourt	16 (1)	0	3	0
J Woodgate	11 (2)	0	2	0
R Keane	16 (9)	3	3	0
M Viduka	33 (0)	11	3	0
H Kewell	26 (1)	8	2	0
L Bowyer	24 (1)	5	6	1
S McPhail	0 (1)	0	0	0
J Wilcox	4 (9)	0	3	0
A Smith	19 (4)	4	6	1
D Mills	28 (0)	1	11	2
E Bakke	20 (7)	2	6	0
S Johnson	12 (2)	0	4	0
D Matteo	32 (0)	0	7	1
M Duberry	3 (1)	0	2	0
D Batty	30 (6)	0	8	0
R Fowler	22 (0)	12	1	0
R Ferdinand	31 (0)	0	0	0
A Maybury	0 (1)	0	1	0

Key Stat: On June 28, Leeds' share price was 5.75p from a high of 35p.

Sponsored by Stan James

LIVERPOOL

Nickname: Reds
Colours: Red
Ground: Anfield

Capacity: 45,362
Tel: 0151 263 2361   www.liverpoolfc.tv

OUR tip for the title here last year, Liverpool came close. They did the league double over United but arguably lost it with soft defeats by Bolton and Villa at the start of the season.

At the summer sales, they hit the ground running, signing Senegal's Salif Diao for £5m from Lens before they defeated France, then snatching compatriot El Hadji Diouf from underneath Valencia's nose within days of that shock. French U-21 midfielder Alou Diarra has arrived on a free from Bayern Munich where he was on the fringes of the first team.

Heskey, Hyypia and Riise have signed new long-term deals, while Gerrard, Murphy, Carragher, Berger, Babbel, and most importantly Houllier, are now fit. Bruno Cheyrou has come from Lille for £4m too. All the pieces are in place. Let the good times roll.

Longest run without loss: 11
Longest run without win: 3

Figaro's forecast:	1st
Your forecast:	

2001/02 Premiership Stats				
	Apps	Gls	YC	RC
S Henchoz	37 (0)	0	4	0
A Xavier	9 (1)	1	1	0
S Hyypia	37 (0)	3	3	0
M Baros	0 (0)	0	0	0
M Babbel	2 (0)	0	0	0
V Smicer	13 (9)	4	2	0
E Heskey	26 (9)	9	3	0
N Anelka	13 (7)	4	0	0
M Owen	25 (4)	19	1	0
J Redknapp	2 (2)	1	1	0
J Dudek	35 (0)	0	0	0
D Murphy	31 (5)	6	4	0
P Berger	12 (9)	1	0	0
D Hamann	31 (0)	1	2	1
S Gerrard	26 (2)	3	5	1
J ArneRiise	34 (4)	7	1	0
P Arphexad	1 (1)	0	0	0
N Barmby	2 (4)	0	1	0
G McAllister	14 (11)	0	0	0
C Kirkland	1 (0)	0	0	0
J Carragher	33 (0)	0	7	0
I Biscan	4 (2)	0	0	0
G Vignal	3 (0)	0	1	0
S Wright	10 (2)	0	2	1
J Litmanen	8 (13)	4	0	0
R Fowler	8 (2)	3	2	0
S Westerveld	1 (0)	0	0	0

Key Stat: Liverpool did the league double over Premiership favourites Man Utd last term.

MANCHESTER CITY

Nickname: Lazer Blues
Colours: Light Blue
Ground: Maine Road

Capacity: 34,996
Tel: 0161 232 3000   www.mcfc.co.uk

CITY fans can't wait to see how Premiership sides handle Benarbia and Berkovic in tandem. There is a waiting list of 14,000 for season tickets, while 20,000 for the 2003/4 season in the new stadium have already been sold as well.

Of seven newcomers, the most intriguing is Vicente Matias Vuoso from Independiente (£4m). Keegan believes the young striker will make the full Argentine side. With Anelka (£13m), Wright-Phillips and Jon Macken, City have pace going forward, and Schmeichel might even help them to the occasional clean sheet.

Marc-Vivien Foe is in on loan from French champions Lyon for a year. Sylvain Distin is another import from PSG (£4m) where he played with Benarbia.

Loss/Win or Win/Loss double results and 2-4, 3-4, 4-3, 4-2 scores could pay.

Longest run without loss: 10
Longest run without win: 3

Figaro's forecast:	6th
Your forecast:	

2001/02 Nationwide Stats

	Apps	Gls	YC	RC
N Weaver	24 (1)	0	0	0
S Pearce	38 (0)	3	5	1
R Edghill	9 (2)	0	3	1
G Wiekens	24 (5)	0	2	0
K Horlock	33 (9)	7	5	1
D Huckerby	30 (10)	20	4	0
J Macken	4 (4)	5	1	0
S Goater	42 (0)	28	3	1
C Negouai	2 (4)	1	0	0
E Berkovic	20 (5)	6	2	1
A-I Haaland	0 (3)	0	0	0
P Ritchie	0 (8)	0	0	0
S Jihai	2 (5)	0	2	0
J Whitley	0 (2)	0	0	0
D Tiatto	36 (1)	1	10	1
C Nash	22 (1)	0	0	0
A Toure	0 (1)	0	0	0
R Dunne	41 (2)	1	4	0
P Wanchope	14 (1)	12	4	1
S Howey	34 (0)	3	4	0
L Mettomo	17 (6)	1	5	0
T Mears	0 (1)	0	0	0
S Wright-Phillips	31 (4)	8	4	0
L Charvet	3 (0)	0	0	0
C Killen	0 (2)	0	0	0
N Jensen	16 (2)	1	1	0
C Shuker	0 (2)	0	0	0
A Benarbia	38 (0)	8	3	1
D Granville	12 (4)	1	2	0
P Dickov	0 (7)	0	0	0
T Grant	2 (1)	0	1	0
D Etuhu	11 (1)	0	4	0
L Mike	1 (1)	0	1	0
S Colosimo	0 (6)	0	0	0

Key Stat: City home win record was the UK's best, no-one scored more either.

Sponsored by Stan James

MANCHESTER UNITED

Nickname: Red Devils
Colours: Red and White
Ground: Old Trafford

Capacity: 67,603
Tel: 0161 872 1661   www.manutd.com

SIR Alex Ferguson blamed "individual errors" for no trophies and six defeats at Old Trafford.

I had assumed the last individual he had in mind in saying that was himself – until, after rummaging in his bin, I came across this crumpled up note: "I humbly apologise for (A) Spending £47m last summer without reinforcing the defence; (B) Spending £28m on Veron when I already had the best midfield quartet in Europe plus Butt in reserve; (C) Reducing Scholes's effectiveness by playing him out of position; (D) Selling Stam and (E) Letting my family persuade me not to retire just as Cloughie did the season before Forest got relegated.

Then I remembered how happy he looked patting Rock Of Gibraltar on the day Arsenal won the Cup, so I put the note back.

Longest run without loss: 9
Longest run without win: 4

Figaro's forecast:	2nd
Your forecast:	

2001/02 Premiership Stats			
	Apps	Gls	YC	RC
F Barthez	32 (0)	0	1	0
G Neville	31 (3)	0	4	0
D Irwin	10 (2)	0	3	0
J S Veron	24 (2)	5	3	0
R Johnsen	9 (1)	1	0	0
L Blanc	29 (0)	1	4	0
D Beckham	23 (5)	11	6	0
N Butt	20 (5)	1	5	0
R van Nistelrooy	29 (3)	23	3	0
R Giggs	18 (7)	7	1	0
P Neville	21 (7)	2	4	0
R Carroll	6 (1)	0	0	0
D May	2 (0)	0	0	0
L Chadwick	5 (3)	0	0	0
R Keane	28 (0)	3	4	1
R van der Gouw	0 (1)	0	0	0
P Scholes	30 (5)	8	9	0
D Yorke	4 (6)	1	0	0
O G Solskjaer	23 (7)	17	3	0
D Forlan	6 (7)	0	0	0
R Wallwork	0 (1)	0	0	0
W Brown	15 (2)	0	0	0
Q Fortune	8 (5)	1	0	0
M Silvestre	31 (4)	0	3	0
M Stewart	2 (1)	0	0	0
J O'Shea	4 (5)	0	1	0
J Stam	1 (0)	0	0	0
A Cole	7 (4)	4	0	0

Key Stat: No team had more shots OFF target: 272!

MIDDLESBROUGH

Nickname: Boro
Colours: Red and White
Ground: Riverside Stadium

Capacity: 35,100
Tel: 01642 877700   www.mfc.co.uk

AFTER their team rounded off the season with a run of five defeats, scoring once, Boro fans may have felt rueful watching Ziege and Juninho playing in the World Cup Final.

Their football wasn't pretty, but it was pretty effective, especially at the back: six of their wins were by 1-0 and they beat Man Utd in Cup and League.

However, they mustered only 12 league goals and managed more than two only once – at home to Derby. Still, signing striker Massimo Maccarone is quite a coup for Steve McClaren.

The Italian scored two great goals against the England U-21s before the World Cup and helped Empoli gain promotion from Serie B. Franck Queudrue has come from Lens for £2.5m too, while Ince and Mustoe have gone to pastures new.

Longest run without loss: 8
Longest run without win: 5

Figaro's forecast:	10th
Your forecast:	

2001/02 Premiership Stats			
	Apps	Gls	YC	RC
M Schwarzer	21 (0)	0	0	1
D Gordon	0 (1)	0	0	0
G Festa	8 (0)	1	1	2
G Southgate	37 (0)	1	0	0
R Mustoe	31 (5)	2	2	0
S Nemeth	11 (10)	3	0	0
P Ince	31 (0)	2	11	1
B Carbone	13 (0)	1	1	0
A Boksic	20 (2)	8	2	0
J Greening	36 (0)	1	5	0
P Okon	1 (3)	0	0	0
M Debeve	1 (3)	0	0	0
M Beresford	0 (1)	0	0	0
J-D Job	3 (1)	0	1	0
U Ehiogu	29 (0)	1	2	2
A Campbell	0 (4)	0	1	0
H Ricard	6 (3)	0	2	0
D Windass	8 (19)	1	2	0
M Wilson	2 (8)	0	1	0
C Marinelli	12 (8)	2	2	0
P Stamp	3 (3)	0	0	0
M Crossley	17 (1)	0	0	0
N Whelan	18 (1)	4	2	0
R Stockdale	26 (2)	1	2	0
C Cooper	14 (4)	2	3	0
J Gavin	5 (4)	0	2	0
L Wilkshire	6 (1)	0	1	0
A Johnston	13 (4)	1	1	0
D Murphy	0 (5)	0	0	0
M Hudson	0 (2)	0	0	0
F Queudrue	28 (0)	2	8	0
C Fleming	8 (0)	0	0	0
B Deane	6 (1)	1	0	0
S Vickers	2 (0)	0	0	0

Key Stat: No team mustered fewer shots – a mere 309 with just 138 on target.

NEWCASTLE UNITED

Nickname: Magpies
Colours: Black and White
Ground: St James' Park

Capacity: 52,173
Tel: 0191 201 8400   www.nufc.co.uk

HAD it not been for the injuries to Bellamy and Dyer, Newcastle might have climbed even higher, though arguably it was their defence that let them down: they had just one clean sheet in their last 13 games.

Central defender Titus Bramble has followed in Dyer's footsteps from Ipswich (for £5m) to plug the gaps, but he won't plug all of them. The other major signing is teenage Portuguese striker Hugo Viana for £8.5m from Lisbon. He is left-footed but Robson intends to play him more in the centre, inside Laurent Robert.

With Jenas, Ameobi and Lua Lua showing signs of adapting to Premiership soccer as the season ended, Shearer can expect more days off this year as he continues his managerial grooming – and we can expect more goals at both ends with the Magpies.

Longest run without loss: 9
Longest run without win: 5

Figaro's forecast: 5th
Your forecast:

2001/02 Premiership Stats				
	Apps	Gls	YC	RC
S Given	38 (0)	0	2	0
R Elliott	26 (1)	1	4	0
N Solano	37 (0)	7	2	0
A O'Brien	31 (3)	2	3	0
C Acuna	10 (6)	3	3	0
J Jenas	6 (6)	0	0	0
K Dyer	15 (3)	3	0	0
A Shearer	36 (1)	24	2	1
C Bassedas	1 (1)	0	0	0
G Speed	28 (1)	5	3	0
A Griffin	3 (1)	0	0	0
C Cort	6 (2)	1	0	0
C Bellamy	26 (1)	9	7	1
A Hughes	34 (0)	0	1	0
L Lua Lua	4 (16)	3	0	0
J McClen	3 (0)	0	0	0
S Ameobi	4 (11)	0	0	0
S Distin	20 (8)	0	4	0
L Robert	34 (2)	8	7	0
N Dabizas	33 (2)	3	6	0
O Bernard	4 (12)	3	1	0
W Barton	4 (1)	0	1	0
R Lee	15 (1)	1	3	0

Key Stat: Newcastle did not have one red card last year.

SOUTHAMPTON

Nickname: Saints
Colours: Red and White
Ground: Friends Provident St Mary's Stadium

Capacity: 32,000
Tel: 01703 220505   www.saintsfc.co.uk

WHEN I look at the final table and see Southampton at 11th I still have to rub my eyes.

Full marks to Gordon Strachan of course. Some neutrals felt that Saints' treatment of David Jones was unsaintly but the appointment of the Scot was a masterstroke. The club overcame injuries to all its main strikers to finish mid-table.

Now the only sale seems likely to be that of Agustin Delgado. Rodrigues, Petrescu and Adam Wallace have been released and Le Tiss retired, but crucially, Wayne Bridge wants to stay.

Anders Svensson's goal for Sweden against Argentina means he'll be nudging James Beattie aside when it comes to free kicks, while fellow international Michael Svensson has joined from Troyes for £2m to strengthen the defence. But 11th? Not again, surely.

Longest run without loss: 6
Longest run without win: 6

Figaro's forecast: 14th

Your forecast:

2001/02 Premiership Stats				
	Apps	Gls	YC	RC
P Jones	36 (0)	0	0	0
J Dodd	26 (3)	0	3	0
W Bridge	38 (0)	0	0	0
C Marsden	27 (1)	3	4	1
C Lundekvam	34 (0)	0	2	1
P Williams	27 (1)	0	5	0
M Le Tissier	0 (4)	0	1	0
M Oakley	26 (1)	1	1	0
J Beattie	23 (5)	12	3	0
K Davies	19 (4)	2	5	0
U Rosler	3 (1)	0	0	0
A Svensson	33 (1)	4	0	0
N Moss	2 (0)	0	0	0
S Ripley	1 (4)	0	0	0
F Benali	0 (3)	0	0	0
M Draper	1 (1)	0	1	0
M Pahars	33 (3)	14	2	0
R Delap	24 (4)	2	3	2
T El Khalej	12 (1)	1	2	1
J Tessem	7 (15)	2	2	0
D Petrescu	0 (2)	0	0	0
G Monk	1 (1)	0	1	0
I Bleidelis	0 (1)	0	0	0
F Fernandes	6 (5)	1	0	0
S McDonald	0 (2)	0	0	0
P Telfer	27 (1)	1	1	0
A Delgado	0 (1)	0	0	0
B Ormerod	8 (10)	1	0	0
D Richards	4 (0)	0	0	0
P Murray	0 (1)	0	0	0

Key Stat: St. Mary's became almost Dellish: they lost one of their last eight homes.

SUNDERLAND

Nickname: Mackems or Black Cats
Colours: Red and White
Ground: Stadium of Light

Capacity: 48,300
Tel: 0191 551 5000 www.sunderland-afc.com

HOW did they stay up? One website wag suggested that if Jim Smith wanted a rest from football, he should go to the Stadium of Light.

The decline was nearly the equal of Ipswich's. Even Leicester scored more. They have cleared out eight: Laslandes, Schwartz, Haas, Varga, Peeters, Mercimek, Macho and Kennedy.

In exchange, by mid-July young midfielder Sean Thornton had arrived from Tranmere, Phil Babb restored to England from Sporting Lisbon and keeper Thomas Myhre had been Bosman'd from Besiktas as back-up for Thomas Sorensen. No wonder the club were coy about the slump in season ticket sales.

Niall Quinn is now player-coach and Adrian Heath the new assistant manager. Peter Reid will need all the assistance he can get.

Longest run without loss: 2
Longest run without win: 7

Figaro's forecast:	18th
Your forecast:	

2001/02 Premiership Stats				
	Apps	Gls	YC	RC
T Sorensen	34 (0)	0	0	0
B Haas	27 (0)	0	7	0
M Gray	35 (0)	0	1	0
C Reyna	17 (0)	3	2	1
S Varga	9 (0)	0	1	0
E Thome	12 (0)	1	3	0
L Laslandes	5 (7)	0	1	0
P Mboma	5 (4)	1	2	0
G McCann	29 (0)	0	8	0
N Quinn	24 (13)	6	3	0
K Phillips	37 (0)	11	3	0
K Kilbane	24 (4)	2	3	0
J Bjorklund	11 (1)	0	2	0
D Bellion	0 (9)	0	0	0
J McAteer	26 (0)	2	8	0
J Craddock	30 (0)	1	3	0
D Williams	23 (5)	0	3	0
K Kyle	0 (6)	0	1	0
S Schwarz	18 (2)	1	7	0
P Thirlwell	11 (3)	0	3	0
G McCartney	12 (6)	0	3	0
T Butler	2 (5)	0	1	0
J Macho	4 (0)	0	0	0
J Arca	20 (2)	1	3	0
A Rae	1 (2)	0	0	0
D Hutchison	2 (0)	0	0	0

Key Stat: Only Man Utd and Arsenal had more players at the World Cup. Strange but true.

Sponsored by Stan James

TOTTENHAM HOTSPUR

Nickname: Spurs
Colours: Blue and White
Ground: White Hart Lane

Capacity: 36,200
Tel: 0208 365 5000   www.spurs.co.uk

DISAPPOINTING. Apart from the Double blow landed by Arsenal, Spurs missed out on Europe after an inept display in the Worthington Cup Final and showed no signs of investing in any important newcomers over the summer.

The squad remains thin while key players like Ferdinand and Sheringham are long in the tooth. To be fair, Ferdinand did have his best spell at the club last season with 15 goals in 33 games.

Belgian U-21 international Jonathan Blondel has signed from Excelsior Mouscron and Milenko Acimovic from Red Star Belgrade on a free, ditto Jamie Redknapp from Liverpool.

There are one or two good signs – Simon Davies has come on a treat and Anderton did OK, but you have to suspect that Man City, Fulham, Middlesboro and Blackburn may overtake them.

Longest run without loss: 4
Longest run without win: 4

| **Figaro's forecast:** | **13th** |
| **Your forecast:** | |

2001/02 Premiership Stats				
	Apps	Gls	YC	RC
N Sullivan	29 (0)	0	0	0
M Taricco	30 (0)	0	4	2
S Freund	19 (1)	0	6	0
G Bunjevcevic	5 (1)	0	0	0
C Perry	30 (3)	0	8	0
D Anderton	33 (2)	3	1	0
T Sherwood	15 (4)	0	5	0
L Ferdinand	22 (3)	9	3	0
T Sheringham	33 (1)	10	4	1
S Rebrov	9 (2)	1	0	0
G Doherty	4 (3)	0	1	0
K Keller	9 (0)	0	0	0
G Poyet	32 (2)	10	6	1
S Iversen	12 (6)	4	1	0
O Leonhardsen	2 (5)	0	0	0
B Thatcher	11 (1)	0	3	0
C Ziege	27 (0)	5	6	0
S Clemence	4 (2)	0	1	0
L King	32 (0)	0	0	0
M Etherington	3 (8)	0	1	0
S Davies	22 (9)	4	0	0
A Gardner	11 (4)	0	4	0
A Thelwell	0 (2)	0	0	0
D Richards	24 (0)	2	3	0

Key Stat: They do need more luck. No team hit the woodwork more times than Spurs last season (16).

109

WEST BROM

Nickname: Baggies
Colours: Black and White
Ground: The Hawthorns

Capacity: 28,000
Tel: 0121 525 8888   www.wba.co.uk

WHILE Manchester City proved the irresistible force, WBA played the role of immovable objects with 27 clean sheets and 17 1-0 wins.

Another immovable object it seems is boss Gary Megson. He's seen off the previous chairman and been told by the new one that his job will be safe if they are relegated. Fair do's: he got them up on a budget of just £2m. Now they are available at 2,500-1 for the title and that is rank bad value. Tidal waves and earthquakes would be needed to demolish everything except the Hawthorns before the title comes there.

The arrival of Man Utd's Worthington Cup stalwart Ronnie Wallwork shows the level of ambition the Baggies are bringing to the Premiership. Any two of Dichio, Jason Roberts, young Scott Dobie and old Bob Taylor up front? Perlease.

Longest run without loss: 9
Longest run without win: 4

| **Figaro's forecast:** | **20th** |
| **Your forecast:** | |

2001/02 Nationwide Stats				
	Apps	Gls	YC	RC
R Hoult	45 (0)	0	1	0
D Lyttle	13 (10)	0	1	0
N Clement	45 (0)	6	2	0
D McInnes	45 (0)	3	5	0
T Butler	14 (4)	0	1	2
P Gilchrist	43 (0)	0	2	0
R Fox	2 (17)	1	0	0
M Appleton	18 (0)	0	4	0
B Taylor	18 (16)	7	2	1
A Johnson	28 (4)	4	2	0
J Roberts	12 (2)	7	3	0
J Quinn	1 (6)	0	2	0
D Dichio	26 (1)	9	4	0
D Moore	31 (1)	2	3	0
I Balis	32 (2)	2	2	0
L Sigurdsson	42 (1)	1	8	0
S Dobie	32 (11)	11	1	0
W Cummings	6 (8)	0	1	0
Jordao	19 (6)	5	3	0
B Jensen	1 (0)	0	0	0
J Chambers	1 (4)	0	0	0
A Chambers	24 (8)	0	6	0
S Varga	3 (1)	0	0	0
T Benjamin	0 (3)	1	0	1
U Rosler	5 (0)	1	2	0

Key Stat: The Baggies conceded only 29 in the league.

Sponsored by Stan James

WEST HAM UNITED

Nickname: The Hammers
Colours: Claret and Blue
Ground: Boleyn Ground

Capacity: 26,309
Tel: 0208 771 2233   www.whufc.co.uk

ALL credit to Glenn Roeder who confounded his critics by guiding the Hammers up the table after a dreadful start. Can they stay up there?

The rehabilitation of captain Steve Lomas and further development of Joe Cole were major plusses, plus the mercurial Di Canio and Kanoute both staying. The trouble is, West Ham remain a selling club. The 18-y-o striker Youssef Sofiane has been signed from Auxerre and Van der Gouw has come in from Man Utd as cover for David James after Shaka Hislop's switch to Portsmouth.

Along with Liverpool, the Hammers boasted the best home defence in the Premiership last year, though perversely theirs was the worst away defensive record – they conceded nearly a goal-a-game more than Leicester. That may remain the pattern.

Longest run without loss: 6
Longest run without win: 5

Figaro's forecast:	**12th**
Your forecast:	

2001/02 Premiership Stats				
	Apps	Gls	YC	RC
S Hislop	12 (0)	0	0	0
D James	26 (0)	0	0	0
T Repka	31 (0)	0	7	2
D Hutchison	24 (0)	1	3	0
V Labant	7 (5)	0	1	0
H Foxe	4 (2)	0	2	0
C Dailly	38 (0)	0	3	0
T Sinclair	34 (0)	5	5	0
P Di Canio	26 (0)	9	5	1
S Lomas	14 (1)	4	3	0
P Kitson	3 (4)	3	0	0
F Kanoute	27 (0)	11	4	0
R Song	5 (0)	0	1	0
J Moncur	7 (11)	0	5	0
N Winterburn	29 (2)	0	4	0
I Pearce	8 (1)	2	3	0
S Minto	5 (0)	0	1	0
M Carrick	30 (0)	2	4	0
R Soma	1 (2)	0	0	0
J Cole	29 (1)	0	5	0
S Byrne	0 (1)	0	0	0
L Courtois	5 (2)	0	0	0
A Camara	0 (1)	0	0	0
S Schemmel	35 (0)	1	6	0
R Garcia	2 (6)	0	0	0
J Defoe	14 (2)	10	0	0
S Todorov	2 (4)	0	2	0
G McCann	0 (3)	0	0	0

Key Stat: The Hammers took points off all six teams that finished above them.

111

BRADFORD

🏠 Nationwide ⚽ 1
FOOTBALL LEAGUE

Nickname: The Bantams
Colours: Claret and Amber
Ground: Valley Parade
Capacity: 18,018
Tel: 01274 773355.

NO money, no players, no hope. That more or less sums up the Bantams as they feel the full force of the collapse of ITV Digital.

The Bantams have gone into administration and their prospects look bleak.

Nicky Law's problems on the field compare as a mere pimple to those facing the board just to keep Bradford in business. They have culled all their top wage earners from the playing staff and face starting the season with a mixture of journeyman footballers and untried youngsters. They struggled to stay out of the relegation battle last season but must view First Division safety as their main aim this term. They are far from certain to achieve that goal.

Longest run without loss: 6
Longest run without win: 6

KEY STAT: They conceded two or more ten games running before Christmas.

Our forecast:	18th
Your forecast:	

BRIGHTON

Nickname: The Seagulls
Colours: Blue and White
Ground: Withdean Stadium
Capacity: 6,000
Tel: 01273 778855

THE Seagulls capped a fine first season back in Division Two, defying many pundits by wrapping up the Championship.

They finished six points clear of second-placed Reading but it was not enough to satisfy manager Peter Taylor who decided to quit the south-coast club.

Several bigger names were touted for the post but Martin Hinshelwood has been appointed from within and Albion fans will be crossing their fingers that he can keep star striker Bobby Zamora at Withdean.

The prolific marksman holds the key to Brighton's season. If he stays then a play-off place is not beyond the realms of possibility. If he departs they could struggle to make an impact.

Longest run without loss: 12
Longest run without win: 5

KEY STAT: Only six teams have won successive titles before.

Our forecast:	16th
Your forecast:	

BURNLEY

Nickname: The Clarets
Colours: Claret and Blue
Ground: Turf Moor
Capacity: 22,500
Tel: 01282 700000

THERE will be no Gazza on show at Turf Moor this season but Clarets fans will be hoping Burnley will be quick out of the blocks again this season.

Stan Ternent's team topped the table during the opening exchanges of last term and although they suffered a mid-season stutter they missed out on a play-off spot by a single goal.

Defender Steve Davis is un-complicated, reliable and consistent he epitomises Burnley. They are a physically uncompromising outfit and don't respect reputations. If Ian Moore and Gareth Taylor continue to find the back of the net they will again have serious play-off aspirations. Promotion, however, is another matter.

Longest run without loss: 10
Longest run without win: 5

KEY STAT: From mid-December, they never scored more than two in a league game.

Our forecast:	8th
Your forecast:	

COVENTRY

Nickname: The Sky Blues
Colours: Sky Blue
Ground: Highfield Road
Capacity: 23,611
Tel: 01203 234000.

MANY Sky Blues fans were expecting Coventry's first season back in the First Division to be their last for a while.

Inconsistency, however, cost manager Gordon Strachan, and then his successor Roland Nielsen, their jobs at Highfield Road.

Fans favourite Gary McAllister has returned to the club from Liverpool to take charge as player-manager. Although he will add steel and guile to the midfield, his management skills are untried, but Eric Black will add experience to the management team.

City have two electric strikers in Julian Joachim and Lee Hughes but the latter will have to find more consistency than last season. Whatever happens they are sure to mount a strong challenge.

Longest run without loss: 6
Longest run without win: 7

KEY STAT: There were no points from their last five games.

Our forecast:	2nd
Your forecast:	

CRYSTAL PALACE

Nickname: The Eagles
Colours: Red and Blue
Ground: Selhurst Park
Capacity: 26,400
Tel: 020 8768 6000.

PALACE'S fearsome strike force will give the Eagles every chance of making a return to the Premiership.

Morrison, Akinbiyi and Freedman are all seasoned goalscorers at this level and will frighten most defenders in the league. Akinbiyi is not expected to return from injury until November but if Morrison starts this season as he did last he will hardly be missed. There are some doubts about Morrison's immediate future but even if he departs there should be funds for a replacement.

Trevor Francis knows the division well and although he came up short at St Andrews, he has arguably a stronger squad at Palace. It would be no surprise if he took the Eagles back into the top flight.

Longest run without loss: 8
Longest run without win: 4

KEY STAT: Together with Coventry, they drew the least in the English league: six

Our forecast:	6th
Your forecast:	

DERBY

Nickname: The Rams
Colours: White and Black
Ground: Pride Park
Capacity: 33,000
Tel: 01332 66750

THE Rams went out of the Premiership with a whimper despite John Gregory's arrival at Pride Park. With just a few weeks to work his magic the task was beyond the former Aston Villa boss.

A lack of goals was their main problem despite the presence of Fabrizio Ravanelli. Much will rest with Malcolm Christie and whether he can realise his huge potential. Christie is not the Rams only genuinely talented youngster; defender Chris Riggot looks set to go all the way to the top.

With experienced players like Rob Lee and Craig Burley in midfield, Derby should be pressing for promotion. However, as Coventry and Watford, found it is not easy to bounce straight back into the Premiership.

Longest run without loss: 3
Longest run without win: 8

KEY STAT: They lost seven of their last eight.

Our forecast:	4th
Your forecast:	

GILLINGHAM

Nickname: The Gills
Colours: Blue and White
Ground: Priestfield Stadium
Capacity: 10,600
Tel: 01634 851854

GILL'S home form ensured they did not become embroiled in the relegation scrap.

However, they conceded far too many goals away from home and although they hit the back of the net often enough they have lost two of their main strikers. Iffy Onuora has departed to Sheffield United while Marlon King is facing a spell eating porridge at HMP's pleasure. Hessenthaler has signed ageing duo Tommy Johnson and Rod Wallace, both were decent enough players in their pomp but those days are distant specks on the horizon for both players.

The squad is experienced but maintaining Division One staus wil be the prioroty at Priestfield. Mid-table obscurity would be a welcome bonus.

Longest run without loss: 8
Longest run without win: 5

KEY STAT: The Gills did not win two in a row in the league last year.

Our forecast:	21st
Your forecast:	

GRIMSBY

Nickname: The Mariners
Colours: Black and White
Ground: Blundell Park
Capacity: 8,900
Tel: 01472 697111

THE Mariners recorded probably the best result in their history when they knocked holders Liverpool out of the Worthington Cup at Anfield. Strangely that result sparked an awful run of results in the league when they won just once in 13 games.

A decent finish to the season lifted them out of the drop zone and ensured they beat the drop – albeit by a single point.

Manager Paul Groves has brought in winger Terry Cooke, joining from Manchester City, but promising youngster Danny Butterfield has departed for the bright lights of Crystal Palace, it could be a wise move. Grimsby look set for another season of dodging the bullets and they will do well to avoid relegation.

Longest run without loss: 4
Longest run without win: 11

KEY STAT: At one stage The Mariners only scored four in 13.

Our forecast:	24th
Your forecast:	

IPSWICH

Nickname: Town
Colours: Blue and White
Ground: Portman Road
Capacity: 30,000
Tel: 01473 400500

AFTER surprising everyone by qualifying for Europe, their second season in the Premiership could hardly have been more different. George Burley's team were "too good to go down" in many people's opinion but go down they did.

A plucky uefa Cup campaign-where they beat Inter Milan at home-may have served as a distraction before Christmas but despite a run of seven wins from eight games after the festive period they could not maintain their form.

Incoming transfer activity has been minimal but Titus Bramble has taken the long road north to Newcastle.

Much will depend on whether George Burley can hold onto the rest of the stars in the squad. If he can, Town will proper.

Longest run without loss: 4
Longest run without win: 11

KEY STAT: They won only one of their last 13.

Our forecast:	1st
Your forecast:	

LEICESTER

Nickname: The Foxes
Colours: Blue and White
Ground: Walkers Stadium
Capacity: 32,000
Tel: 0116 2915000

IT was not so long ago Martin O'Neill was parading silverware to the Filbert Street faithful. The League Cup final victories in 1997 and 2000, as well as O'Neill himself, are now distant memories.

Talented young manager Micky Adams could not save Leicester and the Foxes were dead and buried long before the season drew to a close.

The heart has been ripped out of the side with Robbie Savage departing to Birmingham and fellow midfielder Muzzy Izzet likely to follow – possibly to Middlesbrough. Dennis Wise and Matt Elliott may both be past their best but remain experienced players in a squad short on quality. The Foxes look set for a long hard season

Longest run without loss: 4
Longest run without win: 12

KEY STAT: Even Stockport managed to win more games than the Foxes.

Our forecast:	10th
Your forecast:	

Sponsored by Stan James

MILLWALL

Nickname: The Lions
Colours: Blue and White
Ground: The New Den
Capacity: 20,150
Tel: 020 7232 1222

AFTER winning Division Two the previous year, the Lions continued their progress by making the play-offs. Although they lost out in the semi-finals to eventual winners Birmingham, Millwall's efforts should not be underestimated.

Mark McGhee has moulded a solid squad with a good blend of raw talent and experience. Steve Claridge's cunning was a big plus but just how long the veteran striker is planning on rolling up his sleeves (and his socks down) remains to be seen.

The Lions scored plenty of goals at the New Den, where they had an impressive record, but let themselves down away from home. If they rectify that, the Lions can mix it with the best and the play-offs look a realistic target.

Longest run without loss: 10
Longest run without win: 4

KEY STAT: The Lions conceded only four in their last eight.

Our forecast:	5th
Your forecast:	

NORWICH

Nickname: The Canaries
Colours: Yellow and Green
Ground: Carrow Road
Capacity: 21,995
Tel: 01603 760760

IT was not so long ago East Anglia had two Premiership clubs – now they have two Division One teams.

However, Norwich did their best to swap places with Ipswich and it so very nearly worked. They snatched a place in the play-offs at the eleventh hour and then beat Wolves in the semi-finals to book their place in the "winner takes all" final. Iwan Roberts gave them the lead in the first minute of extra-time in Cardiff but their dreams were finally dashed in a penalty shoot-out. Manager Nigel Worthington is earning himself a reputation as a shrewd operator and, with Roberts a proven goalscorer, they will again be challenging for honours. One just wonders whether their best chance has gone.

Longest run without loss: 8
Longest run without win: 6

KEY STAT: It's 11 games since they've conceded more than one.

Our forecast:	9th
Your forecast:	

NOTTS FOREST

Nickname: Forest
Colours: Red and White
Ground: City Ground
Capacity: 30,602
Tel: 0115 9824444

FOREST'S financial problems have been well documented and the collapse of the ITV Digital contract has done nothing to help the once proud club.

Manager Paul Hart did well to keep them out of the relegation mire but will do well to repeat the trick for the coming season.

Stern John, Jermaine Jenas and Chris Bart-Williams were just three of their better players to leave the club at bargain prices as Forest tried to balance the books.

Those departures have left a severe lack of quality in the City Ground dressing room and it looks like being a trying time this season. Fans will be hoping that there are three clubs with more chance of dropping into Division Two though it is hard to name them.

Longest run without loss: 5
Longest run without win: 6

KEY STAT: Forest have gone nine home games without a win.

Our forecast:	20th
Your forecast:	

PORTSMOUTH

Nickname: Pompey
Colours: Blue and White
Ground: Fratton Park
Capacity: 16,060
Tel: 01705 731204

POMPEY were perhaps the most disappointing team of last season. They announced their intent with several high-profile signings including Robert Prosinecki. The chain-smoking Croat hit nine goals in 30 games but it was not enough to stop Portsmouth sliding down the table to finish 17th.

It cost Graham Rix his job and former West Ham boss Harry Redknapp will need all his experience to turn it round at Fratton Park.

Harry has turned to the tried-and-failed method of bringing in Premiership veterans with inflated egos and even more inflated wages; David Ginola is top of the list. The ambition is there but whether they are going down the right road is another matter.

Longest run without loss: 6
Longest run without win: 8

KEY STAT: No Crouch = ouch! Pompey scored none or one in 13 of their last 14.

Our forecast:	13th
Your forecast:	

PRESTON

Nickname: Lillywhites
Colours: White and Navy
Ground: Deepdale
Capacity: 15,300
Tel: 01772 902020

NORTH END impressed for much of the season and although their promotion campaign eventually faded away they won a lot of friends along the way.

Craig Brown has been handed the reins after David Moyes was poached by Everton late last season. Brown is an astute coach but hardly experienced in Division One.

Preston's last nine home games yielded seven wins and a draw but some indifferent form on the road saw them drop out of the promotion picture.

Clyde Wjinhard has failed to agree a new deal at Deepdale and Sean Gregan's future at the club is also in doubt.

A season of consolidation looks likely.

Longest run without loss: 11
Longest run without win: 4

KEY STAT: They lost seven of last eight aways.

Our forecast:	12th
Your forecast:	

READING

Nickname: The Royals
Colours: Blue and White
Ground: Madjeski Stadium
Capacity: 25,000
Tel: 01189 681100

THE Royals' return to Division One, courtesy of a draw with promotion rivals Brentford, was no more than Alan Pardew's team deserved.

A run of nine draws in the final ten games ended their tilt at the title but Reading still had the best away record in the league. They were no mugs on their own patch either and if players like Jamie Cureton can continue to impress they should hold their own.

It's all quiet on the transfer front, although Adrian Whitbread is expected to be fit for the start of the season after missing eight months through injury.

Reading are a well equipped side who'll hold their own but it's hard to envisage them challenging for promotion, mid-table is the call.

Longest run without loss: 13
Longest run without win: 5

KEY STAT: The Royals drew nine of their last ten.

Our forecast:	17th
Your forecast:	

ROTHERHAM

Nickname: The Millers
Colours: Red and White
Ground: Millmoor Ground
Capacity: 11,510
Tel: 01709 512434

THE Millers clung on to their place in Division One by the width of a cigarette paper.

Goal difference separated them from Crewe with Barnsley just another point behind. Ronnie Moore has a massive task in trying to keep Rotherham in the division. With the coffers all but dry it may well be beyond him.

The likeable Millers boss has announced his intention to bring in new faces, with former Bradford defender Andy Myers top of his shopping list. However, at the time of writing there have been no additions to the Millers squad.

Another season of graft for little reward is the on the cards and it is hard to see them escaping the drop.

Longest run without loss: 5
Longest run without win: 10

KEY STAT: The Merry Millers were tops for draws in the UK last year: 19.

Our forecast:	22nd
Your forecast:	

SHEFFIELD UTD

Nickname: The Blades
Colours: Red and White
Ground: Bramall Lane
Capacity: 30,400
Tel: 0114 221575

THE Blades have been one of the busiest clubs in the close season. As many of their rivals tighten their belts and try to weather the financial storm, United have been out on a recruitment drive.

Striker Iffy Onuora, midfielder Stuart McCall and defender Steve Yates have all arrived at Bramall Lane.

With an average age of 35 it's hardly a long-term fix, although goalkeeper Paddy Kenny and Dutch striker Laurens Ten Heuvel are younger additions to the squad. One thing Neil Warnock's side did not lack last season was fighting spirit – just ask West Brom, three reds in the battle of Bramall Lane. They may well top the disciplinary charts but they are unlikely to claim such a lofty league position.

Longest run without loss: 8
Longest run without win: 5

KEY STAT: They took points off each of the sides in the top ten.

Our forecast:	14th
Your forecast:	

SHEFFIELD WEDNESDAY

Nickname: The Owls
Colours: Blue and White
Ground: Hillsborough
Capacity: 39,859
Tel: 0114 2212121

GONE are the days when the Owls could mix it with the glamour sides of English football.

The Owls were bland and predictable last season and avoided the drop by only a single point.

Terry Yorath is a shrewd coach and has added Chelsea youngster Leon Knight to the squad on a year-long loan. If he plays as well as he did for Huddersfield last year – when he scored 17 goals – he could give the South Yorkshire club a real boost.

With the likes of Sibon and Soltvedt to call on, they can put last season's woeful start, one win in their opening 13 games, behind them. Promotion? No, but the play-offs are a possibility.

Longest run without loss: 5
Longest run without win: 9

KEY STAT: They only scored more than two at home only against relegated teams.

Our forecast:	11th
Your forecast:	

STOKE CITY

Nickname: The Potters
Colours: Red and White
Ground: Britannia Stadium
Capacity: 28,000
Tel: 01782 592222

THE Potters pulled off one of the coups of the summer when they signed talented young manager Steve Cotterill to replace Gudjon Thordarson.

Cotterill guided Cheltenham from the Dr Marten's League to the Second Division in little over six years and is one of the hottest managerial properties around. With a lack of cash around the Nationwide League, the leadership qualities of the respective managers will be paramount. New boy Chris Greenacre was being trailed by a number of clubs and looks a natural goalscorer. His decision to go to the Potters is indicative of their ambition.

Stoke could surprise a few people and if things drop right could find themselves in the play-offs again.

Longest run without loss: 10
Longest run without win: 5

KEY STAT: Their crowd capacity is four times that of Brighton.

Our forecast:	7th
Your forecast:	

WALSALL

Nickname: The Saddlers
Colours: Red, Black and White
Ground: Bescot Stadium
Capacity: 9,000
Tel: 01922 22791

THE Saddlers are in for a bumpy ride. They did well to survive last season when former Wolves boss Colin Lee managed to turn their fortunes around after replacing Ray Graydon.

Although 18th place suggests they avoided the drop with a degree of comfort they were, in fact, only two points ahead of relegated Crewe.

Colin Lee will need all his skills if Walsall are to avoid the drop this season. He has been busy bringing in new faces; Hay, Sonner, Zdrillic and former Southampton forward Dani Rodrigues have been added to the Bescott playing staff but it may not be enough.

They will do well to stay in Division One.

Longest run without loss: 5
Longest run without win: 9

KEY STAT: Surprise! They lost just one of their last ten.

Our forecast:	23rd
Your forecast:	

WATFORD

Nickname: The Hornets
Colours: Yellow, Red and Black
Ground: Vicarage Road
Capacity: 22,000
Tel: 01923 496000

A DISAPPOINTING season for Watford ended with the departure of manager Gianluca Vialli.

A rather less continental figure, reserves chief Ray Lewington, has stepped into his boots and he has a mighty task on his hands if he is to turn the clock back a few years to when ol' turnip head was bossing the Hornets in the Premiership.

Sean Dyche is the only notable signing but promising youngster Paolo Vernazza and Richard Johnson are both set to return from long-term injuries.

Inconsistency cost Watford dear towards the end of the year and, unless Sir Elton can cut a record in aid of the Hornets, they are unlikely to pull themselves clear from the mid-table rabble.

Longest run without loss: 6
Longest run without win: 7

KEY STAT: The Hornets have won only three of their last 12 home games.

Our forecast:	19th
Your forecast:	

Sponsored by Stan James

WIMBLEDON

Nickname: The Dons
Colours: Blue
Ground: Selhurst Park
Capacity: 26,400
Tel: 020 8771 2233

WIMBLEDON– or should we say Milton Keynes Rovers – have been one of the chief victims of the collapse of ITV Digital.

Unable to survive on sparse gates, the Dons have been forced to strip their prize assets.

Kenny Cunningham has already left for Premiership new boys Birmingham and it would no surprise if there weren't a few more players taking the exit door before the season is very old. Stuart Murdoch is hardly the kind of boss to inspire and the former goalkeeping coach's appointment as manager probably had more to do with money than football.

With no cash and fewer fans, team spirit is low and the new stadium may well be hosting Second Division football.

Longest run without loss: 6
Longest run without win: 7

KEY STAT: Only three Div One clubs had lower attendances last season.

Our forecast:	15th
Your forecast:	

WOLVES

Nickname: Wolves
Colours: Amber and Black
Ground: Molineux
Capacity: 28,500
Tel: 01902 655000

Football's "sleeping giants" woke with a roar and then promptly fell back into slumber just before the job was completed.

The Black Country club have everything in place to become an established Premiership club yet they continue to disappoint.

Quite simply Wolves threw away the title, let alone promotion, and they were in no fit state for the play-offs after the torture of the last few weeks. David Jones is an astute manager and the squad have the ability but anyone thinking about taking a short price about Wolves would do well to cast their mind back a few months.

Competitive but unreliable, that's the best way of summing up Wolves.

Longest run without loss: 9
Longest run without win: 4

KEY STAT: They won two out of nine before the play offs.

Our forecast:	3rd
Your forecast:	

BARNSLEY

Nationwide FOOTBALL LEAGUE 2

Nickname: The Tykes
Colours: Red and White
Ground: Oakwell
Capacity: 21,634
Tel: 01224 632328

BARNSLEY fought all the way to the end of last season but four wins in their last 20 games was not good enough to save them.

The Tykes are currently third favourites for the Division Two title and showed with victories over WBA and Wolves what they are capable of. However, money is not washing around Oakwell and Chris Barker has left for Cardiff.

They have, however, brought in Mads Westh, a 20-year-old winger from FC Copenhagen to Oakwell.

The Yorkshire club compete well at home but on the road they were abysmal, with only two wins all season and over 50 goals conceded. Manager Steve Parkin is no mug but has his work cut out to return the Tykes to Division One.

Longest run without loss: 9
Longest run without win: 9

KEY STAT: The Tykes conceded three or more goals in a third of all games.

Our forecast:	8th
Your forecast:	

BLACKPOOL

Nickname: The Seasiders
Colours: Tangerine
Ground: Bloomfield Road
Capacity: 11,000
Tel: 01253 404331

THE Tangerines finished mid-division last time and will have their work cut out to maintain divisional status. Manager Steve McMahon is ambitious but needs to improve the squad at Bloomfield Road. However, the club are not in the position to make significant signings.

The highlight of last season was the 4-1 LDV Vans Final win over Cambridge. More than that, they beat Stoke, Oldham and Huddersfield en route to that final.

Whilst that Cup triumph showed what they can do in a one-off game, the bread and butter of the League was a different matter. Blackpool leaked goals last term, 69 in total, and that frailty must be rectified this season if McMahon is to keep them out of the drop zone.

Longest run without loss: 6
Longest run without win: 6

KEY STAT: They scored four or more nine times.

Our forecast:	16th
Your forecast:	

Sponsored by Stan James

BRENTFORD

Nickname: The Bees
Colours: Red White and Black
Ground: Griffin Park
Capacity: 13,870
Tel: 0208 847 2511

BRENTFORD were a revelation last season, coming agonisingly close to automatic promotion under manager Steve Coppell.

No other team scored more than the Bees and they had the best goal difference in the Division. However, Chairman Ron Noades made it clear before the play-offs that there was no money available to strengthen the squad. That must have been a body blow to players and manager alike, and the tame way in which they lost to Stoke in the final was indicative of that. Coppell has since moved on.

Morale has been further sapped by the departure of prolific striker Lloyd Owusu to Sheffield Wednesday. The Bees will do well to repeat the success of last season.

Longest run without loss: 7
Longest run without win: 5

KEY STAT: The Bees kept nine clean sheets in their last 14 matches.

Our forecast:	12th
Your forecast:	

BRISTOL CITY

Nickname: The Robins
Colours: Red and White
Ground: Ashton Gate
Capacity: 21,500
Tel: 0117 9630630

THE Robins had a gut wrenching choke in the race for promotion last term and finished the season in dreadful shape.

They should have cruised into the play-offs, at least, and the psychological damage that failing to do so could be devastating to them.

City may have lost Tony Thorpe to divisional rivals Luton Town but they still have quality in the squad, with the likes of Tinnion and Matthew Hill, their gifted young centre back. Manager Dave Jones was linked with a move to Brighton but remains at Aston Gate.

City have suffered heartbreak for the past two seasons and may have to settle for more pain this term.

Longest run without loss: 6
Longest run without win: 4

KEY STAT: In 55 League and Cup games, they never scored more than three.

Our forecast:	9th
Your forecast:	

CARDIFF

Nickname: The Bluebirds
Colours: Blue
Ground: Ninian Park
Capacity: 15,000
Tel: 01222 398636

CARDIFF are red hot favourites to finish off a job that should have been completed last season.

The Bluebirds have invested heavily in players and their wage bill must be of some concern to Sam Hammam and Co.

However, it's very much in for a penny in for pound for the Welsh side and they have already been in the market for Chris Barker from Barnsley for £600,000

The form shown by the Welsh side towards the end of the season was outstanding. If they had started the season in the same vein they would have walked Div Two.

Lennie Lawrence is adept at this level and his record since arriving in Cardiff has been outstanding; played 15, won 11, lost one, drawn three.

Longest run without loss: 14
Longest run without win: 5

KEY STAT: They dropped just six points in their last 13 games.

Our forecast:	1st
Your forecast:	

CHELTENHAM

Nickname: The Robins
Colours: Red and White
Ground: Whaddon Road
Capacity: 8,000
Tel: 01242 573558

CHELTENHAM followed in the footsteps of Wycombe in drawing themselves out of the non-league and forging a successful path in the Football League.

Their rise through the leagues has been spectacular and has been done with largely the same group of players, a massive achievement.

The big question for Cheltenham is whether they can continue on the upward curve at a level they have yet to compete at. The architect of their rise from the Doc Marten's League, Steve Cotterill, has moved on to Stoke and this will be a watershed season for the Robins.

They will need to step up significantly if they are to make a mark here.

Longest run without loss: 13
Longest run without win: 7

KEY STAT: Consistency's the key: September-March they did not lose two in a row.

Our forecast:	17th
Your forecast:	

Sponsored by Stan James

CHESTERFIELD

Nickname: The Spireites
Colours: Blue and White
Ground: Recreation Ground
Capacity: 8,800
Tel: 01246 209765

THEY may be one of the oldest clubs in the Football League but in terms of the future there seems little light on the horizon.

Dave Rushbury has been making bullish noises about bringing young Premiership strikers to the Recreation Ground but thus far only midfielder Chris Brandon has been brought in from Torquay.

The need for new striking talent is understandable as this team managed to hit the back of the net on only 18 occasions away from home. Despite that, defeat was avoided 14 times, though ten of those were draws.

They were the losing-most home side in the division and the indications point to a season-long relegation dog fight.

Longest run without loss: 5
Longest run without win: 7

KEY STAT: The Spireites lost five of their last six.

Our forecast:	19th
Your forecast:	

COLCHESTER

Nickname: The U's
Colours: Blue and White
Ground: Layer Road
Capacity: 7,190
Tel: 01206 508800

A SOLID if unspectacular outfit who will realistically be looking at a mid-division finish as successful season.

Steve Whitton has been hoping to lure out-of-contract N. Ireland defender Pat McGibbon to Layer Road from Wigan and the U's could use him; as 76 league goals conceded tells its own story.

Keeper Richard Knight was still in negotiations over a permenent contract while U's defender Joe Dunne will have to delay his return from a knee ligament injury.

On-loan Arsenal duo John Halls and Graham Barratt made the most of their spell at Layer Road last term earning international U-20 call ups, but they are gone.

There are tough times ahead.

Longest run without loss: 5
Longest run without win: 6

KEY STAT: Only two relegated clubs had lower attendances last year.

Our forecast:	20th
Your forecast:	

CREWE

Nickname: The Railwaymen
Colours: Red and White
Ground: Gresty Road
Capacity: 8,900
Tel: 01472 697111

DARIO GRADI has been at the Alexandra Stadium for almost as long as Crewe and relegation from Division One was a bitter pill to swallow for the man committed to nurturing young footballing talent and playing attractive football.

Whether this approach will stand them in good stead in this division remains to bee seen.

The Railwaymen's World Cup star Efe Sodje was linked with a move to Spain but has repeatedly stated his commitment to Crewe and there are some talented younsters coming through at Gresty Road.

However, even given the relative strength of Div One compared to Div Two it's hard to see why a side that managed only 47 League goals all season should prosper in this environment.

Longest run without loss: 4
Longest run without win: 11

KEY STAT: They never won more than two league games running.

Our forecast:	11th
Your forecast:	

HUDDERSFIELD

Nickname: The Terriers
Colours: Blue and White
Ground: McAlpine Stadium
Capacity: 19,600
Tel: 01484 420335

THE Terriers bounced back to finish sixth in the league, best of the previous season's demoted sides but crashed in the play-offs.

New manager Mick Wadsworth has a reputation as a decent coach; he sparked a mini revival at Oldham last term and fans will be hoping he can push the Terriers over the line in the promotion race.

Wadsworth has brought in some loan players from Southampton but there has been a steady stream of talent leaving the McAlpine. Striker Delroy Facey has left for Bolton, with Kevin Gray moving to Tranmere.

Further bad news for Town is that Nathan Clarke is out for several months with an injury picked up towards the end of last season.

Longest run without loss: 10
Longest run without win: 4

KEY STAT: They took just two points off the top four sides.

Our forecast:	4th
Your forecast:	

LUTON

Nickname: The Hatters
Colours: White and Blue
Ground: Kenilworth Road
Capacity: 9,970
Tel: 01582 411622

THE Hatters have been a revelation under Joe Kinnear and the former Dons boss is keen to keep the Luton bandwagon rolling.

They missed the Championship pennant but racked up an incredible 97 points and were scoring for fun; 96 league goals in the season.

Kinnear has shown that he can make the most of limited opportunities and there can be no doubting the ambition of the club. A new stadium could be in place within 18 months.

News on the transfer front has been quiet but Crewe striker Colin Little, Cameroon defender Pierre Njanka and Lens' Xavier Meride have all been on trial.

Bookmakers say the play-offs are in sight, we shall see.

Longest run without loss: 14
Longest run without win: 3

KEY STAT: The Hatters have won their last six aways.

Our forecast:	10th
Your forecast:	

MANSFIELD

Nickname: The Stags
Colours: Amber and Blue
Ground: Field Mill
Capacity: 6,900
Tel: 01623 23567

MANSFIELD finished some way off the leaders in Division Three and unfortunately for the Stags two of their brightest young stars are stalling over signing new contracts.

The loss of the Chris Greenacre to Stoke City will have been a body blow to manager Stuart Watkiss, as is the loss of defensive stalwart Adam Barrett to Bristol Rovers. It's going to be a big ask for the Stags to take that in their stride and prosper in their new environs.

The promotion drive was built on the back of an outstanding home record, with 17 victories at Field Mill.

The away form was patchy with 12 defeats coming on the road but in their favour this is a young side who will at least put up a fight for survival.

Longest run without loss: 7
Longest run without win: 5

KEY STAT: Promoted despite conceding three or more 11 times.

Our forecast:	24th
Your forecast:	

Sponsored by Stan James

NORTHAMPTON

Nickname: The Cobblers
Colours: Claret and White
Ground: Sixfields Stadium
Capacity: 7,650
Tel: 01604 757773

THE Cobblers performed an escape act that Houdini would have been proud of. Rock bottom and detached at the foot of the table, they produced an incredible turnaround in form to rescue themselves and in the end had five points to spare over Bournemouth.

Kevam Briadhurst has brought Paul Harsley to the Sixfields and the young midfielder finished season 2001/02 as top scorer for Halifax on 11, not bad in a team that finished bottom of Div Three.

Further additions have been made with Paul Rickers, (Oldham), and goalkeeper Lee Harper, (Walsall), coming in on on frees.

The club are in a stronger position than last season and may again defy the odds in this division.

Longest run without loss: 4
Longest run without win: 5

KEY STAT: The Cobblers took points off all the promoted teams last season.

Our forecast:	21st
Your forecast:	

NOTTS COUNTY

Nickname: The Magpies
Colours: Black and White
Ground: Meadow Lane
Capacity: 20,300
Tel: 0115 952 9000

THE oldest club in the Football League are in dire financial straits. County boss Billy Deardon is making all the right noises but his hands are tied by the administration order.

Their finishing position of 18th was perilously close to the drop zone and unless fresh impetus can be found the prospects for the club are limited.

County have invited Anthony Fenton – identical twin brother of Meadow Lane favourite Nicky – to join them for pre-season training and another to come in on trial is Maltese international Luke Dimech. However, County are vulnerable to outside predators and it would be no surprise to see some established players moving on. Harder times beckon for County.

Longest run without loss: 5
Longest run without win: 10

KEY STAT: The Magpies won their last five home games.

Our forecast:	22nd
Your forecast:	

OLDHAM

Nickname: The Latics
Colours: Blue and White
Ground: Boundary Park
Capacity: 13,700
Tel: 0161 624 4972

FORMER QPR reserve team manager Iain Dowie is the new man in the hot seat at Boundary Park.

The Latics had a mixed season last year, starting slowly but then threatening to gate crash the play-off party before fading to eighth place.

Oldham will have to convert draws into victories this season. Stalemate was a feature of last season as the Latics drew 34 per cent of their games. Home form was rock solid with 14 victories tucked under their belt but the away win column was the third worst in the division.

Dowie has brought in new blood in the shape of Les Pogliacomi from Parramatta and Clint Hill from Tranmere for £250,000. They should be challenging this term.

Longest run without loss: 8
Longest run without win: 6

KEY STAT: Div Two top scorers with Brentford.

Our forecast:	5th
Your forecast:	

PETERBOROUGH

Nickname: The Posh
Colours: Blue and White
Ground: London Road
Capacity: 15,500
Tel: 01733 63947

IT'S out with the old and in with the new as Posh are in the throes of a boardroom take-over and a period of readjustment can be expected for United.

Peterborough were a tough side to crack at home but their poor away form dragged them dangerously close to the relegation zone.

In goals terms, Posh were the Jekyll and Hyde of the division. There were goals aplenty at London Road, their haul of 46 was only bettered by Oldham, but it was a different matter on their travels when they hit only 18. Only Bury and Port Vale scored less.

Tony Shields has pledged his immediate future to the club and defender Adam Newton has come in on a free from West Ham.

Longest run without loss: 6
Longest run without win: 10

KEY STAT: They won just two of their last 18 aways.

Our forecast:	15th
Your forecast:	

PLYMOUTH

Nickname: The Pilgrims
Colours: Green, White & Black
Ground: Home Park
Capacity: 19,640
Tel: 01752 562561

ARGYLE cruised to the Div Three title breaking the 100-point barrier in their Championship charge.

Home Park was a fortress and ten points were dropped there all season. The Pilgrims weren't too bad on the road either, tasting defeat on only four occasions.

Paul Sturrock has gone north of the border to strengthen the squad, believing that Nathan Lowndes from Livingston will give his side increased attacking options. David Berseford has also been added to the ranks, moving south from Hull. The Pilgrims can compete here as they were head and shoulders above their rivals in Div Three.

Bookmakers fear them and no Div Two side will relish a trip to Home Park.

Longest run without loss: 12
Longest run without win: 4

KEY STAT: Plymouth had the meanest defence in England, conceding a miserly 28 goals.

Our forecast:	7th
Your forecast:	

PORT VALE

Nickname: The Valiants
Colours: White and Black
Ground: Vale Park
Capacity: 22,356
Tel: 01782 814134

BRIAN HORTON could do with some of celebrity fan Robbie William's millions as he prepares his squad for the start of the season.

Walsall's 24-year-old midfielder Dean Keates joined Brett Angell, Phil Charnock and Ian Brightwell in pre-season training, and the four have been involved friendlies but long term the picture is still unclear. One definite starter for Vale this season is Marc Bridge-Wilkinson who has just boosted the club by signing a new two-year contract.

The Valiants had the distinction of being the lowest scorers away from home in Div Two, with 16. If they are to maintain their position in the League, Horton must address those impotency problems.

Longest run without loss: 8
Longest run without win: 7

KEY STAT: Goals are a problem. The Valients scored just six in their last 11 games.

Our forecast:	23rd
Your forecast:	

Sponsored by Stan James

QPR

Nickname: The R's
Colours: Blue and White
Ground: Loftus Road
Capacity: 19,150
Tel: 020 7743 0262

RANGERS flattered to deceive last season, having established themselves in the play-off zone, they then self-destructed in the new year and their challenge for promotion faded away.

Despite having one of the Division's most potent strikers in Andy Thomson, goals were hard to come by. However, with Gallen fit again and a stronger squad in place, Rangers are set fair for a good season. Manager Ian Holloway has brought in Marc Bircham from Millwall and keeper Nick Culkin from Man Utd. Bircham was a target of a number of Premiership and Division One clubs but luckily for the R's the player is a lifelong Rangers fan. With the return of Clark Carlisle from long term injury, Rangers will go well.

Longest run without loss: 7
Longest run without win: 5

KEY STAT: Consistency please! They were in and out of the play-off zone four times.

Our forecast:	2nd
Your forecast:	

STOCKPORT

Nickname: County
Colours: White
Ground: Edgeley Park
Capacity: 12,086
Tel: 0161 286 8888

CARLTON PALMER has been making all the right noises about his team's prospects for the new season mind you, he assured fans that they would not go down.

County were abysmal last season and it will take a mammoth turn around in form for them to stay in Division Two never mind bounce back.

They managed to win only six games home and way all season and four of those victories came when the cause was already lost. The goals against column tells it's own story: 102 goals conceded at an average of 2.2 per game.

There has at least been some good news for the club as County have swooped for young striker Ben Burgess, from Blackburn. Can he turn it round for them? No.

Longest run without loss: 3
Longest run without win: 18

KEY STAT: They lost nine homes in a row at one stage.

Our forecast:	18th
Your forecast:	

SWINDON

Nickname: The Robins
Colours: Red
Ground: County Ground
Capacity: 15,760
Tel: 01793 430430

TOWN were at times quite simply appalling. They did, however, end the weekly pantomime that was the Neil Ruddock show and that done turned their season around.

Andy King has limited resources to work with but has shown he can operate under those constraints. The principal problem for the Robins was a lack of creativity; they relied too much on the long ball and game-breakers are thin on the ground. With only 46 hits on goal Div Two defenders will not be losing too much sleep.

King has made a move for Bolton striker Davis Norris in a proposed year-long deal but has been unable to tie his man down. Trialists Bimbo Fatukonlaner and Stefani Miglioranzi do not whet the appetite.

Longest run without loss: 5
Longest run without win: 4

KEY STAT: The Robins managed to win just two of their last 18 away games.

Our forecast:	14th
Your forecast:	

TRANMERE

Nickname: Rovers
Colours: White
Ground: Prenton Park
Capacity: 16,970
Tel: 0151 608 4194

ROVERS were a match for anyone on their day last season but unfortunately they lacked consistency and dropped points which should have been gimmes for such a relatively talented squad.

That squad is now being torn asunder and if pre-season is anything to go by the omens are looking extremely bleak for Rovers.

Clint Hill has departed for rivals Oldham, always a bad sign, while Joe Murphy has gone to Premiership new boys West Brom.

Their creative jewel in the crown, Jason Koumas, has been consistently linked with other clubs but it looks as if he is finally off. He is reportedly in talks with Everton who seem willing to fork out to secure the talented midfielder.

Longest run without loss: 12
Longest run without win: 5

KEY STAT: They scored twice as many before Christmas (59) as after (27).

Our forecast:	13th
Your forecast:	

134

WIGAN

Nickname: The Latics
Colours: Blue and White
Ground: Springfield Park
Capacity: 7,500
Tel: 01942 244333

PAUL JEWELL has already proved himself at Bradford and although has yet to do it with Wigan they showed last season that they are not far away from what is required.

They made an appalling start to the campaign last term and only managed only two wins in their first 12 games. However, they hit a hot streak mid way through and showed with a 6-1 victory over Stoke and a 4-0 thrashing of Cardiff what they are capable of.

Bristol Rovers striking sensation Nathan Ellington has been added to the squad for £1.2m and if the 21-year-old can fulfil the promise he showed last season he will prove one of the shrewdest buys of the division.

Longest run without loss: 11
Longest run without win: 7

KEY STAT: They are in the top two of the Div Two market for the third year running.

Our forecast:	3rd
Your forecast:	

WYCOMBE

Nickname: The Chairboys
Colours: Blue
Ground: Adams Park
Capacity: 10,000
Tel: 01494 472100

WANDERERS' promotion push fell away last season but Lawrie Sanchez has shown that his side are a decent if underrated outfit. The former Don has been in situ for three summers now and feels that this squad are capable of building on the success of last season.

Striker Jermaine McSporran is going to be injured for a large part of the season but the squad look solid and ex-Crystal Palace striker Richard Harris has moved to Adams Park as a striking option.

Players coming through are striker Craig Faulconbridge and Andy Thomson who came in at the end of last season.

Wycombe are a well organised, extremely fit outfit; there are no easy games against the Chairboys.

Longest run without loss: 9
Longest run without win: 6

KEY STAT: The Chairboys won only two of their last 15 aways.

Our forecast:	6th
Your forecast:	

BOSTON

Nickname: The Pilgrims
Colours: Amber and Black
Ground: York Street
Capacity: 6,643
Tel: 01205 364406

BOSTON have survived the FA inquiry into financial irregularities in as much as they have preserved their league status. They have, however, been deducted four points and fined £100K.

Even with the penalty, United should give a good account of themselves, as the Conference champs normally do. They turned down offers for seven players during last season. Crowds of 5,000 are likely at York Street, and they should take 2,500 fans with them to some away games. Their top scorer Daryl Clare has made 100 league appearances for Northampton, Cheltenham and Grimsby. Matt Hocking has come in from York City and Ben Chapman from Grimsby.

Longest run without loss: 15
Longest run without win: 3

KEY STAT: Arch Conference rivals Dagenham beat them twice last season.

Our forecast:	14th
Your forecast:	

BOURNEMOUTH

Nickname: The Cherries
Colours: Red and White
Ground: Dean Court
Capacity: 10,400
Tel: 01202 395381

PERHAPS the new Stadium should have been called "Finances First", instead of "Fitness First". A year after its completion the club are having to contemplate selling it, to a property company for £4m and then leasing it back, with a Winding Up order on the way because of the struggle to pay wages.

This is what the collapse of the ITV deal means. David Birmingham, James Bittner, James Ford, Willie Huck, Tresor Kandol, Graeme Mathie, Danny Smith and Pascal Tetu have all been released and Richard Hughes sold to Portsmouth for an undisclosed fee. Five players were given trials in the summer, but none had signed as we went to press. It looks like being a long hard winter on the south coast.

Longest run without loss: 5
Longest run without win: 12

KEY STAT: They won one of their last eight, mostly against fellow strugglers.

Our forecast:	22nd
Your forecast:	

BRISTOL ROVERS

Nationwide FOOTBALL LEAGUE 3

Nickname: The Pirates
Colours: Blue and White
Ground: The Memorial Ground
Capacity: 8,500
Tel: 0117 9772000

IT'S unusual for ante-post favourites to finish second from bottom, but Rovers achieved that last season, even though they kicked off with four wins.

They won one and lost 11 of their last 16 and failed to score in ten of their last 19, paying the price for letting striker after striker move on. At least they got a good price for Nathan Ellington so the finances are in reasonable shape and Ray Graydon has brought in a fair batch of new talent. Crewe striker Paul Tait was his seventh signing of the summer with Swindon striker Grazioli amongst the others. Adam Barrett from Mansfield, Kevin Austen from Cambridge and Danny Boxall from Brentford have also joined. Expect a big improvement.

Longest run without loss: 4
Longest run without win: 14

KEY STAT: No side scored fewer away goals than Rovers, who managed just 12.

Our forecast:	5th
Your forecast:	

BURY

Nickname: The Shakers
Colours: Blue and White
Ground: Gigg Lane
Capacity: 11,840
Tel: 0161 764 4881

THAT Bury should figure here at all is something of a miracle given the scale of their money troubles, which they have tackled with some ingenuity, getting fans and businesses to buy or sponsor seats or bricks in the stand and auctioning first team places.

Their injury problems were consistently the worst in the Nationwide last season too and for five or more players to be sidelined every weekend was the norm from October onwards.

Man Utd's decision to stop playing reserve games at Gigg Lane would have cost Bury £35,000 a year, but Bolton's reserves have stepped in as replacements. They have managed to hold on to Jon Newby, their highly rated striker, so it's not all doom and gloom.

Longest run without loss: 6
Longest run without win: 12

KEY STAT: No side scored fewer home goals in Div Two last term.

Our forecast:	15th
Your forecast:	

Sponsored by Stan James

CAMBRIDGE

Nickname: The U's
Colours: Amber and Black
Ground: Abbey Stadium
Capacity: 9,670
Tel: 01223 566500

A MERE seven league wins made relegation inevitable and they ended up 15 points adrift of safety, conceding 93.

The away record was especially dire, with zero wins and 59 goals conceded. That made their achievement in reaching the LDV Trophy Final all the more remarkable.

The Cup run helped the cash flow and now United are buoyed by an investment of £30,000 from supporters group Cambridge Fans Utd.

Ian Ashbee has gone to Hull and Kevin Austin to Bristol Rovers, but Daniel Chillingworth will be fit for the opener after an operation. Watch out for 19-year-old Supporters' Player of Year Adam Tann.

Longest run without loss: 3
Longest run without win: 11

KEY STAT: The U's were unable to keep a single clean sheet in their last 17 league games.

Our forecast:	16th
Your forecast:	

CARLISLE

Nickname: The Cumbrians
Colours: Blue
Ground: Brunton Park
Capacity: 16,651
Tel: 01228 26237

GUESS what. They've got no money – and hence no Safety Certificate for Brunton Park as we went to press.

A 16-man squad, a transfer embargo and no manager spells another troubled season. They did haul themselves up nine places after a run of one goal in six games left them bottom in November, but nearly eight hours without a goal at the end of the season is surely a taste of things to come.

Caretaker boss Billy Barr did his best over the summer trying to hold the fort, but hadn't signed any of the triallists by mid-July. Mick Galloway and Stuart Whitehead have had successful operations, but it's the club that needs to go under the knife for an emergency op. Or an autopsy.

Longest run without loss: 5
Longest run without win: 8

KEY STAT: Just the one away win last season – in League and Cups.

Our forecast:	24th
Your forecast:	

DARLINGTON

Nickname: The Quakers
Colours: Black and White
Ground: Feethams Ground
Capacity: 7,050
Tel: 01325 465097

AT least they have a Sugar Daddy. Boss Tommy Taylor had mixed fortunes at Cambridge and Orient but chairman George Reynolds has great ambitions for the club.

Like Oxford though, it seems they will get the ground sorted before they get the team to match. At least Mr Reynolds has "Darlo" written through him and is more concerned with performance than profit.

Left back Paul Heckingbottom has left for Norwich and been replaced by Matthew Clarke on a free from Halifax. Taylor averaged around 14 new faces a season when he was in charge at Orient so a big turnover is likely. Whether that brings a turnaround remains to be seen. Mr Reynolds deserves better, lads.

Longest run without loss: 7
Longest run without win: 10

KEY STAT: How about more consistency? They never won three in a row.

Our forecast:	6th
Your forecast:	

EXETER

Nickname: The Grecians
Colours: Black and White
Ground: St James Park
Capacity: 10,570
Tel: 01392 254073

CO-CHAIRMAN Uri Geller is making things happen. His son is on the Board and Michael Jackson has visited and been made an honorary Director. Now Geller plans to get Brazil to play in Devon for the club's centenary in 2004 – because he is well known in Brazil and Exeter were the first team to play a competitive match against Brazil in 1914 (Brazil won 2-0). There should be a film: "Bend it like Uri".

They did climb from bottom up to ninth between October and Christmas, so there is potential here. And money. Young striker James Coppinger comes in from Newcastle, while winger Andrew Baird had a successful summer trial and was expected to sign. Gareth Sheldon and Martin Thomas are also new.

Longest run without loss: 6
Longest run without win: 7

KEY STAT: The Grecians had the worst home defence in the division last season.

Our forecast:	9th
Your forecast:	

Sponsored by Stan James

HARTLEPOOL

Nickname: The Pool
Colours: Blue
Ground: Victoria Park
Capacity: 7,230
Tel: 01429 222077

ONE of the many pleasures of watching Soccer Saturday on Sky is to see Jeff Stelling going through the wringer as a goal for or against Hartlepool goes in.

The Monkey Hangers touched bottom in October and November, then won by three or more seven times to reach the play-offs on the last day, before losing to Cheltenham on penalties.

Three play-off defeats in three seasons is testimony to their resilience, but can they go the extra half yard? Their greatest close season success has been keeping manager Chris Turner. Signs from their successful pre-season tour of Holland were very encouraging: SV Nootdorp and Theole were both beaten 12-0 on successive days.

Longest run without loss: 7
Longest run without win: 8

KEY STAT: Only Man City scored more home goals in England last season.

Our forecast:	2nd
Your forecast:	

HULL CITY

Nickname: The Tigers
Colours: Amber and Black
Ground: Boothferry Park
Capacity: 25,000
Tel: 01482 351119

WE hitched our star to this bandwagon last season, only for the wheels and Brian Little to fall off. The First XI now will be entirely different. Those who have backed the Tigers into 11-4 are trusting in Jan Molby's judgement that all the newcomers will blend.

None of Hull's opponents could afford to splash out £220,000 on Lawrie Dudfield, a 22-y-o Leicester reserve; then a similar sum on N. Ireland international Stuart Elliott from Motherwell – from where defender Greg Strong and John Anderson have also come. Other signings are Newcastle midfielder Stuart Green and Richard Appleby. In their new 25,000 seater stadium, they'll take some stopping. Any value has long gone, but they remain the bet.

Longest run without loss: 8
Longest run without win: 9

KEY STAT: Hull were the only Div Three side paying for players.

Our forecast:	1st
Your forecast:	

Sponsored by Stan James

KIDDERMINSTER

Nickname: Harriers
Colours: Red and White
Ground: Aggborough Stadium
Capacity: 6,500
Tel: 01562 823931

KIDDER continue to adjust to life after Jan Molby under new manager Ian Britton and close season reports were encouraging: the spirit in the camp was good and pre-season training tough.

Richie Appleby has joined up with his old boss at Hull but Chesterfield midfielder Shaun Parrish has signed a two-year deal and will form a tough barrier in the centre with Danny Williams.

Full-back Scott Stamps, keeper John Danby and Ian Foster have all signed new contracts too.

Young striker Matt Lewis is interesting Liverpool and Aston Villa but essentially this is a starless squad which Molby felt he had taken as far as they could go. I can't see them proving him wrong.

Longest run without loss: 4
Longest run without win: 8

KEY STAT: A run of four goals in 13 games each side of Xmas scuppered any play-off hopes.

Our forecast:	19th
Your forecast:	

LEYTON ORIENT

Nickname: The O's
Colours: Red and Black
Ground: Brisbane Road
Capacity: 13,850
Tel: 020 8539 2223

FORMER sprint champ John Regis has been helping the Os with pre-season training, but it's the league marathon they need help with: from fourth in mid-September, they hit 23rd in February.

It's not surprising that new manager Paul Brush has behaved like a new broom – 24 players have gone. In have come N. Ireland midfielder Ciaran Toner from Bristol Rovers and striker Lee Thorpe

who's hit ten or more for the last five seasons. Matthew Brazier, signed for £100k in January, is fit from the injury that sidelined him after eight games.

Chairman Barry Hearn plans to develop Brisbane Road into an all-seater stadium but O's fans may be standing up to boo this season.

Longest run without loss: 5
Longest run without win: 10

KEY STAT: Orient conceded three or more goals on 15 occasions last season.

Our forecast:	13th
Your forecast:	

LINCOLN

Nickname: The Red Imps
Colours: Red, White and Black
Ground: Sincil Bank
Capacity: 10,900
Tel: 01522 880011

NEVER mind Ronaldo, Rivaldo and Ronaldhino – the three R's more likely at Sincil Bank this season are Rolled Over, Receivership and Relegation.

They got five points from their last 11 games, scoring only six. Jason Barnett, Grant Brown, Dave Cameron, Steve Holmes and Justin Walker have been released. Ben Futcher from Doncater, Simon Weaver (Nuneaton) and Simon Yeo (Hyde) have all come up from the Conference. Let's hope they won't be back there next season.

They may be in administration, but the Imps have received a Lincoln Council grant of £50,000 for their Red Imps Centre of Excellence. If you want the best communist hobbits, you know where to go.

Longest run without loss: 4
Longest run without win: 11

KEY STAT: A run of four goals in 13 games each side of Xmas scuppered any play off hopes

Our forecast:	23rd
Your forecast:	

MACCLESFIELD

Nickname: The Silkmen
Colours: Blue and White
Ground: Moss Rose
Capacity: 6,027
Tel: 01625 264686

YET another Division Three team which have little grounds for optimism. They last scored more than two on December 8th, but were unbeaten against Plymouth, Hartlepool, Cheltenham and Luton over the last six weeks.

The Silkmen gathered more points from aways than homes last season and no team scored fewer home goals, which is a bit of an insult to groundsman Mark Patterson who won the Division Three Groundsman of the Year title!

Midfielder Rickie Lambert has gone to Stockport, but former Barnsley defender Michael Welsh has signed for a year after impressing manager Dave Moss and Lee Hardy has come in from Oldham for free.

Longest run without loss: 8
Longest run without win: 8

KEY STAT: A run of four goals in 13 games each side of Xmas scuppered any play off hopes.

Our forecast:	20th
Your forecast:	

OXFORD

Nickname: The U's
Colours: Yellow and Blue
Ground: Manor Ground
Capacity: 9,570
Tel: 01865 761503

THAT striker Lee Steele has come from Brighton invites a comparison. The Seagulls have no proper ground, but appointed proven managers and bought players to leap two divisions in two seasons. Oxford dropped two Divisions in three years by spending peanuts on players, but have a wonderful ground which staged England v Brazil U17s in July.

It hurts fans even more that Chairman Kassam made £6m profit on the old Manor Ground yet is being sued by Oxford Council for £500k. The U's have brought in Matt Robinson from Reading and David McNiven, a Scottish U-21 international from Oldham. Northampton midfielder James Hunt is U's other new boy. Just seven players to go Mr K.

Longest run without loss: 4
Longest run without win: 7

KEY STAT: They won only one of their last ten.

Our forecast:	11th
Your forecast:	

ROCHDALE

Nickname: The Dale
Colours: Blue, Red and White
Ground: Spotland
Capacity: 6,450
Tel: 01706 44648

CLEARLY contenders – the squad is stronger and the finances sound. The manager is now a rookie though. John Hollins refused a new contract so Paul Simpson will try to keep Spotland in the spotlight and he will be playing for them too after his success at Blackpool.

By mid-July there were two recruits: Huddersfield midfielder Chris Beech and Lee Hodges from Scunthorpe. Dale were actually top most of September and enjoyed two more No. 1 days before dropping into the play off zone.

They were undone by a sloppy home performance against Rushden in the play offs but remain a useful side, having done the double over Luton and beaten both Mansfield and Plymouth.

Longest run without loss: 9
Longest run without win: 5

KEY STAT: How about more support at Spotland? The average crowd: 3,411.

Our forecast:	3rd
Your forecast:	

143

RUSHDEN & DIAMONDS

Nickname: Diamonds
Colours: Red, White and Blue
Ground: Nene Park
Capacity: 6,553
Tel: 01933 652000

YET another Conference Champion who did that division proud and were denied successive promotions only by previous Conference Champions.

After a poor start – they collected only three points from their first nine games – they slumped to 22nd. Then came a run of 11 without defeat and they were back in business.

Brett Angell has been released, but they still have their main man and leading scorer, Onandi Lowe, who finished with ten goals in the last seven games of the regular season.

Fellow Jamaican international Paul Hall is another quality Diamond geezer who gets goals. They don't have Hull's resources or support but they will be right up there.

Longest run without loss: 7
Longest run without win: 7

KEY STAT: The Diamonds failed to score in only one of their last 21 games.

Our forecast:	4th
Your forecast:	

SCUNTHORPE

Nickname: The Iron
Colours: Claret and Blue
Ground: Glanford Park
Capacity: 9,185
Tel: 01724 848077

THE Iron saved their worst run of the season for the end: two points from five games, three of which were against teams in the bottom half of the table. An injury to Peter Beagrie didn't help.

Prior to that they had scored in 22 successive games and hovered around the play-off zone since the end of October. The Iron scored more away goals than champions Plymouth last season and only two other sides scored more at home. Paul Wheatcroft has joined from Bolton Wanderers on a free, but they will miss Gareth Sheldon who has gone to Exeter City and Lee Hodges who has joined Rochdale. Brian Laws has done an excellent job but, with limited resorces at Glanford Park, mid-table beckons.

Longest run without loss: 10
Longest run without win: 5

KEY STAT: The Irons took points off every other top half team in Division Three.

Our forecast:	12th
Your forecast:	

Sponsored by Stan James

SHREWSBURY

Nickname: The Shrews
Colours: Blue and White
Ground: Gay Meadow
Capacity: 8,000
Tel: 01743 360111

LAST year we told you this lot would improve because of the quality of their youngsters and manager Kevin Ratcliffe has promised more of the likes of Welsh youth internationals Bragoli, March and Ross Stevens.

The absence in March and April of top scorer Luke Rodgers (only one scored more in Div Three) and skipper Nigel Jemson cost them a play-off spot. They failed to score in five of their last 11.

Pete Wilding and former Forest star Ian Woan have all signed one-year deals. Tretton and Rioch have been released while keeper Mark Cartwright has returned to the States; David Walsh is his likely replacement. They won't be champions but they should kick on.

Longest run without loss: 4
Longest run without win: 4

KEY STAT: The Shrews did the league double over Champions Plymouth.

Our forecast:	7th
Your forecast:	

SOUTHEND

Nickname: The Shrimpers
Colours: Blue
Ground: Roots Hall
Capacity: 12,300
Tel: 01702 304050

MORE ground and money troubles, I'm afraid. The lease on Roots Hall runs out in March and new stadium plans have been scuppered.

Their turnover of £2.9m is the third highest in the division, but they are still losing £6,000 a week, so it's hard to see them challenging. Last season's charge lasted three games: two wins and a draw took them to second at the start but then they descended to mid-table and never looked like escaping.

The club were given a pre-season boost when keeper Darryl Flahavan turned down several lucrative offers and signed up for a further year. He's likely to get plenty of practice playing behind Southend's back line.

Longest run without loss: 6
Longest run without win: 6

KEY STAT: The Shrimpers could not score in four of their last five games.

Our forecast:	18th
Your forecast:	

Sponsored by Stan James

SWANSEA

Nickname: The Swans
Colours: Black, Red and White
Ground: Vetch Field
Capacity: 11,500
Tel: 01792 474114

THE transfer embargo may have been lifted but mascot Cyril & Co. are likely to remain ugly ducklings for a while yet.

Perhaps the most significant departure is that of striker Mamade Sidibe, but the club has also released a further ten of last seaons squad.

In coming frees include Matt Murphy and Paul Reid from Bury, Michael Jackson, Jonathan Keaveny, David Moss (Falkirk), Andrew Marsh, David Smith (Grimsby) and James Thomas.

Who knows whether this mix will work any better than the old. The defence was a shambles at the end as they conceded 17 in five games and had a run of nine games conceding two or more at one stage.

Longest run without loss: 6
Longest run without win: 8

KEY STAT: Only Halifax, who were relegated, conceded more away goals than the Swans.

Our forecast:	17th
Your forecast:	

TORQUAY

Nickname: The Gulls
Colours: Yellow and Blue
Ground: Plainmoor
Capacity: 6,000
Tel: 01803 328666

GULLS fans must have feared the worst when their side lost their first three without scoring, but by the first week in October they had dragged themselves into the top half. However, a run of six defeats pitched them down to 23rd before Halifax and six clean sheets saved their bacon.

There is absolutely no reason to expect anything different this time. New manager Leroy Rosenior has promised that the squad will be much fitter but his hands will remain tied by frugal chairman Mike Bateson – whose latest offer to buy Plainmoor, rebuilding the decrepit "stand", has been spurned by the Torbay District Council yet again. Matt Hockley has signed a new one- year deal. Yawn.

Longest run without loss: 6
Longest run without win: 12

KEY STAT: The Gulls average crowd was 2,563. Only two clubs were lower.

Our forecast:	21st
Your forecast:	

WREXHAM

Nickname: The Robins
Colours: Red and White
Ground: Racecourse Ground
Capacity: 9,200
Tel: 01978 262129

A 5-1 defeat at Huddersfield pitched the Dragons into the relegation pit at the end of October and they were never able to haul themselves out.

A key factor was the way injury and loss of form reduced the effectiveness of striker Lee Trundle: after that 5-1, they failed to score in ten of the next 16 games. Dennis Smith was brought in to manage the club but he could not stop the rot. The good news is that there are so many financially stricken clubs in the basement now that an instant return to Division Two is possible.

The squad remains largely intact with Player of the Year Jim Whitley staying. Dan Bennett has gone to Singapore AF for free, which seems a good swap to me.

Longest run without loss: 4
Longest run without win: 7

KEY STAT: They conceded three or more in nearly a third of their games.

Our forecast:	8th
Your forecast:	

YORK

Nickname: The Minstermen
Colours: Red and Blue
Ground: Bootham Crescent
Capacity: 9,500
Tel: 01904 624447

DICING with death at the beginning of the year when they stayed 23rd for a month, York responded well to the arrival of a new owner and ended up just one point short of the top half, losing only one of their last 12 at home in the league.

Now ex-Watford and AC Milan man Luther Blisset has come in as club coach, to work alongside manager Terry Dolan and assistant Adie Shaw. There's not a lot of new talent – left-sided defender Tom Cowan has come on a free from Cambridge – but there is hope.

They have suffered one financial blow in that Leeds United have decided to stop playing their reserve games at Bootham Crescent. However, I still expect them to push for a play-off place.

Longest run without loss: 5
Longest run without win: 7

KEY STAT: City conceded just two in their last six games.

Our forecast:	10th
Your forecast:	

Sponsored by Stan James

147

CELTIC

Nickname: The Bhoys
Colours: Green and White
Ground: Celtic Park

Capacity: 60,294
Tel: 0141 556 2611 www.celticfc.co.uk

O'NEILL dodged the Leeds banana skin, but notably failed to make any public pledge of his future to Celtic.

That's worrying for the Bhoys, as it suggests this most dedicated of managers feels he has achieved everything he can at the club.

A treble in his first season was outstanding but the Champions League is the grail and the Bhoys were unable to deliver a significant blow.

By the time they next face Rangers, it'll be 11 months since Celtic won an Old Firm game. They're the better of the two at pushing around the SPL minnows but look like coming off second-best in the games that matter this season.

David Fernandez is an excellent signing and the race for the title will be close – but, unlike the bookies, we make their chances odds-against.

Longest run without loss: 9
Longest run without win: 12

Figaro's forecast: 2nd

Your forecast:

2001/02 SPL Stats	Apps	Gls	YC	RC
D Agathe	20 (0)	1	1	0
B Balde	22 (0)	2	2	0
T Boyd	9 (0)	0	1	0
S Crainey	10 (5)	0	1	0
R Douglas	35 (0)	0	0	0
J Gould	1 (0)	0	0	0
S Guppy	10 (6)	0	1	0
J Hartson	26 (5)	19	4	0
C Healy	2 (2)	0	1	0
J Kennedy	1 (0)	0	0	0
D Kharin	2 (1)	0	0	0
P Lambert	33 (1)	5	3	0
H Larsson	33 (0)	29	0	0
N Lennon	32 (1)	1	5	0
S Lynch	1 (0)	2	0	0
S Maloney	3 (13)	5	1	0
J McNamara	9 (11)	0	0	0
J Mjallby	35 (0)	3	2	1
L Moravcik	16 (7)	6	5	0
S Petrov	26 (2)	6	3	0
B Petta	12 (6)	0	4	0
J Smith	3 (8)	1	0	0
C Sutton	18 (0)	4	3	0
M Sylla	7 (2)	1	2	0
O Tebily	8 (3)	0	0	0
A Thompson	22 (3)	6	8	1
J Valgaeren	20 (0)	2	3	1
M Wieghorst	2 (1)	0	0	0

Key Stat: Celtic won 18 of their 19 home games in the SPL, they drew the other one.

Sponsored by Stan James

RANGERS

Nickname: The Gers
Colours: Blue, White and Black
Ground: Ibrox

Capacity: 50,500
Tel: 0141 427 8500   www.rangers.co.uk

WHEN Alex McLeish took over from Dick Advocaat at Ibrox, Rangers were already 12 points adrift. They were eventually beaten by 18 points – should we take this as a sign that he failed to make an impact, or that he slowed the decline?

He joined the club in the middle of a season that already looked distinctly unpromising, 18 months after they last won a trophy. They'd already lost twice to Celtic, including a humiliating 2-0 defeat at Ibrox.

Over the next five months, he steered them to victory in both Cups. The Gers were undefeated in four further encounters with their hated rivals and lost only twice in 30 matches.

Rangers will mount a strong challenge for the title this season. The squad looks strong and they should probably be favourites.

Longest run without loss: 28
Longest run without win: 2

Figaro's forecast: 1st

Your forecast:

2001/02 SPL Stats				
	Apps	Gls	YC	RC
L Amoruso	28 (0)	4	2	1
S Arveladze	21 (1)	11	0	0
M Ball	5 (2)	0	2	0
J Brighton	1 (0)	0	0	0
C Burke	1 (1)	1	0	0
C Caniggia	16 (8)	5	1	0
B Dodds	5 (6)	2	0	0
A Dowie	0 (1)	0	0	0
B Ferguson	21 (1)	1	2	0
T Flo	25 (5)	18	2	0
S Hughes	12 (5)	1	1	0
Jim Gibson	0 (1)	0	0	0
A Johnston	1 (0)	0	0	0
A Kanchelskis	6 (4)	1	1	0
S Klos	36 (0)	0	1	0
B Konterman	26 (0)	2	5	0
R Latapy	14 (2)	5	0	0
P Lovenkrands	10 (9)	2	1	0
R Malcolm	6 (1)	0	0	0
A McGregor	2 (0)	0	0	0
K Miller	0 (3)	0	0	0
M Mols	8 (7)	2	0	0
C Moore	18 (0)	3	4	1
Neil McCann	13 (12)	6	1	1
C Nerlinger	7 (1)	1	1	0
A Numan	28 (2)	1	1	0
T Penttila	0 (1)	0	0	0
C Reyna	10 (0)	2	1	0
F Ricksen	31 (0)	4	5	1
M Ross	19 (2)	0	3	0
T Vidmar	23 (1)	1	2	0
S Wilson	6 (0)	0	0	0
R de Boer	19 (6)	8	1	0

Key Stat: Eventual uefa Cup winners Feyenoord were one of only two sides to defeat Rangers in that 30-match run.

ABERDEEN

Nickname: The Dons
Colours: Red
Ground: Pittodrie
Capacity: 21,634
Tel: 01224 632328

DONS fans devotedly think of their team as the third force in Scottish football, but last season was their first top-half finish since 1996.

Manager Skovdahl has wrought steady improvement. Successive finishes of 12th, seventh and fouth lead to an obvious conclusion.

Their home form last season was easily the best outside the Old Firm, while their away performances let them down.

D'Jaffo and Deloumeaux are uninspiring transfers but equally there have been no hugely significant departures and Aberdeen will continue to hold their own.

They lack Livingston's determined investment, though, and may have to accept that they're no longer even the best of the rest.

Our forecast:	4th
Your forecast:	

DUNDEE

Nickname: The Dark Blues
Colours: Dark Blue
Ground: Dens Park
Capacity: 14,177
Tel: 01382 826104

THE flamboyant Bonetti party is over and it's time for the hangover at Dens Park.

The last time new manager Jim Duffy assumed control, he took them straight down to the First, where they were stuck for the remaining two years of his command. Without him, they won the league and have been fixtures in the SPL since.

Duffy has not been a senior coach in the four years that followed.

Dundee's best six players (Rae, Caballero, Sara, Nemsadze, Carranza and Wilkie) are all for sale while the signing of Novo from relegated Raith does not inspire.

The immediate future for the Dark Blues looks black.

Our forecast:	11th
Your forecast:	

DUNDEE UNITED

Nickname: The Terrors
Colours: Orange and Black
Ground: Tannadice
Capacity: 14,209
Tel: 01382 833166

ONE of the last two teams to wrest the title away from the Old Firm, the Terrors have been readily tamed in recent seasons. We even forecast them for the drop last year. It's to their credit that they improved their consistency and achieved mid-table obscurity last term.

It's been a long time since they looked anything other than a bottom-half club and, with little sign of any great change ahead of the coming season, it's impossible to work up any enthusiasm for them. With respect, new signing Allan Smart is not the stuff that dreams are made of.

They continue to do well as a Cup side, though, making the quarters and round five of last season's tournaments.

Our forecast:	9th
Your forecast:	

DUNFERMLINE

Nickname: The Pars
Colours: Black and White
Ground: East End Park
Capacity: 12,500
Tel: 01383 724295

IN achieving promotion to the SPL behind St Mirren, the Pars won ten of their 18 away games. In each of their seasons in the top flight, by contrast, they've managed only three from 19.

Judged simply on last season's home form, Dunfermline would be entitled to call themselves a better side than Hearts or Kilmarnock. Since September, only the Old Firm have beaten them at East End Park. The Pars have spent the summer on tour in New Zealand, where they played the national side, beating them once.

Whether they can translate this antipodean form to places like Rugby Park is by no means a sure thing, but they merit respect.

Our forecast:	7th
Your forecast:	

HEARTS

Nickname: Hearts
Colours: Claret and White
Ground: Tynecastle Park
Capacity: 18,300
Tel: 0131 337 6132

CRAIG LEVEIN is not proving a great success at Tynecastle. Jim Jefferies was a hard act to follow. He steered Hearts through their best season of recent years, to a clear third in the SPL and a Scottish Cup in 1997-98.

In that year, Hearts averaged 1.86 points per game, which was still 1.5 in the season Levein took over, but has since dropped to 1.37 and most recently 1.26.

In fairness, the club is badly affected by the current cash-flow crisis in Scotland and posted an annual loss of over £3m last autumn. Now, with new signings De Vries and Twaddle injured out of the first part of the season, it looks like they'll have to contend with bad luck as well.

Our forecast:	6th
Your forecast:	

HIBERNIAN

Nickname: Hibees
Colours: Green and White
Ground: Easter Road
Capacity: 17,500
Tel: 0131 661 2159

FRANCK SAUZEE was the fans' choice for manager when Alex McLeish left for Rangers, but he was ill-prepared, winning one match out of 15.

Bobby Williamson's credentials were clearer and his arrival had an electrifying effect – Hibs won their next two matches 3-0. His nine games in charge brought five wins, a draw and no defeat by more than a single goal.

The manager has the ability to make a solid team with limited materials, an essential attribute for any Easter Road coach.

Williamson won the Cup with Killie in '97 and could conjure a Cup run out of Hibs (Cup finalists last year), though their league performance is likely to be dour.

Our forecast:	5th
Your forecast:	

Sponsored by Stan James

KILMARNOCK

Nickname: Killie
Colours: Blue and White
Ground: Rugby Park
Capacity: 18,128
Tel: 01563 525184

THE loss of Bobby Williamson was a massive blow for Killie fans. He was there for 11 years, leading the stripes to their first Cup final for 37 years (in which they beat Falkirk) and their first League Cup final for 39 years (losing to Celtic).

After failure at Bradford, Jim Jefferies will be regarded with suspicion. Although he did well with Hearts, it's the inglorious circumstances of his departure which are remembered.

The manager has promised new faces and it's to be hoped that he means it because, in league terms, Killie were treading water last season. Unless freshened up, they're in danger of a malaise which the arrival of Jambo rejects like Stevie Fulton will do nothing to prevent.

Our forecast:	8th
Your forecast:	

Sponsored by Stan James

LIVINGSTON

Nickname: Livvy Lions
Colours: Black
Ground: Almondvale Stadium
Capacity: 7,500
Tel: 01506 417000

FINANCIAL security and a co-ordinated management drive have provided this club with secure foundations.

It's only six years since they won Division Three in their first season, having discarded their previous identity as Meadowbank Thistle. As Livvy, they've yet to finish in the bottom half of any league they've contested.

Last season, they showed they could mix it with the Old Firm, holding Celtic to a draw and getting four points from their two home games with Rangers.

David Fernandez has gone, but Sergio Berti looks a good signing, while the club may be rewarded for a late change of heart about dumping stiker David Bingham.

Our forecast:	3rd
Your forecast:	

MOTHERWELL

Nickname: The Well
Colours: Amber and Claret
Ground: Fir Park
Capacity: 13,742
Tel: 01698 333333

ADMINISTRATION means straightened times at Fir Park. Nineteen players were axed after the club's parlous financial position became clear and those who remain have had to take wage cuts.

Takeover talk has gone rather quiet in the wake of Airdrie's death and resurrection (through the cannibalising of Clydebank).

Kevin Twaddle, Stuart Elliott and Eric Deloumeaux are no longer on the playing staff and it's clear that any good offers for any players will have to be considered.

New boss Terry Butcher can be relied on to instill some fighting spirit, but Motherwell's "happy few" may not be numerous enough to guarantee 11 fit men throughout the season.

Our forecast:	12th
Your forecast:	

PARTICK THISTLE

Nickname: The Jags
Colours: Red and Yellow
Ground: Firhill Stadium
Capacity: 6,250
Tel: 0141 579 1971

HAVING won two titles in a row, the Jags are ambitious to make a mark, but would settle for SPL survival.

This is a capable squad who do well in front of their own fans; they were unbeaten at home in all competitions last season, while there were only two league losses at Firhill the year before.

They even have respectable form against some top-flight op-position. Although Rangers scored within ten minutes and went on to win their Cup semi-final 3-0, Partick had beaten Dundee at Dens Park to get there.

They lack Livingston's solid finances and can't hope to cut a similar swathe, but Partick won't go straight down.

Our forecast:	10th
Your forecast:	

BELL'S
SCOTTISH FOOTBALL LEAGUE
Partick Thistle FC

FIRST
DIVISION
CHAMPIONS
2001/02

PARTICK THISTLE: Can they do a "Livvy" in the Scottish Premier League?

Sponsored by Stan James

EVERY week in the Outlook you will find articles analysing football stats but perhaps the most important thing that every punter should analyse before striking a bet is himself. Sort that out and you can become more alert at spotting how precisely the bookies are trying to manipulate you.

You need to do this because one of the most potent weapons in the bookies' armoury these days is psychology.

If someone asks you, "Why do you gamble?" the knee-jerk reaction is to say, "I want to make money!", yet if you ask yourself the same question in private, the answer might not be so simple.

Let's consider two different types of bet, both relatively new and increasingly popular – especially with bookmakers – because they are extremely profitable and they exploit a recurrent weakness of punters perfectly.

Twenty years ago, if a Second Division manager lost his job and you wanted to put a fiver on his replacement, most bookies would have looked at you as though were mad and would not have framed a price.

Now, however, the price lists hit the wires seconds after a sacking or resignation is announced. They must have them pre-prepared: eight or nine years ago Ron Atkinson appeared on all of them, then it was Dave Bassett and now of course if the club is a big one, it's Martin O'Neill.

Look closely at the lists and they always contain names of men the clubs would never want or can't afford, or men under contract, or men who wouldn't dream of going to that club. Yet presumably some people bet on them simply because they are on the list and are thus by definition "candidates" even before anyone has asked them if they want the job.

What the bookies have cottoned on to is the need that all punters have to be proved right and the fact that football journalists these days deal more in speculation or saying what they think should happen rather than reporting what has happened. With transfer windows coming in for the Premiership and maybe the Nationwide, this will only get worse.

So this summer the back pages lined up Martin O'Neill, then Mick McCarthy, then Gus Hiddink for David O'Leary's job and the bookies lined their wallets with money punted by thousands of people who did not have a clue about what was really going on but simply hitched their star to the latest bandwagon.

All the bookies have to do is engineer their prices according to trends set by people who are, in respect of what they are betting on, complete ignoramuses. Unless you really are an insider, you will win only if you

Sponsored by Stan James

make a lucky guess.

In your heart of hearts though, are you really out to make money or are you more anxious to seem "in the know" with your mates? It's a macho thing isn't it – a way of saying "I know more about football than you do!" Get it wrong and you just keep quiet.

The second bet works on punters in a much simpler way. It's the Scorecast, combining first goalscorer plus correct score, a related contingency bet unheard of ten years ago. This appeals very basically to the punter's greed simply because of the size of the prices.

The fact is that ANY of the odds quoted in this market are rank bad value in that the probability of the event is much less than the odds suggest. Perhaps one or two punters doing this may suspect they're being fleeced. They are right.

Quite how they are being worked on is interesting though. The most striking feature of the teletext screens, shop posters or web pages carrying these odds is the sheer quantity of prices on show – nearly all big ones, too. It's like a giant box of chocs and the impression created is that maybe ALL the possible options are on display.

In fact of course, only a tiny fraction of the possible permutations are on offer. Discounting goalkeepers but including substitutes, there are 26 possible scorers in a game and, if we allow each side up to six goals and ignore 5-5 or 6-6 (though they have happened), 34 most likely possible scores. So the full set of possibilities is 884
Sponsored by Stan James

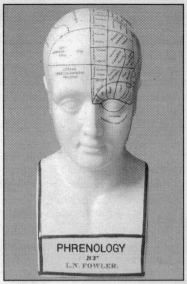

FIGARO SAYS: Know thy self

(and theoretically over 1,000).

So when you dazzled by a display of, say, 30 juicy prices, just remember you are being shown around only three per cent of the possible outcomes. About one quarter of all UK games are draws and one in nine end 0-0, and that result ensures the bookie is like a croupier sweeping the chips off a roulette table because the ball's dropped in zero.

Draws are not the only Scorecast skinner either: games where the side scoring first eventually loses is another. With international Scorecasts too, the layout of the prices is devised so it appeals to punters who bet on what they WANT to happen: OWEN – ENGLAND 2-0: 16-1.

Keep a good eye out then for the Hidden Persuaders – and monitor their dialogue with your inner self.

FA Premiership Ante-post

	Bet365	Coral	Hills	Lads	S James	S Sc
Manchester United	6-4	11-8	11-8	5-4	11-8	6-4
Arsenal	7-4	7-4	13-8	7-4	9-5	7-4
Liverpool	10-3	3	10-3	3	3	10-3
Leeds United	14	14	16	14	12	12
Chelsea	14	12	16	18	16	14
Newcastle United	25	28	28	33	33	22
Tottenham	80	100	80	100	100	80
Manchester City	125	150	100	125	150	125
Aston Villa	150	125	125	150	200	150
Fulham	250	200	200	100	200	250
West Ham	300	250	150	250	300	200
Blackburn	350	200	150	200	300	200
Middlesbrough	500	250	100	200	300	400
Everton	750	500	300	500	400	400
Charlton	1000	1250	350	350	750	1000
Sunderland	750	750	250	500	750	1500
Southampton	1000	1000	300	500	750	750
Bolton	1500	1500	500	500	1500	2000
Birmingham	1500	1500	750	500	1000	1000
West Brom	2500	2500	1000	1000	2500	2000

Nationwide First Division Ante-post

	Bet365	Coral	Hills	Lads	S James	S Sc
Ipswich	9-2	9-2	10-3	4	7-2	4
Wolves	9-2	9-2	9-2	4	5	5
Derby County	7	6	5	6	6	7
Leicester City	9	12	9	7	8	7
Coventry City	12	12	14	14	14	11
Norwich	14	12	20	16	16	18
Millwall	14	12	14	12	14	14
Preston	16	14	20	16	16	16
Watford	14	25	20	25	25	25
Burnley	20	25	22	25	25	25
Reading	20	33	40	25	33	33
Portsmouth	20	16	18	16	18	25
Wimbledon	25	40	25	40	28	25
Crystal Palace	25	20	22	16	20	25
Brighton	33	40	50	33	50	40
Sheffield Utd	33	40	33	40	25	40
Stoke City	33	33	50	33	33	28
Sheffield Wed	33	33	33	50	33	40
Notts Forest	40	33	40	40	33	33
Bradford City	40	40	66	50	50	50
Gillingham	50	50	66	66	50	40
Rotherham	125	100	200	125	200	150
Grimsby	150	125	200	200	250	200
Walsall	150	100	125	150	80	80

Sponsored by Stan James

Nationwide Second Division Ante-post

	Bet365	Coral	Hills	Lads	S James	S Sc
Cardiff City	9-4	9-4	11-4	5-2	11-4	3
Wigan Athletic	6	13-2	5	7	8	9
Barnsley	9	16	11	10	11	10
Bristol City	12	14	11	10	14	12
Luton Town	12	14	11	10	10	14
Huddersfield	12	14	14	16	14	12
Stockport	16	20	22	25	28	25
Crewe	16	18	14	14	11	9
QPR	16	16	12	12	14	16
Plymouth	18	14	16	12	22	25
Oldham	20	18	16	16	20	25
Tranmere	20	20	18	25	25	25
Brentford	22	18	20	25	28	22
Wycombe	25	28	33	33	22	25
Blackpool	25	33	25	25	25	18
Notts County	25	40	33	33	25	33
Port Vale	33	40	33	33	28	22
Peterborough	40	40	40	50	33	50
Swindon	40	40	40	40	33	50
Northampton	50	33	50	50	40	50
Chesterfield	50	40	100	100	33	50
Cheltenham	66	40	40	66	66	28
Colchester	66	66	125	100	80	50
Mansfield Town	66	66	80	50	100	50

Nationwide Third Division Ante-post

	Bet365	Coral	Hills	Lads	S James	S Sc
Hull City	4	7-2	7-2	4	5	7-2
Rushden & Diamonds	7	6	6	11-2	7	8
Bournemouth	11	12	12	14	14	14
Wrexham	12	14	9	10	10	16
Bristol Rovers	14	12	12	12	10	16
Hartlepool	14	12	12	12	14	14
Scunthorpe	14	12	14	12	14	14
Kidderminster	14	16	18	16	20	8
York City	14	40	22	33	18	28
Rochdale	16	16	12	12	12	14
Oxford Utd	20	20	16	25	18	25
Darlington	18	18	22	20	25	20
Boston United	20	16	20	20	22	22
Shrewsbury	20	22	22	20	20	18
Cambridge	20	22	25	20	22	20
Bury	20	25	28	25	22	22
Leyton Orient	20	28	25	20	25	33
Swansea City	22	16	28	25	25	40
Southend	25	28	28	25	25	22
Maclesfield	33	28	40	33	28	25
Carlisle	33	33	50	33	50	50
Lincoln	33	66	66	66	80	50
Exeter	40	40	40	50	40	50
Torquay	50	50	66	50	66	50

Sponsored by Stan James

Bank of Scotland Premier League

	Bet365	Coral	Hills	Lads	S James	Sry
Celtic	1-2	4-7	**8-13**	1-2	8-15	4-7
Rangers	**6-4**	5-4	6-5	11-8	11-8	5-4
Hearts	100	250	250	250	**300**	200
Livingston	150	250	200	150	**400**	250
Aberdeen	**250**	200	150	150	**250**	**250**
Hibernian	350	400	200	**500**	**500**	250
Kilmarnock	500	500	500	500	**750**	500
Dundee Utd	500	500	**1000**	500	**1000**	**1000**
Dundee	500	750	750	750	**1000**	**1000**
Partick	750	**2000**	1000	1000	**2000**	1000
Dunfermline	1000	1000	1000	750	**2000**	1000
Motherwell	1500	2000	2000	**2500**	**2500**	1000

Bell's Scottish Division One

	Bet365	Coral	Hills	Lads	S James	Suy
St Johnstone	-	-	**11-4**	5-2	-	7-4
Ayr	-	-	3	9-4	-	**4**
Falkirk	-	-	9-2	**6**	-	**4**
Ross Co	-	-	**6**	9-2	-	**6**
Inverness CT	-	-	7	**9**	-	**9**
St Mirren	-	-	10	8	-	**8**
Clyde	-	-	10	**12**	-	9
Queen Of South	-	-	10	**16**	-	14
Alloa	-	-	14	**25**	-	**25**
Arbroath	-	-	20	**25**	-	**25**

Bell's Scottish Division Two

	Bet365	Coral	Hills	Lads	S James	Sur
Raith	-	-	**5-2**	5-2	-	9-4
Forfar	-	-	10-3	**5**	-	**5**
Airdrie	-	-	4	7-2	-	**5**
Berwick	-	-	**11-2**	**6**	-	9-2
Brechin	-	-	7	6	-	**8**
Stenhousemuir	-	-	7	**12**	-	9
Stranraer	-	-	9	**12**	-	10
Hamilton	-	-	**11**	7	-	**7**
Dumbarton	-	-	20	14	-	**20**
Cowdenbeath	-	-	**20**	16	-	**20**

Bell's Scottish Division Three

	Bet365	Coral	Hills	Lads	S James	Sur
Peterhead	-	-	2	3	-	**7-2**
Morton	-	-	**5-2**	9-4	-	7-4
Montrose	-	-	4	**5**	-	4
Queen's Park	-	-	7	**10**	-	11-2
Gretna	-	-	9	10	-	**14**
Albion	-	-	**10**	9-2	-	**10**
Elgin	-	-	11	10	-	**16**
East Fife	-	-	12	14	-	**16**
East Stirling	-	-	16	20	-	**16**
Stirling	-	-	20	14	-	**16**

Sponsored by Stan James

Sponsored by Stan James

	Yellow	Red	Games	Pts/Match
M. Riley	74	9	17	56.76
P. Dowd	20	2	5	50
C. Foy	19	1	5	43
G. Barber	81	5	22	42.5
E. Wolstenholme	42	3	11	45
C. Wilkes	40	3	12	39.58
B. Knight	39	2	11	40
U. Rennie	42	1	16	27.81
J. Winter	51	2	20	28
A. Wiley	68	2	23	31.74
R. Styles	70	1	18	40.28
N. Barry	43	3	17	29.71
M. Halsey	64	4	21	35.24
P. Jones	40	1	14	30.36
A. D'Urso	75	9	23	42.39
S. Dunn	55	3	19	32.89
M. Messias	16	0	5	32
P. Durkin	56	3	21	30.24
G. Poll	59	5	24	29.79
D. Pugh	35	0	10	35
M. Dean	44	2	14	35
S. Bennett	55	5	19	35.53
D. Gallagher	40	2	16	28.13
D. Elleray	38	3	17	26.76
Total	**1,166**	**71**		

Total includes Premiership games only.

Points are awarded on the basis of ten points for a yellow card and 25 for a red, the usual practice in spread betting.

Sponsored by Stan James

	Yellow	Red	Av. Points
Arsenal	71	6	22.63
Aston Villa	44	2	12.89
Blackburn	59	4	18.16
Bolton	58	7	19.87
Charlton	63	3	18.55
Chelsea	69	3	20.13
Derby	73	3	21.18
Everton	57	3	16.97
Fulham	55	2	15.79
Ipswich	44	1	12.24
Leeds	69	5	21.45
Leicester	76	5	23.29
Liverpool	41	3	12.76
Man Utd	53	1	14.61
Middlesbrough	53	7	18.55
Newcastle	51	2	14.74
Southampton	36	5	12.76
Sunderland	68	1	18.55
Tottenham	59	5	18.82
West Ham	66	3	19.34

Total includes Premiership games only.

Points are awarded on the basis of ten points for a yellow card and 25 for a red, the usual practice in spread betting.

Sponsored by Stan James

	Score First	Clean sheets	Shots	Fouls
Arsenal	**30 (22)**	14	513	615
Aston Villa	15 (12)	9	431	556
Blackburn	14 (11)	8	420	608
Bolton	15 (8)	7	382	588
Charlton	12 (8)	12	366	559
Chelsea	20 (15)	15	455	546
Derby	12 (7)	7	312	551
Everton	13 (10)	11	388	**637**
Fulham	13 (9)	15	391	547
Ipswich	14 (8)	8	433	520
Leeds United	23 (16)	**18**	449	625
Leicester City	10 (3)	7	310	611
Liverpool	26 (23)	**18**	426	471
Man Utd	23 (20)	13	**544**	490
Middlesbrough	16 (11)	12	323	552
Newcastle Utd	14 (11)	9	477	558
Southampton	16 (12)	9	386	593
Sunderland	12 (10)	11	415	616
Tottenham	23 (12)	8	429	514
West Ham Utd	21 (15)	13	427	570

Values include Premiership games only.

Figure in brackets shows games won when scoring first goal.

Values in bold are the most impressive for each stat category.

Sponsored by Stan James

	To Concede			To Score		
	Avg	Home	Away	Avg	Home	Away
Arsenal	95	68	**155**	43	**40**	46
Liverpool	**114**	**122**	107	51	52	50
Man Utd	76	101	61	**39**	43	**36**
Newcastle	66	74	59	46	43	50
Leeds	92	81	107	65	55	78
Chelsea	90	81	101	52	**40**	74
West Ham	60	**122**	40	71	53	107
Aston Villa	73	101	57	74	78	71
Tottenham	65	71	59	70	53	101
Blackburn	67	86	55	62	52	78
Southampton	63	78	53	74	74	74
Middlesbrough	73	66	81	98	74	143
Fulham	78	107	61	95	81	114
Charlton	70	57	90	90	74	114
Everton	60	74	50	76	66	90
Bolton	55	55	55	78	86	71
Sunderland	67	107	49	118	95	155
Ipswich	53	71	43	83	86	81
Derby	54	66	46	104	86	132
Leicester	53	50	57	114	114	114

Values include Premiership games only and are shown as minutes totals.

Values in bold are the most impressive for each rate.
Sponsored by Stan James

165

Outlook Index
It's all relative in the Euro leagues

REGULAR readers of the *Racing & Football Outlook* will be more than familiar with our exclusive *Index* ratings in which, for every team in the English, Scottish and top European leagues, we seek to eliminate the usual reliance on the league tables for a value of a team's worth. The *Index* instead provides a consistent indicator as to a side's true strength relative to every other team in the league.

Alex Deacon

One of the more unique features of the *Index* is that it not only enables cross divisional comparison between sides, so that you can for example accurately forecast domestic Cup matches, but also allows for direct comparisons between the strength of sides across all of the leagues featured in the RFO. Thus regardless of nationality a European "league" table is created.

Since its inception, this comparative feature has generated a generous level of profits in both European club competitions, chiefly by exploiting the misconceptions that exist in comparing teams from different national leagues.

The natural tendency is for the majority of supporters or punters from certain leagues to over-emphasise the strength of the sides in their own league and to underrate others. For example, there is a tendency for punters in this country to subscribe to the theory that the German Bundesliga is not particularly strong. This is in spite of the fact that the league provided two finalists for last season's European club finals and that with regard to the *Index* the league has nine sides in excess of the 900 mark. That watermark highlights a team as potential championship challengers in that division.

Compare that with Italy and England who have eight and six clubs rated at 900 or above respectively and whatever the truth exactly is, it is almost certainly not suggestive of a weaker German league.

Sponsored by Stan James

Of course, you don't need the *Index* to tell you this; taken as a whole the results from this and last season's European club competitions suggest as much themselves.

What the *Index* does is to provide an objective consistent framework from which to accurately quantify any difference that does exist between sides.

Throughout the past two seasons the main debate in this area has concentrated primarily on the fact that the overall strength of the Spanish

"What the Index does is to provide an objective consistent framework from which to accurately quantify any difference that does exist between sides"

top flight appears, from the *Index* at least, to be significantly above the overall level of ability in the top flights in Italy, England or Germany.

While any sane person would have little reason to disagree with the fact that, at the present time, the Primera Liga contains probably the best team in Europe in Real Madrid, the extent to which the *Index* emphasises the strength in depth of the Primera Liga has vexed a good many. This is despite results bearing out the hypothesis suggested by the *Index*.

Comparing the values of sides in the top flights of the competitions covered in the *Index* is obviously only a preliminary point of analysis. It does
Sponsored by Stan James

nevertheless provide a snapshot that is at least consistent with itself rather than by formation on grounds of random patriotism or just plain stupidity.

On the assumption that the Primera Liga is the strongest league and putting the other leagues alongside it, it is not difficult on first inspection to find fault with the fact that in terms of relative strength the entire Spanish top flight fits into the top six positions of the Premiership.

Does this mean that the *Index* rates bottom-ranked Real Zaragoza as better than seventh-placed West Ham? Yes it does and converting the *Index* value to one of an equivalent goal superiority value it's possible to say that they're just under one-tenth of a goal better.

Utilising the *Index*'s consistent and objective approach, there are few who would deny with much conviction that at the end of last season Real Madrid were not worth the 0.15-0.2 goal supremacy against Man United, on a neutral ground, that the *Index* suggests.

Given the consistency that underlies the *Index* compilation method, if the Real/Man Utd figure seems reasonably accurate, then it follows that the initially hard-to-swallow comparison between other teams must also be accurate.

The problem is that, in the majority of these hypothetical "X is better than Y" arguments, we are never provided with the actual matches that would prove the point in the way that we are with the numerous examples of matches between the sides at the top of their national divisions.

League tables are, quite simply, one of the most deceptive tools a punter can employ in making selections each week, showing as they do the state of a competition at any given point in time.

In their usual format they reveal nothing as to the quality of the opponents each side has met until then. That's where the Outlook Index comes in, showing as it does the relative strength of each side determined by the results of over 38,000 matches and weighted by the strength of the opposition.

Detailed 60-match form is also given for each side so that any trends in a side's playing strength can be readily identified.

Each week of the football season, the Outlook will print updated Index ratings, with the best analysis to help your football betting.

FA BARCLAYCARD PREMIERSHIP 2001-2002

	Curr	Previous match form										Home	Away	Trend
		1-6	7-12	13-18	19-24	25-30	31-36	37-42	43-48	49-54	55-60	Home	Away	Trend
Arsenal	969	961	947	936	930	929	927	932	931	929	939	957	926	14
Liverpool	955	955	942	927	936	934	921	922	910	913	908	942	922	8
Man Utd	946	946	944	936	921	934	940	958	972	973	970	932	944	4
Leeds	915	912	916	928	928	932	929	923	905	888	886	900	904	-2
Newcastle	914	918	920	913	906	894	892	879	873	892	895	928	870	-1
Chelsea	909	916	916	914	914	916	921	912	910	905	896	931	857	-4
West Ham	885	883	870	871	867	866	858	862	873	885	898	936	830	7
Tottenham	879	880	874	880	888	880	873	873	873	876	880	923	836	0
Aston Villa	877	871	888	889	892	905	899	894	894	884	898	904	853	-3
So'ton	876	878	888	885	870	871	886	884	888	877	867	883	849	-3
Blackburn	874	863	850	853	864	866	859	856	858	850	841	900	842	12
Middlesbro	872	884	879	871	875	873	868	878	873	873	860	865	880	-4
Charlton	864	868	877	878	875	870	875	876	876	874	860	877	853	-6
Sunderland	863	867	871	880	888	888	894	894	904	918	910	908	852	-6
Ipswich	862	864	874	876	860	872	890	901	890	885	886	890	849	-4
Everton	862	864	858	860	870	873	871	865	869	866	872	899	850	0
Fulham	860	859	866	878	877	867	862	862	861	854	858	888	832	-4
Bolton	856	863	860	859	865	868	872	855	854	857	858	866	860	-3
Leicester	842	832	830	844	850	844	851	857	884	887	899	884	856	5
Derby	832	835	844	844	848	848	859	862	865	855	856	868	828	-5

Sponsored by Stan James

NATIONWIDE DIV ONE 2001-2002

Previous match form

	Curr	1-6	7-12	13-18	19-24	25-30	31-36	37-42	43-48	49-54	55-60	Home	Away	Trend
Man City	875	866	868	860	845	838	836	842	842	838	845	882	846	8
WBA	861	852	837	831	829	826	824	821	812	821	824	854	847	14
Birmingham	832	828	824	820	818	810	819	828	824	826	854	862	806	6
Wolves	831	835	845	832	824	831	828	816	802	803	808	841	826	-3
Preston	825	824	825	826	829	839	827	822	827	821	818	845	807	0
Norwich	823	814	808	812	814	810	809	813	793	790	799	876	800	8
Millwall	822	810	827	827	817	813	804	790	792	780	785	855	786	2
Burnley	814	814	822	828	844	829	828	835	820	805	794	834	801	-5
Wimbledon	812	822	820	817	810	813	824	818	832	827	818	838	830	-4
Gillingham	806	804	804	809	806	793	788	796	799	795	791	850	783	1
Coventry	802	819	830	823	830	843	848	839	847	852	843	860	804	-14
Sheff Utd	798	806	805	809	810	798	802	804	809	810	817	836	794	-5
C Palace	793	792	801	804	795	804	812	788	783	780	784	836	798	-2
Walsall	792	781	766	766	764	772	765	766	773	762	764	846	773	14
Bradford	791	792	795	796	810	815	818	839	835	831	835	830	805	-3
Grimsby	790	788	774	768	766	772	780	802	792	784	776	849	784	9
Watford	790	799	799	803	814	799	797	796	798	802	808	818	807	-7
Nottm For	789	795	804	808	804	809	818	806	804	811	816	841	812	-8
Barnsley	789	784	783	794	783	768	772	782	790	805	795	858	778	3
Portsmouth	786	791	787	782	796	804	796	798	780	782	791	844	783	-1
Sheff Wed	785	792	788	787	783	789	785	797	806	807	794	814	819	-2
Rotherham	783	787	790	787	793	786	775	772	779	778	781	854	767	-3
Crewe	783	779	790	790	795	796	804	796	801	803	794	836	783	-2
Stockport	746	742	732	740	753	769	780	783	800	798	785	790	784	5

NATIONWIDE DIV TWO 2001-2002

Previous match form

	Curr	1-6	7-12	13-18	19-24	25-30	31-36	37-42	43-48	49-54	55-60	Home	Away	Trend
Brighton	788	780	769	764	760	759	745	737	726	725	720	821	748	11
Cardiff	781	768	750	743	738	734	726	717	708	715	725	820	767	18
Reading	779	786	788	793	778	775	766	778	782	783	780	808	772	-5
Huddersfield	772	781	781	777	768	772	779	792	796	793	787	821	774	-4
Brentford	767	765	750	740	753	768	760	746	726	732	732	830	747	9
QPR	762	760	758	767	766	755	766	772	777	774	784	841	764	1
Stoke	760	763	758	766	782	784	780	767	765	757	769	818	746	-2
Wigan	752	750	749	745	741	731	725	741	750	751	762	765	770	3
Oldham	752	747	752	750	745	740	747	746	733	728	729	804	736	3
Bristol City	749	751	764	770	767	753	762	762	749	754	754	813	758	-7
Swindon	734	734	734	730	726	733	739	732	727	735	740	800	760	2
Wycombe	732	726	737	740	742	747	743	734	728	717	722	790	733	-1
Notts Co	728	720	697	700	718	725	736	747	745	740	751	778	755	13
Tranmere	727	739	752	764	765	748	749	746	751	760	772	829	734	-15
Colchester	726	720	721	728	736	728	731	738	732	732	727	778	738	2
Port Vale	723	730	745	734	722	732	728	737	749	756	754	794	743	-7
Blackpool	719	722	722	720	721	723	717	705	698	694	709	784	741	-1
Peterboro	718	714	712	714	720	730	738	727	727	728	723	789	714	3
North'ton	717	716	711	702	688	694	696	696	709	722	734	770	736	6
Chesterfield	714	720	725	729	726	710	717	712	713	732	737	763	726	-6
Wrexham	706	702	711	704	704	711	720	729	738	741	744	770	739	1
Bour'mouth	705	709	714	725	730	752	750	752	766	755	738	764	735	-7
Bury	701	710	716	718	722	714	702	708	728	734	735	790	727	-9
Cambridge	687	681	680	690	689	698	711	705	714	714	708	766	707	3

Sponsored by Stan James

NATIONWIDE DIV THREE 2001-2002

Previous match form

	Curr	1-6	7-12	13-18	19-24	25-30	31-36	37-42	43-48	49-54	55-60	Home	Away	Trend
Luton	748	741	723	715	720	712	714	708	702	707	716	767	778	14
Plymouth	744	738	732	720	714	711	693	679	667	680	677	802	721	10
Rushden	718	719	710	709	716	727	724	734	506	0	0	758	728	3
Hartlepool	714	702	696	705	698	690	686	695	714	714	717	762	728	10
Cheltenham	710	720	722	714	701	690	692	683	688	690	682	757	732	-5
Rochdale	703	700	701	696	694	711	709	703	691	685	685	757	718	3
Scunthorpe	699	700	698	690	698	694	678	675	679	691	684	774	706	2
Mansfield	695	691	706	706	698	700	690	686	675	662	664	781	688	-2
Shrewsbury	682	677	679	677	681	680	683	682	663	652	652	755	691	3
Kidd'minster	681	684	688	691	694	677	667	670	676	676	689	758	702	-4
Macclesfield	678	673	672	661	663	652	664	668	670	679	675	722	735	6
Southend	676	675	668	674	672	663	669	677	676	676	677	757	694	3
York	672	666	659	660	650	657	660	664	668	668	655	757	694	8
Swansea	664	673	679	663	676	673	672	680	688	689	694	752	705	-6
L. Orient	664	661	654	654	674	685	686	701	690	685	684	754	686	4
Torquay	664	668	654	655	652	664	670	662	660	656	660	746	692	3
Carlisle	662	669	674	675	662	652	654	655	660	656	646	756	664	-6
Darlington	661	652	653	667	656	658	666	669	658	676	671	759	673	4
Exeter	658	666	670	676	681	665	654	650	657	657	646	754	691	-8
Hull	655	664	685	698	702	717	721	717	711	706	694	742	684	-17
Bristol Rov	650	658	659	680	678	680	704	719	719	722	727	752	693	-9
Lincoln	647	645	658	659	662	664	658	658	657	654	659	721	687	-4
Oxford Utd	647	659	663	664	664	664	670	675	673	674	674	734	692	-9
Halifax	634	634	626	640	646	651	654	654	659	648	647	718	687	0

BANK OF SCOTLAND SCOTTISH PREMIER 2001-2002

Previous match form

	Curr	1-6	7-12	13-18	19-24	25-30	31-36	37-42	43-48	49-54	55-60	Home	Away	Trend
Celtic	932	930	931	928	930	921	914	922	917	906	900	928	895	2
Rangers	910	910	906	900	902	904	900	891	905	905	899	914	876	3
Livingston	826	819	834	836	836	812	798	794	792	797	787	830	788	-1
Hearts	826	822	826	826	815	826	830	830	829	833	835	826	802	2
Aberdeen	826	829	821	821	824	813	809	816	809	795	794	848	779	1
Kilmarnock	815	819	823	827	821	829	831	827	830	833	848	826	806	-4
Dundee Utd	812	804	801	799	806	803	805	787	776	764	760	813	811	7
Dunfermline	808	816	810	801	784	786	798	806	819	812	806	853	767	0
Dundee	808	810	806	809	814	822	827	822	812	820	819	820	804	0
Hibernian	805	804	801	812	827	840	837	843	858	860	856	854	769	-1
Motherwell	790	793	799	795	798	799	802	811	820	823	825	814	788	-3
St Johnstne	761	762	763	773	775	777	786	802	805	822	827	766	799	-3

Outlook Index Ratings

BELL'S SCOTTISH DIV ONE 2001-2002

Previous match form

	Curr	1-6	7-12	13-18	19-24	25-30	31-36	37-42	43-48	49-54	55-60	Home	Away	Trend
Ross Co	751	744	730	712	714	710	712	718	731	725	709	740	769	14
Partick	749	751	760	753	738	726	712	710	707	698	690	781	733	-2
Ayr	746	747	746	744	745	765	777	772	760	753	754	768	726	1
Clyde	743	743	734	734	732	729	735	718	721	721	720	795	727	4
Inverness	740	736	736	735	744	743	745	760	754	751	744	799	700	3
St Mirren	733	738	740	756	769	770	783	768	762	769	782	778	728	-8
Airdrie	732	736	752	768	752	747	726	729	726	714	707	754	750	-11
Arbroath	730	728	715	705	702	692	683	685	682	668	664	768	704	9
Falkirk	723	722	733	745	746	752	765	768	775	786	806	754	760	-6
Raith	704	710	708	697	707	720	715	720	722	740	754	766	708	-1

BELL'S SCOTTISH DIV TWO 2001-2002

Previous match form

	Curr	1-6	7-12	13-18	19-24	25-30	31-36	37-42	43-48	49-54	55-60	Home	Away	Trend
QOTS	699	690	676	665	664	664	651	663	665	653	650	734	716	14
Alloa	691	692	690	687	688	700	702	708	702	709	706	741	676	1
Berwick	676	666	668	666	653	648	655	672	668	662	661	690	718	8
Hamilton	664	670	666	671	657	666	672	669	661	672	671	724	678	-2
Cowd'beath	662	658	652	650	659	644	647	652	643	651	641	717	694	5
Forfar	661	666	653	660	654	648	643	632	633	627	629	712	690	1
Stranraer	656	648	653	667	668	672	668	659	662	675	671	697	681	1
Clydebank	652	661	671	672	674	666	666	653	646	652	664	714	675	-10
Morton	651	653	659	668	678	690	715	707	702	706	714	700	699	-6
Sten'muir	628	637	650	642	650	651	639	632	643	647	652	716	674	-10

BELL'S SCOTTISH DIV THREE 2001-2002

Previous match form

	Curr	1-6	7-12	13-18	19-24	25-30	31-36	37-42	43-48	49-54	55-60	Home	Away	Trend
Brechin	637	646	654	654	646	644	644	638	640	635	630	710	651	-8
Albion	626	619	609	601	595	583	576	583	577	585	580	664	684	11
Dumbarton	622	616	612	613	612	610	608	612	608	588	580	668	654	6
Peterhead	605	605	610	613	609	610	601	602	609	602	611	644	629	-2
Montrose	600	596	586	584	594	591	574	562	562	554	558	662	649	7
Q. Park	590	584	591	597	583	594	618	633	637	652	658	671	656	1
Elgin	587	586	574	575	569	560	557	543	546	560	577	643	612	6
East Fife	583	584	591	589	600	591	603	612	626	637	634	664	640	-3
Stirling	573	580	594	607	610	629	642	637	642	640	638	675	625	-13
East Stirling	571	576	566	565	577	576	571	582	584	572	577	649	611	1

Sponsored by Stan James

GERMAN BUNDESLIGA 2001-2002

	Previous match form												
	Curr	1-6	7-12	13-18	19-24	25-30	31-36	37-42	43-48	49-54	55-60	Home	Away	Trend
B Munich	952	945	942	948	964	949	944	942	952	944	957	974	913	4
Dortmund	944	938	938	942	933	926	918	912	913	908	896	944	897	4
Leverkusen	936	942	935	943	953	938	931	933	940	951	950	957	895	-3
Hertha	931	933	926	922	916	907	912	914	918	922	929	957	875	3
Schalke	928	941	938	924	923	924	920	914	909	912	900	956	877	-4
W. Bremen	919	913	917	935	924	911	918	919	914	899	891	938	887	0
K'lautern	906	912	924	928	922	924	905	918	916	911	910	936	880	-9
Stuttgart	905	897	893	900	908	904	897	892	888	887	900	915	874	5
1860 M'nich	903	900	904	903	888	893	894	896	901	900	913	902	887	2
Wolfsburg	890	880	876	875	857	891	902	909	913	912	914	901	874	10
Hamburg	883	889	892	883	881	885	898	894	888	900	916	946	844	-3
Cottbus	874	880	871	864	870	891	882	878	881	883	887	922	843	1
Nurnberg	870	862	873	863	866	878	892	886	875	879	887	908	868	3
Cologne	868	857	854	868	872	891	897	903	895	898	879	912	864	6
M'gladbach	867	874	860	853	860	861	855	857	858	858	864	905	849	2
Freiburg	866	864	885	897	910	912	921	907	900	890	880	904	852	-10
Hansa	834	731	883	885	884	886	895	897	890	889	895	932	811	8
St Pauli	830	840	848	836	840	843	850	867	872	883	878	877	852	-7

SPANISH LA LIGA 2001-2002

	Previous match form												
	Curr	1-6	7-12	13-18	19-24	25-30	31-36	37-42	43-48	49-54	55-60	Home	Away	Trend
Valencia	970	959	948	941	942	943	937	944	951	952	962	975	918	14
Real Madrid	958	965	961	968	964	957	965	976	974	976	966	996	906	-4
Deportivo	957	953	945	948	957	967	970	958	964	967	960	1002	908	5
Barcelona	951	943	937	936	938	952	946	943	952	957	953	977	910	8
Celta	942	947	943	948	942	957	957	949	938	916	915	975	915	-2
Malaga	929	935	926	925	923	926	934	933	927	922	924	950	912	0
R. Sociedad	928	919	905	898	897	889	904	907	902	896	899	963	908	14
Mallorca	922	918	918	928	936	938	960	957	950	939	938	961	903	1
R Vallecano	918	903	900	896	882	875	882	894	897	916	922	942	908	13
Betis	917	922	922	916	912	921	905	899	907	907	916	948	882	-1
Seville	915	899	900	906	898	891	884	885	896	892	894	931	914	10
Espanyol	907	910	918	911	913	913	918	926	925	918	915	967	870	-3
Villarreal	906	905	910	905	917	924	932	923	920	919	906	955	888	-1
Alaves	905	913	917	934	941	927	918	918	929	924	930	924	909	-10
R Valladolid	902	908	921	916	915	905	904	907	920	928	927	962	861	-8
Osasuna	898	900	909	906	904	913	906	901	890	880	890	930	903	-4
Las Palmas	896	907	904	905	905	906	905	906	911	924	922	944	873	-6
Ath Bilbao	894	904	920	920	922	910	901	908	918	928	922	930	902	-13
Tenerife	892	887	888	893	891	894	891	896	903	906	909	955	886	3
R Zaragoza	887	896	902	907	912	913	911	920	926	927	937	956	872	-9

Sponsored by Stan James

Outlook Index Ratings

ITALIAN SERIE A 2001-2002

	Curr	1-6	7-12	13-18	19-24	25-30	31-36	37-42	43-48	49-54	55-60	Home	Away	Trend
						Previous match form								
Juventus	977	970	969	964	965	976	978	968	965	962	956	992	939	6
Roma	966	962	967	973	962	957	962	959	962	950	940	1000	898	1
Inter	945	950	947	952	946	935	920	921	916	914	914	948	935	-2
Lazio	938	933	930	947	950	950	963	962	962	952	960	983	906	1
Milan	931	926	924	931	928	927	926	933	931	942	940	979	902	3
Chievo	921	916	914	924	920	917	454	0	0	0	0	928	896	3
Parma	911	906	907	901	906	922	930	938	934	923	937	939	901	4
Atalanta	905	903	892	893	896	884	887	898	903	900	898	928	905	6
Bologna	899	907	910	897	894	894	885	899	897	893	899	945	848	-3
Perugia	898	895	895	890	882	886	886	892	892	895	890	948	867	4
Torino	898	904	898	883	880	872	878	875	876	870	882	932	861	2
Brescia	893	890	886	884	897	903	902	883	870	867	856	930	882	4
Piacenza	887	880	875	865	855	856	854	862	868	874	888	913	862	10
Udinese	875	872	879	877	879	879	881	882	892	904	922	895	904	0
Verona	871	878	886	894	895	891	886	872	884	888	898	939	842	-9
Lecce	857	864	870	875	884	893	883	878	892	892	886	894	876	-8
Fiorentina	842	853	862	869	875	886	895	906	904	923	921	925	851	-12
Venezia	828	832	844	846	844	848	861	875	876	880	881	899	840	-7

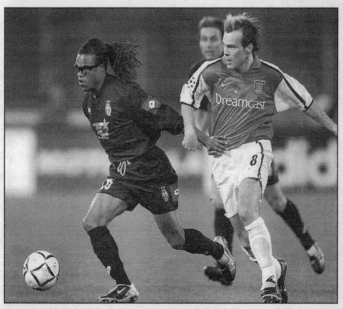

CHAMPIONS LEAGUE: Dual champs Juve and Arsenal are in

Reds and Rams can rampage

AT least 1,000 footballers lost their jobs in England and Scotland over the summer but that ill wind could blow punters plenty of good: with so many clubs in or near administration the number who can win their respective divisions has shrunk.

It's not just the minnows feeling the pinch, either: Leeds and Chelsea have massive eight-figure debts, yet their options are severely limited because the European clubs to whom they might sell are feeling the pinch too.

So clubs that two years ago you would have earmarked to take advantage of transitional seasons for both Arsenal and Man Utd (both rebuilding their defence) could be out of the running.

Newcastle emerged from the depths last season to mount a surprise challenge that stopped only because Dyer and Bellamy picked up injuries.

This time the likeliest surprise package must be Manchester City who are clearly superior to the side dragged up by Joe Royle two years ago. With Schmeichel then Benarbia and Berkovic then Anelka, it truly has a diamond at its heart and it should be as exciting as the Newcastle team Keegan brought up from Division One in 1993.

The trouble is that while City have the stars, they don't have the squad. **LIVERPOOL** had the squad already and they have spent the summer strengthening

Sponsored by Stan James

MICHAEL OWEN: A Premiership winner's medal in 2002/03?

it which is why they are our confident vote to go one step further this time. Their internationals generally had a better World Cup than Arsenal's.

Given how relegated Premiership sides so often bounce back straight away, it has surprised me that the attention paid to Ipswich and Leicester has seen **DERBY** open up at 7-1 for Division One even though their companions in woe have been quick to offload players like Bramble and Savage. You could of course say that nobody wanted Derby's, although Poom

was in demand.

Of course Ipswich deserve to be favourites because of their recent experience at this level, but on a strictly value basis, Derby get the vote here – and so do **Portsmouth**, who can emerge from the depths just as West Brom did last year. The collapse of ITV Digital hit Division One clubs the hardest, but Pompey have the resources to withstand the blow.

Lower down, the clubs we picked last year start hot favourites and while we shall go with the flow and pick **HULL**, the

Sponsored by Stan James

WE'RE BACK: Rangers have been rejuvenated by Alex McLeish

only Division Three club to spend any summer money and now surely the biggest fish in a rapidly shrinking pond, I'm not that keen on Cardiff at a prohibitive 7-2. There remain question marks about the Bluebird defence.

It has become a tradition now for teams promoted from the basement to go through Division Two like a dose of salts and **Plymouth** have emerged like Brighton did with extraordinary credentials in defence. They don't have a spearhead like Zamora, but they have to be the Handicap pick. For the Division Two title the value lies in **QPR** as both Brentford and Bristol City look likely to go backwards.

In the Scottish two horse race, recent Old Firm games

Sponsored by Stan James

suggest that **RANGERS** should not be so far behind Celtic on the lists. McLeish has settled in impressively at Ibrox.

The best Scottish bet has to be **AIRDRIE UTD** or Phoenixonians as they should be known. The old Airdrie pushed Partick hard even though they were on their way down and out. Starting a division lower with sound finances, the new side could develop an unstoppable momentum.

A little series of ante-post pieces in the Outlook last spring incidentally enjoyed great success and we shall be doing more stats analysis in the paper this season in the confident hope of more.

THE BETS

PREMIERSHIP: 4 pts **LIVERPOOL** - general 7-2; Handicap: **Manchester City**.

DIVISION ONE: 2 pts **DERBY** 7-1 Bet365; 1 pt e/w **Portsmouth** 25-1 Betabet or Paddy Power. Handicap: **Portsmouth**.

DIVISION TWO: 2 pts e/w **QPR** - general 16-1; Handicap: **Plymouth**.

DIVISION THREE: 3 pts **HULL** 5-1 Tote; 1 pt e/w **Hartlepool** 14-1 Tote; 1 pt e/w **Rochdale** 16-1 Bet365. Handicap: **Exeter**.

SCOTTISH PREMIER: 2 pts **RANGERS** 6-4 Bet365.

SCOTTISH ONE: 1 pt **AYR UTD**

Sponsored by Stan James

QPR: Division 2 joy for the R's

3-1 Hills.

SCOTTISH TWO: 2 pts **AIRDRIE UTD** 11-2 Blue Square.

SCOTTISH THREE: 1 pt **ALBION** 10-1 with Hills.

ACCA: Cover any 2, any 3 and any 4 of **Liverpool, Derby, QPR, Hull** and **Airdrie Utd** = 25 bets. Stake 1/5 point per bet plus 1 point on all five.

FA BARCLAYCARD PREMIER DIVISION

Pos		P	Home W	D	L	F	A	Away W	D	L	F	A	Pts	Goal Diff
1.	Arsenal	38	12	4	3	42	25	14	5	0	37	11	87	+43
2.	Liverpool	38	12	5	2	33	14	12	3	4	34	16	80	+37
3.	Man. Utd.	38	11	2	6	40	17	13	3	3	47	28	77	+42
4.	Newcastle	38	12	3	4	40	23	9	5	5	34	29	71	+22
5.	Leeds	38	9	6	4	31	21	9	6	4	22	16	66	+16
6.	Chelsea	38	11	4	4	43	21	6	9	4	23	17	64	+28
7.	West Ham	38	12	4	3	32	14	3	4	12	16	43	53	-9
8.	Aston Villa	38	8	7	4	22	17	4	7	8	24	30	50	-1
9.	Tottenham	38	10	4	5	32	24	4	4	11	17	29	50	-4
10.	Blackburn	38	8	6	5	33	20	4	4	11	22	31	46	+4
11.	Southampton	38	7	5	7	23	22	5	4	10	23	32	45	-8
12.	Middlesbro	38	7	5	7	23	26	5	4	10	12	21	45	-12
13.	Fulham	38	7	7	5	21	16	3	7	9	15	28	44	-8
14.	Charlton	38	5	6	8	23	30	5	8	6	15	19	44	-11
15.	Everton	38	8	4	7	26	23	3	6	10	19	34	43	-12
16.	Bolton	38	5	7	7	20	31	4	6	9	24	31	40	-18
17.	Sunderland	38	7	7	5	18	16	3	3	13	11	35	40	-22
18.	Ipswich	38	6	4	9	20	24	3	5	11	21	40	36	-23
19.	Derby	38	5	4	10	20	26	3	2	14	13	37	30	-30
20.	Leicester	38	3	7	9	15	34	2	6	11	15	30	28	-34

NATIONWIDE LEAGUE DIVISION I

Pos		P	Home W	D	L	F	A	Away W	D	L	F	A	Pts	Goal Diff
1.	Man. City	46	19	3	1	63	19	12	3	8	45	33	99	+56
2.	WBA	46	15	4	4	36	11	12	4	7	25	18	89	+32
3.	Wolves	46	13	4	6	33	18	12	7	4	43	25	86	+33
4.	Millwall	46	15	3	5	43	22	7	8	8	26	26	77	+21
5.	Birmingham	46	14	4	5	44	20	7	9	7	26	29	76	+21
6.	Norwich	46	15	6	2	36	16	7	3	13	24	35	75	+9
7.	Burnley	46	11	7	5	39	29	10	5	8	31	33	75	+8
8.	Preston	46	13	7	3	45	21	7	5	11	26	38	72	+12
9.	Wimbledon	46	9	8	6	30	22	9	5	9	33	35	67	+6
10.	Crystal Pal.	46	13	3	7	42	22	7	3	13	28	40	66	+8
11.	Coventry	46	12	4	7	33	19	8	2	13	26	34	66	+6
12.	Gillingham	46	12	5	6	38	26	6	5	12	26	41	64	-3
13.	Sheff. Utd.	46	8	8	7	34	30	7	7	9	19	24	60	-1
14.	Watford	46	10	5	8	38	30	6	6	11	24	26	59	+6
15.	Bradford	46	10	1	12	41	39	5	9	9	28	37	55	-7
16.	Nottm F.	46	7	11	5	26	21	5	7	11	24	30	54	-1
17.	Portsmouth	46	9	6	8	36	31	4	8	11	24	41	53	-12
18.	Walsall	46	10	6	7	29	27	3	6	14	22	44	51	-20
19.	Grimsby	46	9	7	7	34	28	3	7	13	16	44	50	-22
20.	Sheff. Weds.	46	6	7	10	28	37	6	7	10	21	34	50	-22
21.	Rotherham	46	7	13	3	32	29	3	6	14	20	37	49	-14
22.	Crewe	46	8	8	7	23	32	4	5	14	24	44	49	-29
23.	Barnsley	46	9	9	5	37	33	2	6	15	22	53	48	-27
24.	Stockport	46	5	1	17	19	44	1	7	15	23	58	26	-60

Sponsored by Stan James

Pos		P	Home W	D	L	F	A	Away W	D	L	F	A	Pts	Goal Diff
1.	Brighton	46	17	5	1	42	16	8	10	5	24	26	90	+24
2.	Reading	46	12	7	4	36	20	11	8	4	34	23	84	+27
3.	Brentford	46	17	5	1	48	12	7	6	10	29	31	83	+34
4.	Cardiff	46	12	8	3	39	25	11	6	6	36	25	83	+25
5.	Stoke	46	16	4	3	43	12	7	7	9	24	28	80	+27
6.	Huddersfield	46	13	7	3	35	19	8	8	7	30	28	78	+18
7.	Bristol C.	46	13	6	4	38	21	8	4	11	30	32	73	+15
8.	QPR	46	11	10	2	35	18	8	4	11	25	31	71	+11
9.	Oldham	46	14	6	3	47	27	4	10	9	30	38	70	+12
10.	Wigan	46	9	6	8	36	23	7	10	6	30	28	64	+15
11.	Wycombe	46	13	5	5	38	26	4	8	11	20	38	64	-6
12.	Tranmere	46	10	9	4	39	19	6	6	11	24	41	63	+3
13.	Swindon	46	10	7	6	26	21	5	7	11	20	35	59	-10
14.	Port Vale	46	11	6	6	35	24	5	4	14	16	38	58	-11
15.	Colchester	46	9	6	8	35	33	6	6	11	30	43	57	-11
16.	Blackpool	46	8	9	6	39	31	6	5	12	27	38	56	-3
17.	Peterboro	46	11	5	7	46	26	4	5	14	18	33	55	+5
18.	Chesterfield	46	9	3	11	35	36	4	10	9	18	29	52	-12
19.	Notts Co.	46	8	7	8	28	29	5	4	14	31	42	50	-12
20.	Northampton	46	9	4	10	30	33	5	3	15	24	46	49	-25
21.	Bournemouth	46	9	4	10	36	33	1	10	12	20	38	44	-15
22.	Bury	46	6	9	8	26	32	5	2	16	17	43	44	-32
23.	Wrexham	46	7	7	9	29	32	4	3	16	27	57	43	-33
24.	Cambridge U.	46	7	7	9	29	34	0	6	17	18	59	34	-46

Pos		P	Home W	D	L	F	A	Away W	D	L	F	A	Pts	Goal Diff
1.	Plymouth	46	19	2	2	41	11	12	7	4	30	17	102	+43
2.	Luton	46	15	5	3	50	18	15	2	6	46	30	97	+48
3.	Mansfield	46	17	3	3	49	24	7	4	12	23	36	79	+12
4.	Cheltenham	46	11	11	1	40	20	10	4	9	26	29	78	+17
5.	Rochdale	46	13	8	2	41	22	8	7	8	24	30	78	+13
6.	Rushden & D	46	14	5	4	40	20	6	8	9	29	33	73	+16
7.	Hartlepool	46	12	6	5	53	23	8	5	10	21	25	71	+26
8.	Scunthorpe	46	14	5	4	43	22	5	9	9	31	34	71	+18
9.	Shrewsbury	46	13	4	6	36	19	7	6	10	28	34	70	+11
10.	Kidderminstr	46	13	6	4	35	17	6	3	14	21	30	66	+9
11.	Hull	46	12	6	5	38	18	4	7	12	19	33	61	+6
12.	Southend	46	12	5	6	36	22	3	8	12	15	32	58	-3
13.	Macclesfield	46	7	7	9	23	25	8	6	9	18	27	58	-11
14.	York	46	11	5	7	26	20	5	4	14	28	47	57	-13
15.	Darlington	46	11	6	6	37	25	4	5	14	23	46	56	-11
16.	Exeter	46	7	9	7	25	32	7	4	12	23	41	55	-25
17.	Carlisle	46	11	5	7	31	21	1	11	11	18	35	52	-7
18.	Leyton O.	46	10	5	7	37	25	3	6	14	18	46	52	-16
19.	Torquay	46	8	6	9	27	31	4	9	10	19	32	51	-17
20.	Swansea	46	7	8	8	26	26	6	4	13	27	51	51	-24
21.	Oxford Utd	46	8	7	8	34	28	3	7	13	19	34	47	-9
22.	Lincoln	46	8	4	11	25	27	2	12	9	19	35	46	-18
23.	Bristol R.	46	8	7	8	28	28	3	5	15	12	32	45	-20
24.	Halifax	46	5	9	9	24	28	3	3	17	15	56	36	-45

Sponsored by Stan James

Pos		P	Home W	D	L	F	A	Away W	D	L	F	A	Pts	Goal Diff
1.	Boston	42	12	5	4	53	24	13	4	4	31	18	84	+42
2.	Dagenham & R	42	13	6	2	35	20	11	6	4	35	27	84	+23
3.	Yeovil	42	6	7	8	27	30	13	6	2	39	23	70	+13
4.	Doncaster	42	11	6	4	41	23	7	7	6	27	23	67	+22
5.	Barnet	42	10	4	7	30	19	9	6	6	34	29	67	+16
6.	Morecambe	42	12	5	4	30	27	5	6	10	33	40	62	-4
7.	Farnborough	42	11	3	7	38	23	7	4	10	28	31	61	+12
8.	Margate	42	7	9	5	33	22	7	7	7	26	31	58	+6
9.	Telford	42	8	6	7	34	31	6	9	6	29	27	57	+5
10.	Nuneaton	42	9	3	9	33	27	7	6	8	24	30	57	-2
11.	Stevenage	42	10	4	7	36	30	5	6	10	21	30	55	+5
12.	Scarborough*	42	9	6	6	27	22	5	8	8	28	41	55	+5
13.	Northwich	42	9	4	8	32	34	7	3	11	25	36	55	+1
14.	Chester	42	7	7	7	26	23	8	2	11	28	28	54	+4
15.	Southport	42	9	6	6	40	26	4	8	9	13	23	53	+4
16.	Leigh RMI	42	6	4	11	29	29	9	4	8	27	29	53	-2
17.	Hereford	42	9	6	6	28	15	5	4	12	22	38	52	-3
18.	Forest G.	42	7	7	7	28	32	5	8	8	26	44	51	-22
19.	Woking	42	7	5	9	28	29	6	4	11	31	41	48	-11
20.	Hayes	42	6	2	13	27	45	7	3	11	26	35	44	-27
21.	Stalybridge	42	7	6	8	26	32	4	4	13	14	37	43	-29
22.	Dover	42	6	5	10	20	25	5	1	15	21	40	39	-24

*Scarborough deducted 1 point

Pos		P	Home W	D	L	F	A	Away W	D	L	F	A	Pts	Goal Diff
1.	Kettering	42	12	4	5	42	22	15	2	4	38	19	87	+39
2.	Tamworth	42	16	5	0	46	13	8	8	5	35	27	85	+41
3.	Havant	42	14	4	3	47	23	8	5	8	27	27	75	+24
4.	Crawley	42	12	3	6	39	22	9	7	5	28	26	73	+19
5.	Newport AFC	42	10	6	5	32	20	9	3	9	29	28	66	+13
6.	Tiverton	42	10	4	7	34	23	7	6	8	36	40	61	+7
7.	Moor Green	42	10	6	5	39	27	8	1	12	25	35	61	+2
8.	Worcester	42	9	7	5	40	25	7	5	9	25	29	60	+11
9.	Stafford	42	13	2	6	42	26	4	7	10	28	36	60	+8
10.	Ilkeston	42	8	6	7	35	30	6	8	7	28	35	58	-3
11.	Weymouth	42	9	4	8	28	27	6	7	8	31	40	56	-8
12.	Hinckley	42	10	5	6	35	26	4	8	9	29	36	55	+2
13.	Folkestone	42	10	5	6	29	28	4	7	10	22	33	54	-10
14.	Cambridge C.	42	7	7	7	27	29	5	9	7	33	41	52	-10
15.	Welling	42	8	7	6	43	34	5	5	11	26	32	51	+3
16.	Hednesford	42	9	4	8	37	32	6	2	13	22	38	51	-11
17.	Bath	42	9	3	9	36	33	4	8	9	20	32	50	-9
18.	Chelmsford	42	8	6	7	33	33	4	5	11	30	42	50	-12
19.	Newport IOW	42	6	7	8	17	26	6	5	10	21	35	48	-23
20.	Kings Lynn	42	6	8	7	23	23	5	5	11	21	34	46	-13
21.	Merthyr	42	8	7	6	37	31	4	1	16	16	40	44	-18
22.	Salisbury	42	4	5	12	22	34	2	3	16	13	53	26	-52

Sponsored by Stan James

UNIBOND PREMIER DIVISION

Pos		P	Home W	D	L	F	A	Away W	D	L	F	A	Pts	Goal Diff
1.	Burton	44	17	5	0	59	12	14	6	2	47	18	104	+76
2.	Vauxhall M.	44	16	3	3	50	26	11	5	6	36	29	89	+31
3.	Lancaster	44	14	4	4	44	26	9	5	8	36	31	78	+23
4.	Worksop	44	13	4	5	40	22	10	5	7	34	29	78	+23
5.	Emley	44	15	4	3	43	24	7	5	10	26	30	75	+15
6.	Accrington	44	10	7	5	47	27	11	2	9	42	37	72	+25
7.	Runcorn	44	11	2	9	36	26	10	6	6	40	27	71	+23
8.	Barrow	44	10	7	5	40	25	9	3	10	35	34	67	+16
9.	Altrincham	44	11	3	8	33	28	8	6	8	33	30	66	+8
10.	Bradford Pk.	44	11	2	9	45	37	6	4	12	28	39	57	-3
11.	Droylsden	44	11	3	8	32	34	6	5	11	33	44	59	-13
12.	Blyth Sp.	44	9	8	5	30	24	5	8	9	29	38	58	-3
13.	Frickley**	44	10	4	8	37	37	6	7	9	26	32	58	-6
14.	Gateshead	44	7	8	7	24	30	7	6	9	34	41	56	-13
15.	Whitby	44	7	5	10	33	39	8	3	11	28	37	53	-15
16.	Hucknall T.	44	6	5	11	25	35	8	4	10	24	33	51	-19
17.	Marine	44	7	7	8	36	38	4	10	8	26	33	50	-9
18.	Burscough	44	9	4	9	40	38	6	1	15	29	48	50	-17
19.	Gainsborough	44	9	5	8	36	30	4	5	13	25	46	49	-15
20.	Colwyn Bay	44	7	6	9	27	39	5	5	12	22	43	47	-33
21.	Bishop A	44	5	6	11	22	30	7	3	12	24	34	45	-18
22.	Hyde	44	5	7	10	29	37	5	3	14	32	50	40	-26
23.	Bamber Br.**	44	5	4	13	23	40	2	6	14	15	48	30	-50

**Frickley and Bamber Bridge deducted 1 point

RYMAN PREMIER DIVISION

Pos		P	Home W	D	L	F	A	Away W	D	L	F	A	Pts	Goal Diff
1.	Gravesend	42	14	4	3	43	18	17	2	2	47	15	99	+57
2.	Canvey Islnd.	42	15	3	3	55	25	15	2	4	53	16	95	+67
3.	Aldershot	42	12	4	5	44	23	10	3	8	32	28	73	+25
4.	Braintree	42	15	2	4	37	20	8	2	11	29	41	73	+5
5.	Purfleet	42	11	8	2	39	20	8	7	6	28	24	72	+23
6.	Grays	42	12	5	4	33	21	8	5	8	32	34	70	+10
7.	Chesham	42	11	7	3	40	27	8	3	10	29	26	67	+16
8.	Hendon	42	10	3	8	26	22	9	2	10	40	33	62	+11
9.	Billericay	42	8	6	7	32	34	8	7	6	27	26	61	-1
10.	St Albans	42	9	5	7	29	25	7	4	10	42	35	57	+11
11.	Hitchin	42	7	4	10	31	39	8	6	7	42	42	55	-8
12.	Sutton Utd.	42	8	9	4	33	26	5	6	10	29	37	54	-1
13.	Heybridge	42	7	6	8	34	40	8	3	10	34	45	54	-17
14.	Kingstonian	42	10	4	7	34	27	3	9	9	16	29	52	-6
15.	Boreham Wood	42	6	4	11	24	36	9	2	10	26	26	51	-12
16.	Maidenhead	42	9	3	9	27	30	6	2	13	24	33	50	-12
17.	Bedford	42	10	1	10	39	32	2	11	8	25	37	48	-5
18.	Basingstoke	42	8	5	8	28	31	3	10	8	22	37	48	-18
19.	Enfield	42	4	4	13	20	44	7	5	9	28	33	42	-29
20.	Hampton	42	5	8	8	26	32	4	5	12	25	39	40	-20
21.	Harrow	42	2	5	14	26	54	6	5	10	24	35	34	-39
22.	Croydon	42	5	3	13	24	40	2	2	17	12	53	26	-57

Sponsored by Stan James

Pos		P	Home W	D	L	F	A	Away W	D	L	F	A	Pts	Goal Diff
1.	Celtic	38	18	1	0	51	9	15	3	1	43	9	103	+76
2.	Rangers	38	14	4	1	42	11	11	3	2	40	16	85	+55
3.	Livingston	38	9	5	5	23	17	7	5	5	27	30	58	+3
4.	Aberdeen	38	12	2	5	31	19	4	5	10	20	30	55	+2
5.	Kilmarnock	38	7	6	6	24	26	6	4	9	20	28	49	-10
6.	Hearts	38	8	6	5	30	27	6	3	10	22	30	48	-5
7.	Dundee Utd.	38	8	3	8	18	30	5	5	9	20	29	46	-21
8.	Dunfermline	38	9	2	8	25	24	3	5	11	16	40	45	-23
9.	Dundee	38	8	5	6	23	24	4	3	12	18	31	44	-14
10.	Hibernian	38	8	5	6	30	25	5	4	10	16	26	41	-5
11.	Motherwell	38	8	8	3	30	25	3	2	14	19	44	40	-20
12.	St Johnstone	38	2	3	15	11	32	3	3	12	13	30	21	-38

Pos		P	Home W	D	L	F	A	Away W	D	L	F	A	Pts	Goal Diff
1.	Partick	36	12	6	0	38	15	7	3	8	23	23	66	+23
2.	Airdrie Utd.	36	8	6	4	31	19	7	5	6	28	21	56	+19
3.	Ayr	36	8	4	6	25	16	5	8	6	28	28	52	+9
4.	Ross County	36	10	2	6	33	21	5	8	6	18	22	52	+8
5.	Clyde	36	8	6	4	27	21	5	4	9	24	15	49	-5
6.	Inv. CT	36	11	3	4	47	22	2	5	10	13	29	48	+9
7.	Arbroath	36	9	5	4	22	28	3	10	5	20	31	48	-17
8.	St Mirren	36	6	8	4	19	19	5	3	10	24	34	45	-10
9.	Falkirk	36	5	5	8	24	36	4	9	5	25	37	39	-24
10.	Raith	36	7	5	6	31	25	1	6	11	19	37	35	-12

Pos		P	Home W	D	L	F	A	Away W	D	L	F	A	Pts	Goal Diff
1.	Queen of Sth	36	12	2	4	33	19	8	5	5	31	23	67	+22
2.	Alloa	36	8	8	2	35	17	7	6	5	20	16	59	+22
3.	Forfar	36	8	2	7	25	25	7	6	2	26	22	53	+4
4.	Clydebank	36	8	8	4	25	23	6	7	5	19	22	51	-1
5.	Hamilton	36	9	5	4	26	15	4	10	4	23	29	48	+5
6.	Berwick	36	7	4	8	19	28	6	5	7	25	24	47	-8
7.	Stranraer	36	6	7	5	19	25	3	10	5	21	26	45	-3
8.	Cowdenbeath	36	5	8	5	27	28	3	9	6	22	23	44	-2
9.	Stenhsmuir	36	3	8	7	15	25	5	4	9	18	32	36	-24
10.	Morton	36	3	8	7	20	28	4	6	8	28	35	35	-15

Pos		P	Home W	D	L	F	A	Away W	D	L	F	A	Pts	Goal Diff
1.	Brechin	36	12	4	2	38	14	10	3	5	29	24	73	+29
2.	Dumbarton	36	10	4	4	30	22	8	3	7	29	26	61	+11
3.	Albion	36	8	5	5	28	23	8	6	4	23	19	59	+9
4.	Peterhead	36	9	2	4	36	26	7	2	9	27	26	56	+11
5.	Montrose	36	9	2	7	25	20	6	7	9	18	19	54	+4
6.	Elgin	36	9	3	6	26	20	4	5	9	19	27	47	-2
7.	E. Stirling	36	8	1	9	27	27	4	3	11	24	31	40	-7
8.	East Fife	36	6	4	8	23	26	5	3	10	16	30	40	-17
9.	Stirling	36	6	4	8	23	29	3	6	9	22	39	37	-23
10.	Queen's Park	36	4	6	8	17	21	5	2	11	21	32	35	-15

Sponsored by Stan James

Pos		P	Home W	D	L	F	A	Away W	D	L	F	A	Pts	Goal Diff
1.	Juventus	34	13	3	1	38	11	7	8	2	26	12	71	+41
2.	Roma	34	13	4	0	33	8	6	9	2	25	16	70	+34
3.	Inter Milan	34	11	3	3	33	17	9	6	2	29	18	69	+27
4.	AC Milan	34	7	8	2	25	14	7	5	5	22	19	55	+14
5.	Chievo	34	9	5	3	30	21	5	7	5	27	31	54	+5
6.	Lazio	34	10	6	1	38	18	4	5	8	12	19	53	+13
7.	Bologna	34	12	2	3	28	17	3	5	9	12	23	52	0
8.	Perugia	34	10	4	3	24	15	3	3	11	14	31	46	-8
9.	Atalanta	34	6	6	5	22	23	6	3	8	19	27	45	-9
10.	Parma	34	8	6	3	22	15	4	2	11	21	32	44	-4
11.	Torino	34	7	5	5	23	18	3	8	6	14	21	43	-2
12.	Piacenza	34	8	1	8	30	18	3	8	6	19	25	42	+6
13.	Brescia	34	5	8	4	28	26	4	5	8	15	26	40	-9
14.	Udinese	34	4	5	8	19	26	7	2	8	22	26	40	-11
15.	Verona	34	9	3	5	23	18	2	3	12	18	35	39	-12
16.	Lecce	34	3	6	8	19	24	3	4	10	17	32	28	-20
17.	Fiorentina	34	3	6	8	16	23	2	1	14	13	40	22	-34
18.	Venezia	34	2	6	9	17	26	1	3	13	13	35	18	-31

Pos		P	Home W	D	L	F	A	Away W	D	L	F	A	Pts	Goal Diff
1.	Valencia	38	14	4	1	28	8	7	8	4	23	19	75	+24
2.	Deportivo	38	13	4	2	40	13	7	4	8	25	28	68	+24
3.	Real Madrid	38	14	5	0	48	14	5	4	10	21	30	66	+25
4.	Barcelona	38	12	5	2	44	17	6	5	8	21	20	64	+28
5.	Celta Vigo	38	10	5	4	36	21	6	7	6	28	25	60	+18
6.	Real Betis	38	11	5	3	26	13	4	9	6	16	21	59	+8
7.	Alaves	38	10	1	8	22	21	7	2	10	19	23	54	-3
8.	Seville	38	7	6	6	26	18	7	5	7	25	22	53	+11
9.	Malaga	38	8	7	4	24	20	5	7	7	20	24	53	0
10.	Ath. Bilbao	38	6	7	6	23	29	8	4	7	31	37	53	-12
11.	R Vallecano	38	11	3	5	27	19	2	7	10	19	33	49	-6
12.	Valladolid	38	9	4	6	24	20	4	5	10	21	38	48	-13
13.	Sociedad	38	8	6	5	31	22	5	2	12	17	32	47	-6
14.	Espanyol	38	12	2	5	34	20	1	6	12	13	36	47	-9
15.	Villarreal	38	9	6	4	30	21	2	4	13	16	34	43	-9
16.	Mallorca	38	7	5	7	24	23	4	5	10	16	29	43	-12
17.	Osasuna	38	6	6	7	19	21	4	6	9	17	28	42	-13
18.	Las Palmas	38	7	8	4	23	17	2	5	12	17	33	40	-10
19.	Tenerife	38	6	5	8	21	30	4	3	12	11	28	38	-26
20.	Real Zaragoza	38	6	7	6	21	23	3	3	13	14	31	37	-19

Sponsored by Stan James

GERMAN BUNDESLIGA

Pos		P	Home W	D	L	F	A	Away W	D	L	F	A	Pts	Goal Diff
1.	B Dortmund	34	12	3	2	31	12	9	4	4	31	21	70	+29
2.	B Leverkusen	34	14	1	2	46	13	7	5	5	31	25	69	+39
3.	B Munich	34	12	5	0	42	10	8	3	6	23	15	68	+40
4.	Hertha Berlin	34	13	2	2	40	13	5	5	7	21	25	61	+23
5.	Schalke	34	13	2	2	38	14	5	5	7	14	22	61	+16
6.	W Bremen	34	11	2	4	29	21	6	3	8	25	22	56	+11
7.	Kaiserslautern	34	11	4	2	39	21	6	1	10	23	32	56	+9
8.	VfB Stuttgart	34	8	5	4	25	16	5	6	6	22	27	50	+4
9.	1860 Munich	34	8	3	6	31	33	7	2	8	28	26	50	0
10.	Wolfsburg	34	9	3	5	34	18	4	4	9	23	31	46	+8
11.	SV Hamburg	34	7	6	4	35	25	3	4	10	16	32	40	-6
12.	B M'gladbach	34	6	5	6	21	21	3	7	7	20	32	39	-12
13.	Cottbus	34	8	4	5	27	21	1	4	12	9	39	35	-24
14.	H Rostock	34	6	6	5	20	18	3	1	13	15	36	34	-19
15.	Nuremberg	34	7	3	7	21	23	3	1	13	13	34	34	-23
16.	Freiburg	34	6	5	6	25	26	1	4	12	12	38	30	-27
17.	FC Cologne	34	5	5	7	16	21	2	3	12	10	40	29	-35
18.	St Pauli	34	4	4	9	19	28	0	6	11	18	42	22	-33

FRENCH CHAMPIONNAT

Pos		P	Home W	D	L	F	A	Away W	D	L	F	A	Pts	Goal Diff
1.	Lyon	34	14	3	0	42	7	6	3	8	20	25	66	+30
2.	Lens	34	10	7	0	33	7	8	3	6	22	23	64	+25
3.	Auxerre	34	10	3	4	26	18	6	8	3	22	20	59	+10
4.	Paris St-G.	34	8	8	1	26	9	7	5	5	17	15	58	+19
5.	Lille	34	11	3	3	25	13	4	8	5	14	19	56	+7
6.	Bordeaux	34	10	4	3	22	12	4	4	9	12	19	50	+3
7.	Troyes	34	9	5	3	27	12	4	3	10	13	23	47	+5
8.	Sochaux	34	9	3	5	29	17	3	7	7	12	23	46	+1
9.	Marseille	34	10	5	2	25	13	1	6	10	9	26	44	-5
10.	Nantes	34	8	4	5	25	16	4	3	10	10	25	43	-6
11.	Bastia	34	9	1	7	25	15	3	4	10	13	29	41	-6
12.	Rennes	34	9	4	4	25	17	2	4	11	15	34	41	-11
13.	Montpellier	34	7	8	2	21	9	2	5	10	7	22	40	-3
14.	Sedan	34	6	9	2	22	13	2	6	9	13	26	39	-4
15.	Monaco	34	8	7	2	29	16	1	5	11	7	25	39	-5
16.	Guingamp	34	8	5	4	19	17	1	3	13	15	40	35	-23
17.	Metz	34	7	2	8	20	19	2	4	11	11	28	33	-16
18.	Lorient	34	6	5	6	23	22	1	5	11	20	42	31	-21k

Sponsored by Stan James

	Arsenal	Aston Villa	Blackburn	Bolton	Charlton	Chelsea	Derby	Everton	Fulham	Ipswich	Leeds	Leicester	Liverpool	Man Utd	Middlesboro	Newcastle	Southampton	Sunderland	Tottenham	West Ham
Arsenal	*	3-2	3-3	1-1	2-4	2-1	1-0	4-3	4-1	2-0	1-2	4-0	1-1	3-1	2-1	1-3	1-1	3-0	2-1	2-0
Aston Villa	1-2	*	2-0	3-2	1-0	1-1	2-1	0-0	2-0	2-1	0-1	0-2	1-2	1-1	0-0	1-1	2-1	0-0	1-1	2-1
Blackburn	2-3	3-0	*	1-1	4-1	0-0	0-1	1-0	3-0	2-1	1-2	0-0	1-1	2-2	0-1	2-2	2-0	0-3	2-1	7-1
Bolton	0-2	3-2	1-1	*	0-0	2-2	1-3	2-2	0-0	4-1	0-3	2-2	2-1	0-4	1-0	0-4	0-1	0-2	1-1	1-0
Charlton	0-3	1-2	0-2	1-2	*	2-1	1-0	1-2	1-1	3-2	0-2	2-0	0-2	0-2	0-0	1-1	0-1	2-2	3-1	4-4
Chelsea	1-1	1-3	0-0	5-1	0-1	*	2-1	3-0	3-2	2-1	2-0	2-0	4-0	0-3	2-2	1-1	2-4	4-0	4-0	5-1
Derby	0-2	3-1	2-1	1-0	1-1	1-1	*	3-4	0-1	1-3	0-1	2-3	0-1	2-2	0-1	2-3	1-0	0-1	1-0	0-0
Everton	0-1	3-2	1-2	3-1	0-3	0-0	1-0	*	2-1	1-2	0-0	2-2	1-3	0-2	2-0	1-3	2-0	1-0	1-1	5-0
Fulham	1-3	0-0	2-0	3-0	0-0	1-1	0-0	2-0	*	1-1	0-0	0-0	0-2	2-3	2-1	3-1	2-1	2-0	0-2	0-1
Ipswich	0-2	0-0	1-1	1-2	0-1	0-0	3-1	0-0	1-0	*	1-2	2-0	0-6	0-1	1-0	0-1	1-3	5-0	2-1	2-3
Leeds	1-1	1-1	3-1	0-0	0-0	0-0	3-0	3-2	0-1	2-0	*	2-2	0-4	3-4	1-0	3-4	2-0	2-0	2-1	3-0
Leicester	1-3	2-2	2-1	0-5	1-1	2-3	0-3	0-0	0-0	1-1	0-2	*	1-4	0-1	1-2	0-0	0-4	1-0	2-1	1-1
Liverpool	1-2	1-3	4-3	1-1	2-0	1-0	2-0	1-1	0-0	5-0	1-1	1-0	*	3-1	2-0	3-0	1-1	1-0	1-0	2-1
Man Utd	0-1	1-0	2-1	1-2	0-0	0-3	5-0	4-1	3-2	4-0	1-1	2-0	0-1	*	0-1	3-1	6-1	4-1	4-0	0-1
Middlesboro	0-4	2-1	1-3	1-1	0-0	0-2	5-1	1-0	2-1	0-0	2-2	1-0	1-2	0-1	*	1-4	1-3	2-0	1-1	2-0
Newcastle	0-2	3-0	2-1	3-2	3-0	1-2	1-0	6-2	1-1	2-2	3-1	1-0	0-2	4-3	3-0	*	3-1	1-1	0-2	3-1
Southampton	0-2	1-3	1-2	0-0	1-0	0-2	2-0	0-1	1-1	3-3	3-1	2-2	2-0	1-3	1-1	3-1	*	2-0	1-0	2-0
Sunderland	1-1	1-1	1-0	1-0	2-2	0-0	1-1	1-0	1-1	1-0	2-0	2-1	0-1	1-3	0-1	0-1	1-1	*	1-2	1-0
Tottenham	1-1	0-0	1-0	3-2	0-1	2-3	3-1	1-1	4-0	1-2	2-1	2-1	1-0	3-5	2-1	1-3	2-0	2-1	*	1-1
West Ham	1-1	1-1	2-0	2-1	2-0	2-1	4-0	1-0	0-2	3-1	0-0	1-0	1-1	3-5	1-0	3-0	2-0	3-0	0-1	*

Sponsored by Stan James

NATIONWIDE DIV ONE 2001-2002 RESULTS

	Barnsley	Birmingham	Bradford	Burnley	Coventry	Crewe	Crystal P	Gillingham	Grimsby	Man City	Millwall	Norwich	Notts F	Portsmouth	Preston	Rotherham	Sheffield U	Sheffield W	Stockport	WBA	Walsall	Watford	Wimbledon	Wolves
Barnsley	*	1-3	3-3	1-1	1-1	2-0	1-4	4-1	0-0	0-3	1-1	0-2	2-1	1-4	2-1	1-1	1-1	3-0	2-2	3-2	4-1	2-0	1-1	1-0
Birmingham	1-0	*	4-0	1-3	2-0	3-1	1-0	2-1	4-0	1-2	4-0	4-0	1-1	1-1	0-1	2-2	2-0	2-0	2-1	0-1	1-0	3-2	1-1	2-2
Bradford	4-0	1-3	*	2-3	2-1	2-0	1-2	5-1	3-2	0-2	1-2	4-0	2-1	3-1	0-1	3-0	1-2	0-2	2-4	0-2	2-0	4-3	3-3	0-3
Burnley	3-3	0-1	1-1	*	1-0	3-3	1-0	5-1	1-0	2-4	0-0	1-1	2-1	1-1	2-1	3-0	2-0	1-2	3-2	0-2	5-2	1-0	3-2	2-3
Coventry	4-0	1-1	4-0	0-2	*	1-0	2-0	1-2	0-1	4-3	0-1	2-1	0-0	2-0	2-2	2-0	1-0	2-0	0-0	0-1	2-1	0-2	3-1	0-1
Crewe	2-0	0-0	2-2	1-2	1-6	*	0-0	3-1	2-0	1-3	1-0	1-0	0-3	1-1	2-2	2-0	2-2	0-2	4-1	1-1	2-1	1-0	0-4	1-4
Crystal P	1-0	0-0	2-0	1-2	1-3	4-1	*	3-1	5-0	2-1	1-3	3-2	1-1	0-0	2-0	2-0	0-1	4-1	4-1	0-1	2-0	0-2	4-0	0-2
Gillingham	3-0	1-1	0-4	2-2	1-2	1-0	3-0	*	2-1	1-3	1-0	0-2	3-1	2-0	5-0	2-1	0-1	2-1	3-3	2-1	2-0	0-0	0-0	2-3
Grimsby	1-0	3-1	0-1	3-1	0-1	1-0	5-2	1-2	*	0-2	2-2	0-2	3-1	2-0	2-2	0-2	1-0	0-0	3-1	0-0	3-0	0-3	6-2	1-1
Man City	5-1	3-0	3-1	5-1	4-2	3-2	3-0	4-1	4-0	*	2-0	2-0	0-0	3-1	2-2	3-0	2-1	4-0	2-2	1-0	3-0	1-0	0-4	1-0
Millwall	3-1	1-1	3-1	2-1	3-2	2-0	3-0	1-2	3-1	2-3	*	4-0	3-3	1-0	2-1	2-2	2-0	1-2	2-0	1-0	2-2	1-0	0-1	1-0
Norwich	2-1	0-1	1-4	2-1	2-0	2-2	2-1	2-1	1-1	2-0	0-0	*	1-0	0-0	3-0	0-0	2-1	2-0	2-0	2-0	1-1	3-1	2-1	2-0
Nottm F	0-0	0-0	1-0	1-0	2-1	2-2	4-2	2-2	0-0	1-1	1-2	2-0	*	0-1	1-1	2-0	1-0	0-1	2-1	0-1	2-3	0-0	0-0	2-2
Portsmouth	4-4	1-1	0-1	1-1	1-0	2-4	4-2	2-1	4-2	2-1	3-0	4-0	3-2	*	0-1	2-1	3-0	0-0	6-0	1-2	1-1	0-1	1-2	2-3
Preston	2-2	1-0	1-1	2-3	4-0	2-2	2-1	0-2	0-0	2-1	1-0	4-0	3-2	2-0	*	2-1	3-0	4-2	3-2	1-0	1-1	1-1	1-1	1-2
Rotherham	1-1	2-2	1-1	1-1	0-0	2-2	2-3	3-2	1-1	1-2	0-0	1-1	2-1	1-0	1-0	*	1-1	1-1	3-2	2-1	2-0	1-1	3-2	0-3
Sheff Utd	3-1	4-0	2-2	3-0	0-1	1-0	1-3	0-0	3-1	1-3	3-2	2-1	0-0	4-3	2-2	2-2	*	0-0	3-0	0-3	0-1	0-2	0-1	2-2
Sheff Wed	1-3	0-1	1-1	0-2	2-1	1-0	1-3	0-2	0-0	2-6	1-1	0-5	1-3	2-3	1-2	1-2	0-0	*	5-0	0-3	2-1	2-1	0-1	2-2
Stockport	3-1	0-3	1-0	4-1	0-2	0-1	0-1	1-0	3-3	4-0	0-4	2-1	0-1	0-1	0-2	0-1	1-2	3-1	*	1-2	0-2	2-1	1-2	1-4
WBA	2-1	1-0	1-0	0-2	0-2	4-1	0-1	0-1	0-1	0-0	0-2	2-0	1-0	5-0	2-0	0-1	0-1	1-1	4-0	*	1-0	1-1	0-1	1-1
Walsall	3-0	1-2	2-2	1-0	0-1	2-1	2-2	1-0	4-0	2-0	1-4	0-1	2-1	0-0	1-2	3-2	0-3	3-1	1-0	2-1	*	0-3	2-1	0-3
Watford	3-0	3-3	0-0	1-2	3-0	2-0	0-2	3-1	2-0	1-2	1-4	2-1	1-2	3-0	2-0	3-2	1-1	3-1	1-0	1-2	2-1	*	3-0	1-1
Wimbledon	0-1	3-1	1-2	0-0	0-1	2-0	1-1	3-1	2-2	2-1	1-0	0-1	1-0	3-3	2-3	1-0	1-1	1-1	3-1	0-1	2-2	0-0	*	0-1
Wolves	4-1	2-1	3-1	3-0	3-1	1-4	0-2	1-4	1-1	1-0	1-0	0-0	1-0	2-2	1-2	0-3	0-0	0-0	2-2	0-1	3-0	1-0	1-0	*

Sponsored by Stan James

NATIONWIDE DIV TWO 2001-2002 RESULTS

	Blackpool	Bournem'th	Brentford	Brighton	Bristol C	Bury	Cambridge	Cardiff	Chesterf'ld	Colchester	H'dersfield	N'thampton	Notts Co	Oldham	Peterboro	Port Vale	QPR	Reading	Stoke	Swindon	Tranmere	Wigan	Wrexham	Wycombe
Blackpool	*	4-3	1-3	2-2	5-1	0-1	1-1	1-1	1-0	2-1	1-2	1-2	0-0	0-2	2-2	4-0	2-2	0-2	2-2	1-0	1-1	3-1	3-0	2-2
Bournemouth	0-1	*	0-2	1-1	1-3	3-2	2-2	1-3	3-1	0-1	2-3	5-1	4-2	3-2	0-2	0-0	1-2	1-0	3-1	0-0	0-2	2-0	3-0	1-2
Brentford	2-0	1-0	*	4-0	2-2	5-1	2-1	2-1	0-0	4-1	3-0	2-0	2-1	3-0	2-1	2-0	0-0	3-1	1-0	2-0	4-0	0-1	3-0	1-2
Brighton	4-0	2-1	1-2	*	4-0	2-1	4-3	1-0	2-2	4-1	1-0	2-0	2-1	3-0	2-1	0-0	0-1	1-1	1-1	3-1	1-0	2-2	0-0	1-0
Bristol C	2-1	1-0	0-2	0-1	*	2-0	2-0	1-1	3-0	3-1	1-1	1-3	3-2	1-1	1-0	1-1	2-0	3-3	0-1	0-3	2-0	2-1	1-0	0-1
Bury	1-1	2-1	2-0	0-2	2-0	*	2-2	3-0	2-1	1-3	0-0	2-1	0-4	1-1	2-0	1-1	1-2	1-1	0-2	1-2	0-1	0-2	2-2	1-1
Cambridge U	0-3	2-2	2-1	0-0	2-2	2-2	*	2-1	4-1	1-2	0-1	3-3	0-2	1-1	0-0	0-1	2-1	2-2	0-2	1-2	2-1	2-2	0-2	2-0
Cardiff	2-2	2-2	3-1	1-1	0-3	3-1	2-1	*	2-1	1-1	1-2	2-0	2-1	3-1	0-2	1-0	1-1	2-2	2-0	3-0	1-1	2-2	3-2	0-1
Chesterfield	2-1	2-1	0-1	1-2	1-3	1-0	2-1	2-1	*	3-6	3-3	2-2	2-1	4-2	0-1	1-1	2-3	0-2	1-2	4-0	0-2	1-2	3-2	0-0
Colchester	1-1	1-2	1-1	1-1	2-1	2-0	2-0	0-2	3-6	*	0-3	3-1	0-1	2-1	2-1	2-0	3-1	2-0	1-3	1-3	2-1	2-2	2-1	0-0
Huddersfield	2-4	1-2	1-1	1-4	0-0	1-0	3-1	0-1	1-2	0-3	*	2-0	2-2	0-1	3-1	1-0	1-0	0-1	0-0	2-0	4-1	0-0	5-1	2-4
Northampton	1-3	1-0	1-0	2-0	0-3	1-2	2-1	2-2	0-2	2-3	2-0	*	0-2	2-1	2-1	1-3	2-2	0-1	0-0	1-2	3-0	0-2	4-1	2-1
Notts Co	1-0	2-0	0-0	2-2	2-0	1-2	2-1	1-7	1-1	1-1	1-1	0-3	*	0-2	1-0	0-2	1-0	3-4	2-1	0-3	1-1	1-3	2-2	3-0
Oldham	2-1	3-3	3-2	2-0	0-1	4-0	2-2	1-1	1-1	4-1	1-1	4-2	4-1	*	2-0	2-0	1-0	0-1	1-2	3-1	5-0	1-1	3-1	2-1
Peterboro	3-2	6-0	1-1	0-1	4-1	2-1	1-0	1-1	1-1	3-1	1-2	2-0	0-1	2-2	*	3-0	4-1	1-2	1-1	2-0	1-1	0-2	2-3	3-0
Port Vale	1-1	0-0	2-1	0-1	1-0	1-0	5-0	0-2	4-1	3-1	1-1	0-1	4-2	3-2	4-1	*	1-0	0-2	1-0	1-1	1-2	1-0	1-3	3-1
QPR	2-0	1-1	0-0	0-0	1-0	3-0	0-0	2-1	0-0	2-2	3-2	0-1	3-2	1-1	4-1	4-1	*	0-0	4-0	0-2	4-1	1-1	2-1	1-0
Reading	3-0	2-2	1-2	0-0	3-2	1-1	1-0	1-2	0-1	3-0	1-0	0-0	2-1	2-2	2-2	2-0	1-0	*	1-3	2-0	1-2	1-1	2-0	0-2
Stoke	2-0	2-2	3-2	2-0	1-2	4-0	5-0	1-0	3-0	0-1	1-1	2-1	1-0	2-2	1-0	3-0	0-1	2-0	*	1-3	2-2	2-2	1-0	1-0
Swindon	1-0	0-0	2-0	3-1	1-2	5-0	2-0	0-3	2-1	3-0	0-1	2-0	4-2	1-0	0-0	0-1	2-3	0-0	0-3	*	2-2	1-1	3-1	1-1
Tranmere	4-0	0-0	1-0	0-0	3-1	2-0	6-1	0-1	0-0	2-1	1-0	3-0	1-1	2-2	1-0	3-1	1-2	2-2	2-2	2-2	*	1-2	5-0	2-1
Wigan	0-1	0-0	1-0	1-1	1-0	6-1	4-1	4-0	1-1	2-3	1-0	3-0	1-1	1-0	2-1	0-1	1-0	0-2	6-1	1-0	1-2	*	2-3	1-0
Wrexham	1-1	2-1	0-3	1-2	0-2	1-0	5-0	1-3	0-1	1-1	3-2	3-2	2-1	3-3	1-2	1-3	1-0	0-2	0-1	2-2	1-1	2-0	*	0-0
Wycombe	1-4	1-1	5-3	1-1	2-1	0-2	2-0	0-1	0-0	0-0	2-4	2-1	3-0	2-1	3-0	3-1	1-0	0-2	1-0	1-1	2-1	1-0	5-2	*

Sponsored by Stan James

NATIONWIDE DIV THREE 2001-2002 RESULTS

	Bristol R	Carlisle	Cheltenham	Darlington	Exeter	Halifax	Hartlepool	Hull	Kidderm'ter	Leyton O	Lincoln	Luton	Maclesf'd	Mansfield	Oxford Utd	Plymouth	Rochdale	Rushden	Scunthorpe	Shrewsbury	Southend	Swansea	Torquay	York
Bristol R	*	0-0	1-2	1-0	0-0	2-0	0-1	1-1	2-1	5-3	1-2	3-2	0-2	0-1	1-1	1-2	0-2	0-3	1-1	0-0	2-1	4-1	1-0	2-2
Carlisle	1-0	*	0-0	1-3	1-0	0-0	0-2	0-0	1-0	6-1	2-2	0-2	3-2	0-1	2-1	0-2	1-2	3-0	3-0	0-1	0-0	3-1	2-0	2-1
Cheltenham	0-0	2-0	*	0-0	3-1	2-1	3-0	1-0	2-1	1-1	2-1	1-1	4-1	2-3	2-0	0-0	1-1	1-1	3-3	1-0	1-1	2-2	2-2	4-0
Darlington	1-0	2-2	0-2	*	4-0	5-0	1-1	1-0	2-0	3-0	2-1	3-2	0-1	0-1	1-0	1-4	1-0	0-0	2-1	3-3	2-2	0-0	1-3	3-1
Exeter	1-0	1-0	0-2	4-2	*	0-0	0-2	1-3	2-1	0-0	1-1	2-2	0-1	0-1	3-2	2-3	1-2	1-1	0-4	3-3	2-1	0-3	0-0	3-1
Halifax	0-0	2-2	4-1	2-2	1-1	*	0-2	0-1	1-0	0-0	3-0	2-4	0-0	1-0	0-2	0-2	2-4	1-0	0-0	1-2	1-1	0-1	2-0	1-1
Hartlepool	1-1	3-1	0-1	1-2	2-0	3-0	*	4-0	1-1	3-1	1-1	1-2	0-0	1-1	0-1	1-0	5-1	5-1	3-2	2-2	5-1	7-1	4-1	3-0
Hull	0-0	0-1	5-1	1-2	2-0	3-0	1-1	*	2-1	1-1	1-1	0-4	4-1	1-1	3-0	1-0	2-1	2-1	0-1	3-0	0-0	2-1	1-0	4-0
Kidderminstr	2-0	2-2	0-0	1-0	3-1	3-0	3-2	*	2-1	0-1	1-1	0-4	1-1	4-1	0-0	0-0	4-1	3-0	1-0	3-0	2-0	0-2	1-0	4-1
Leyton O	3-1	0-0	0-2	0-0	1-1	3-1	3-2	2-1	*	0-1	5-0	1-4	2-0	1-1	3-0	0-0	4-2	2-1	0-0	2-4	2-1	2-2	1-2	1-2
Lincoln	0-1	3-1	0-1	1-1	0-0	1-2	2-0	1-3	0-1	2-0	*	0-1	2-0	1-4	3-0	0-1	1-1	2-4	3-2	1-2	0-1	3-0	0-0	1-3
Luton	3-0	1-1	2-1	5-2	3-0	5-0	0-1	1-0	1-0	3-0	1-1	*	0-0	5-3	1-1	2-0	0-1	1-0	2-3	1-0	2-0	3-0	5-1	2-1
Macclesfield	2-1	1-1	1-0	1-1	3-0	5-0	0-1	0-0	1-0	3-0	0-1	4-1	*	0-1	0-1	0-1	0-1	0-0	4-3	0-1	0-0	1-3	0-2	2-1
Mansfield	2-0	2-0	2-1	4-2	0-1	2-0	3-0	4-2	1-1	3-2	2-1	4-1	0-1	*	2-1	0-3	3-1	1-4	2-1	3-1	0-0	3-0	2-0	1-1
Oxford Utd	0-0	1-1	3-0	1-2	1-2	6-1	1-2	1-0	1-1	1-1	2-1	1-2	3-2	0-2	*	1-1	1-2	3-2	0-1	0-1	2-0	0-1	1-1	2-2
Plymouth	1-0	3-0	2-0	1-0	3-0	3-0	1-0	1-0	2-1	3-0	2-0	2-1	1-0	1-0	4-2	*	1-2	1-0	2-1	1-0	0-0	3-1	2-2	1-0
Rochdale	2-1	1-1	2-2	3-1	2-0	2-0	0-0	3-2	2-0	3-0	2-2	1-0	3-1	3-1	2-1	1-3	*	0-0	4-3	1-0	0-1	2-0	2-0	5-4
Rushden & D	3-1	3-1	1-0	2-1	0-1	2-1	0-1	4-2	1-1	1-0	0-0	1-1	1-1	3-1	2-1	2-3	1-1	*	2-1	3-0	0-1	4-0	0-0	3-0
Scunthorpe	1-2	2-1	1-2	7-1	3-4	4-0	1-0	1-0	1-0	4-1	1-1	0-2	4-0	0-0	1-0	0-1	2-1	1-1	*	3-1	2-0	2-2	1-0	1-0
Shrewsbury	0-1	1-0	2-1	3-0	0-1	3-0	1-3	4-0	2-1	1-0	1-1	0-2	1-1	3-0	1-0	3-1	1-0	0-2	2-2	*	2-0	3-0	1-0	3-2
Southend	2-1	3-2	0-1	1-0	3-1	4-1	0-0	2-0	1-0	1-2	1-1	1-2	3-0	1-0	2-2	0-1	4-2	0-0	2-2	3-3	*	4-2	0-1	1-0
Swansea	2-1	0-0	2-2	2-0	4-2	0-2	0-1	2-1	2-1	0-1	0-0	1-3	0-0	2-0	0-0	0-1	0-0	1-1	0-0	2-1	3-2	*	2-2	0-1
Torquay	2-1	2-1	0-1	2-1	0-2	2-4	1-0	2-1	1-4	1-1	2-0	0-1	1-2	0-0	3-3	0-1	3-0	1-1	0-2	2-1	2-1	1-2	*	1-1
York	3-0	0-0	1-3	2-0	2-3	1-0	1-0	2-1	0-1	2-1	2-0	1-0	1-0	3-1	1-0	0-0	0-1	0-1	0-2	1-1	2-1	0-2	1-1	*

Sponsored by Stan James

NATIONWIDE CONFERENCE 2001-2002 RESULTS

	Barnet	Boston	Chester	Dagenham	Doncaster	Dover	Farnboro	Forest G	Hayes	Hereford	Leigh RMI	Margate	Morecambe	Northwich	Nuneaton	Scarboro	Southport	Stalybridge	Stevenage	Telford	Woking	Yeovil
Barnet	*	0-1	3-1	4-0	0-2	2-0	0-3	0-1	3-1	2-0	1-1	4-1	1-0	1-0	0-1	1-1	0-0	1-2	0-3	0-0	3-0	2-3
Boston	1-1	*	0-1	1-2	2-2	4-2	4-0	6-1	4-1	3-4	2-1	0-1	2-1	3-2	4-1	2-2	0-0	4-1	0-0	3-1	4-0	4-0
Chester	1-0	1-2	*	0-1	1-1	3-0	1-0	2-3	3-1	2-0	1-1	0-3	1-1	1-1	1-0	0-0	0-2	0-0	5-1	2-2	0-2	1-1
Dagenham &R	1-1	1-0	3-0	*	1-0	1-0	2-1	1-1	1-1	1-0	0-1	4-1	3-2	2-0	2-0	4-2	1-1	2-1	1-0	1-5	3-1	1-1
Doncaster	2-3	0-1	2-0	0-0	*	2-1	1-1	5-1	5-2	4-0	2-0	1-0	3-3	2-2	2-2	4-3	1-0	0-1	2-0	1-0	2-0	1-2
Dover	2-2	3-2	1-0	0-1	0-1	*	2-1	1-2	3-2	0-1	0-0	0-0	1-1	2-1	1-2	0-2	0-1	1-0	0-1	0-1	2-2	1-2
Farnborough	2-1	0-2	1-1	1-2	0-1	1-0	*	3-0	1-0	4-2	3-0	4-1	2-1	4-1	2-1	4-2	0-1	2-0	6-1	1-1	3-1	1-2
Forest G	2-2	0-3	0-2	2-4	0-2	2-1	3-0	*	1-2	1-1	1-2	3-3	4-3	2-0	1-2	2-2	2-1	0-2	0-0	1-1	0-1	1-3
Hayes	0-2	0-2	1-3	2-4	1-5	2-1	1-0	1-1	*	4-1	2-1	2-4	2-3	2-1	1-2	1-2	1-0	0-0	0-1	1-4	4-3	1-1
Hereford	2-1	0-1	1-0	1-0	0-0	3-0	0-3	1-1	2-1	*	0-1	3-0	3-1	1-2	1-1	1-2	0-0	3-0	0-2	0-1	2-2	0-4
Leigh RMI	3-3	1-2	3-0	2-0	1-4	1-2	3-0	1-2	0-1	0-1	*	2-2	0-2	1-0	0-1	6-0	1-2	1-0	1-1	3-1	3-1	0-2
Margate	0-1	1-1	0-0	1-1	1-1	0-1	4-2	0-0	1-1	2-2	1-2	*	0-1	1-2	1-1	1-1	2-0	8-0	1-2	3-1	3-3	0-1
Morecambe	1-0	0-0	0-3	1-1	1-1	2-1	1-1	1-1	1-0	2-2	1-3	1-1	*	1-2	1-0	2-0	2-2	1-0	2-1	2-1	1-0	0-1
Northwich	0-3	1-2	3-1	1-2	2-1	2-1	1-2	2-0	2-1	1-0	0-3	2-1	2-1	*	3-0	1-1	3-1	3-1	0-3	2-2	0-3	1-5
Nuneaton	2-3	1-1	1-3	2-0	2-3	3-0	1-1	2-2	1-0	2-0	2-1	0-0	0-2	3-0	*	1-0	3-0	1-1	2-1	1-2	0-2	1-3
Scarborough	3-0	2-0	2-0	0-0	2-3	1-1	1-0	2-1	0-2	3-2	2-5	0-1	1-1	0-1	1-2	*	2-0	3-1	2-1	3-0	0-3	1-2
Southport	0-1	2-3	3-2	2-2	1-0	0-2	2-5	5-1	2-3	1-1	5-0	1-2	1-1	1-2	1-1	2-3	*	3-1	1-1	0-0	2-0	0-0
Stalybridge	1-1	2-1	0-4	2-3	1-0	0-2	1-1	2-1	1-0	0-2	0-1	2-2	3-1	5-1	4-2	2-0	0-0	*	3-1	0-2	3-1	1-2
Stevenage	3-2	1-2	2-1	1-3	0-0	1-3	1-2	4-1	1-1	3-1	0-1	3-1	3-1	1-1	2-2	3-0	2-1	2-0	*	1-1	0-2	0-3
Telford	1-2	2-2	0-3	1-4	1-1	4-3	0-1	0-0	1-2	0-1	1-1	1-1	4-1	1-0	0-2	2-2	1-1	3-1	2-0	*	3-3	0-0
Woking	1-3	0-2	2-1	0-2	3-1	4-0	3-2	2-2	2-1	1-0	1-1	1-2	1-3	0-3	0-0	2-2	2-0	1-1	2-1	1-1	*	3-0
Yeovil	1-2	0-1	0-1	3-3	1-1	2-0	0-1	2-2	2-1	2-1	2-1	1-2	1-1	2-3	2-1	2-1	0-0	0-2	2-1	1-1	1-3	*

Sponsored by Stan James

DR MARTENS PREMIER DIV 2001-2002 RESULTS

	Bath	Cambridge	Chelmsford	Crawley	Folkestone	Havant	Hednesford	Hinkley	Ilkeston	Kettering	Kings Lynn	Merthyr	Moor Green	Newport A	Newport I	Salisbury	Stafford	Tamworth	Tiverton	Welling	Weymouth	Worcester
Bath	*	1-1	1-1	1-2	2-0	2-5	3-4	1-2	1-1	0-1	0-1	4-2	0-2	2-1	0-1	1-0	4-3	1-2	4-2	2-1	2-1	4-0
Cambridge C	1-3	*	1-1	0-1	0-0	2-1	2-1	3-2	1-1	2-1	2-1	2-2	0-1	1-2	2-0	1-3	1-1	1-1	1-3	2-0	2-2	0-2
Chelmsford	1-3	0-3	*	2-2	2-1	0-3	1-1	0-2	6-1	0-2	2-2	2-1	0-2	3-1	3-0	3-2	0-0	1-1	2-2	1-2	2-1	2-1
Crawley	3-0	4-3	3-3	*	2-1	3-0	4-1	1-0	2-0	0-2	1-0	2-1	1-2	0-1	2-0	4-0	1-2	1-2	3-0	2-4	0-0	1-0
Folkestone	1-1	1-0	2-1	1-1	*	1-1	1-0	1-3	0-2	2-3	1-2	1-0	1-0	3-1	2-2	2-0	2-1	3-3	0-3	0-0	1-3	2-1
Havant	3-0	4-1	4-1	2-0	2-2	*	2-1	5-0	2-2	1-3	0-0	4-0	3-1	1-3	2-1	2-0	2-1	0-2	3-3	1-0	3-2	1-0
Hednesford	1-0	1-1	1-2	0-0	2-2	2-1	*	2-1	3-2	2-1	1-0	3-0	1-2	3-2	1-2	6-0	3-3	1-2	2-1	1-1	2-4	0-3
Hinckley	2-2	2-2	2-0	0-1	2-1	2-4	4-0	*	2-2	2-1	0-0	1-0	3-1	0-2	0-0	2-1	3-0	1-0	3-4	1-0	3-2	0-0
Ilkeston	3-3	1-1	3-3	0-0	2-4	2-0	2-0	1-1	*	0-2	3-1	1-0	2-1	0-1	1-2	0-1	2-2	2-1	0-2	3-2	2-2	1-2
Kettering	0-0	1-2	4-2	1-3	3-1	3-1	1-1	2-1	1-2	*	3-0	3-0	2-1	1-2	1-1	4-0	1-0	1-1	0-0	3-1	4-1	4-1
Kings Lynn	1-1	1-3	3-0	2-2	1-1	1-1	1-0	1-1	0-1	0-3	*	0-1	1-0	4-2	3-1	2-1	2-0	1-1	0-1	1-2	0-0	0-0
Merthyr	3-1	1-2	3-1	3-1	1-0	2-1	3-1	2-2	2-3	0-2	3-1	*	1-2	1-1	1-4	3-2	2-0	3-2	1-2	4-4	0-1	1-2
Moor Green	0-0	1-2	3-0	1-1	1-2	2-0	1-4	1-1	1-1	1-2	4-0	1-0	*	1-2	0-0	1-1	1-1	2-1	1-1	2-1	2-3	0-0
Newport AFC	1-0	2-2	0-3	1-2	1-1	0-1	0-1	0-2	3-0	0-2	2-1	3-0	2-1	*	1-1	0-0	2-2	1-1	1-1	2-1	0-0	1-1
Newport IOW	2-1	1-0	1-3	0-3	0-1	2-0	0-1	0-0	2-1	1-2	0-0	2-3	2-1	0-4	*	0-0	1-0	0-4	3-0	1-1	2-3	1-1
Salisbury	0-1	1-1	2-1	1-1	2-0	0-2	1-0	1-1	1-1	2-3	0-3	1-2	5-0	0-2	1-0	*	1-4	1-2	0-3	0-1	2-1	1-1
Stafford	2-1	3-0	1-0	0-0	1-2	1-1	3-0	4-2	1-2	1-0	3-2	1-0	3-4	2-1	5-1	3-0	*	0-1	6-2	2-1	3-0	1-1
Tamworth	1-1	2-2	0-1	1-2	1-1	0-1	2-0	2-1	1-1	1-1	4-1	2-0	2-0	2-0	3-0	5-0	1-0	*	3-2	1-0	3-0	1-1
Tiverton	3-1	5-0	2-4	2-3	0-1	1-2	4-1	1-1	3-2	3-2	1-1	1-3	1-1	2-0	0-2	5-1	3-3	2-2	*	0-2	0-1	1-3
Welling	4-0	4-4	2-1	1-1	1-2	0-1	0-4	1-1	1-0	1-1	1-1	1-0	0-1	0-0	4-0	5-1	3-2	3-3	1-1	*	1-1	1-2
Weymouth	0-0	4-2	2-1	1-2	1-1	0-1	0-1	1-1	1-0	2-3	2-1	4-1	3-2	2-1	0-2	6-0	0-1	3-3	2-1	1-1	*	3-3
Worcester	0-1	1-2	1-1	3-0	1-1	0-0	0-1	4-3	2-2	1-1	3-1	1-0	3-2	0-0	4-0	1-2	1-2	0-2	4-2	2-1	3-3	*

191

UNIBOND PREMIER DIV 2001-2002 RESULTS

	Accrington	Altrincham	Bamber B	Barrow	Bishop A	Blyth S	Bradford P	Burscough	Burton	Colwyn B	Droylsden	Emley	Frickley	Gainsboro	Gateshead	Hucknall T	Hyde	Lancaster	Marine	Runcorn	Vauxhall M	Whitby	Worksop
Accrington	*	0-0	2-0	0-3	1-1	0-0	5-1	3-0	3-3	3-0	5-2	0-1	1-1	1-1	2-1	1-2	4-1	3-2	3-1	1-1	2-3	2-3	5-0
Altrincham	3-1	*	4-3	2-1	1-1	2-1	1-0	0-3	0-2	4-0	2-2	1-2	0-2	1-1	3-1	2-0	1-2	2-3	1-0	0-2	0-1	1-0	2-0
Bamber B	0-1	1-1	*	1-0	1-2	0-1	2-1	2-3	0-1	1-2	3-3	2-1	0-2	1-0	1-4	1-4	1-3	1-1	0-1	1-6	1-3	3-0	0-0
Barrow	0-4	2-2	1-0	*	3-1	4-1	2-3	1-0	1-2	1-1	1-2	1-1	3-1	3-0	4-1	6-1	0-0	1-1	0-1	2-1	1-2	2-0	1-0
Bishop A	1-2	2-1	2-0	1-2	*	1-1	0-0	2-1	1-1	1-2	1-2	1-0	1-1	0-1	1-2	0-2	0-2	1-1	0-0	1-3	3-4	1-0	1-2
Blyth S	1-1	0-3	3-1	1-1	2-1	*	4-1	0-2	0-1	2-0	0-0	1-3	0-0	0-1	2-1	1-2	2-0	1-0	0-0	2-2	0-1	2-1	2-2
Bradford P	1-2	4-1	5-2	2-0	0-2	2-2	*	0-2	1-4	5-0	3-1	2-1	3-0	2-0	3-5	0-1	3-1	1-0	2-3	3-1	1-3	2-1	2-2
Burscough	3-2	0-2	5-0	5-0	1-0	1-2	0-2	*	0-0	4-0	6-2	1-1	3-0	3-1	2-2	1-3	0-2	0-6	1-1	1-3	2-3	3-1	1-5
Burton	3-1	1-1	1-1	4-0	3-0	1-1	3-0	0-0	*	1-0	1-0	2-1	4-0	4-2	5-1	2-0	5-1	3-0	0-0	1-3	2-1	5-1	1-0
Colwyn Bay	3-0	2-5	0-0	0-5	1-2	1-1	1-2	2-2	1-3	*	1-0	3-2	1-1	1-2	5-1	5-1	4-4	5-1	0-0	1-0	3-2	1-1	0-3
Droylsden	1-5	2-0	0-0	2-0	1-0	0-0	2-2	1-0	0-7	1-0	*	4-2	2-1	0-1	2-2	3-0	2-1	4-4	3-3	0-1	2-3	1-1	0-2
Emley	0-3	2-1	5-0	2-0	1-2	2-1	1-0	1-1	2-1	3-2	1-0	*	2-1	1-2	0-1	3-0	5-1	1-2	1-1	0-1	1-1	5-1	1-1
Frickley	1-3	3-1	2-0	2-3	2-1	2-1	4-1	3-1	0-5	2-0	3-1	3-2	*	3-1	0-0	0-1	2-2	1-4	3-3	2-4	1-0	1-4	1-1
Gainsborough	5-2	1-3	5-0	0-1	1-1	1-5	0-7	2-2	3-2	2-1	3-1	2-2	2-1	*	1-1	0-0	1-0	3-2	3-0	1-4	2-1	2-0	0-2
Gateshead	0-0	0-2	1-1	0-0	1-0	1-1	0-0	1-3	1-4	1-2	1-0	2-0	0-0	1-0	*	4-1	1-0	2-4	0-0	0-2	1-2	2-0	0-3
HucknallT	1-3	0-0	1-1	2-1	2-3	2-1	1-0	2-0	1-1	1-0	2-4	2-0	1-0	1-4	0-0	*	4-1	3-1	2-4	0-2	1-1	0-1	0-3
Hyde	2-4	3-2	0-1	1-2	1-3	3-1	2-0	1-1	1-0	1-1	3-3	0-4	1-0	1-4	0-0	1-1	*	2-1	2-2	1-2	1-1	0-1	3-3
Lancaster	1-0	1-1	4-1	3-3	1-0	4-2	4-0	0-2	3-0	2-1	2-0	2-3	0-1	1-1	2-1	0-2	4-2	*	2-1	0-1	2-0	1-1	2-1
Marine	2-5	1-0	3-3	1-3	2-3	0-2	4-0	5-2	0-6	0-0	4-4	2-0	5-2	2-0	2-0	1-0	4-2	1-0	*	1-1	2-0	2-3	2-1
Runcorn	1-0	0-1	1-3	1-2	3-1	1-2	0-2	1-1	1-3	1-1	1-0	2-0	1-1	4-0	2-1	2-1	2-1	2-0	2-1	*	2-0	0-3	1-1
Vauxhall M	1-2	2-1	1-0	2-0	3-0	2-2	2-1	2-3	3-2	3-2	3-1	2-1	3-1	4-0	4-1	3-2	3-1	2-1	4-1	3-2	*	4-1	3-2
Whitby	2-1	2-3	1-0	2-4	2-1	2-2	1-1	3-1	1-3	2-2	1-2	1-2	1-3	0-4	2-3	2-1	2-1	0-2	2-1	2-2	1-2	*	0-2
Worksop	5-0	1-2	2-0	0-1	2-1	3-0	3-2	3-1	0-1	2-1	1-0	1-1	4-0	4-0	2-1	1-0	3-2	0-1	2-1	1-1	3-3	2-0	*

Sponsored by Stan James

RYMAN PREMIER DIV 2001-2002 RESULTS

	Aldershot	Basingstke	Bedford	Billericay	Boreh'm W	Braintree	Canvey I	Chesham	Croydon	Enfield	Gravesend	Grays	Hampton	Harrow	Hendon	Heybridge	Hitchin	Kingstonian	Maidenh'd	Purfleet	St Albans	Sutton Utd
Aldershot	*	2-2	4-0	1-1	0-2	4-0	1-3	1-0	2-0	3-1	1-2	0-1	4-1	2-1	2-1	3-3	1-2	3-0	4-1	4-1	1-1	1-0
Basingstoke	1-1	*	1-1	0-1	1-0	1-2	0-4	1-1	1-0	2-0	1-4	0-2	1-1	2-1	2-1	1-3	2-3	2-1	1-2	2-2	3-1	3-0
Bedford	1-2	3-0	*	3-4	2-0	2-0	1-3	2-0	3-2	2-2	0-1	4-0	4-1	3-4	0-5	5-2	0-1	2-1	1-2	1-0	0-1	0-1
Billericay	2-0	2-0	0-0	*	0-1	2-4	0-3	0-0	2-0	3-2	1-3	3-2	2-0	1-1	4-6	1-2	1-1	1-1	2-2	2-0	1-5	0-1
Boreham Wood	1-3	0-0	1-0	1-1	*	0-3	0-3	2-1	1-1	3-2	0-2	2-2	2-0	1-2	1-2	2-4	2-1	1-3	2-1	1-0	0-1	1-2
Braintree	2-0	3-2	2-1	1-0	2-0	*	2-1	2-0	1-1	2-3	0-2	2-3	3-2	0-0	2-0	2-0	0-1	1-0	2-1	2-2	2-1	3-0
Canvey Island	1-3	5-1	3-3	3-0	2-0	3-2	*	2-1	3-0	3-1	0-2	1-2	3-2	5-0	3-1	6-1	5-3	2-0	2-0	3-0	2-1	1-1
Chesham	2-1	1-1	1-1	2-0	1-0	4-1	1-5	*	2-1	0-0	2-2	3-5	2-1	5-0	0-2	3-0	5-5	0-0	1-0	3-0	3-2	2-0
Croydon	1-2	1-3	3-3	0-0	0-5	0-4	1-5	0-1	*	0-2	3-4	1-0	0-0	2-1	1-3	2-3	1-2	4-0	0-2	0-1	3-2	1-2
Enfield	1-1	3-0	1-0	0-2	0-1	1-2	0-3	0-1	3-1	*	1-5	1-2	0-2	1-2	0-6	4-2	0-5	2-2	0-2	0-1	0-0	2-2
Gravesend	2-1	0-0	4-1	1-0	0-1	3-0	0-1	1-4	6-1	3-0	*	2-0	2-1	2-2	3-0	1-1	2-0	2-0	3-2	0-0	3-2	3-1
Grays	3-1	0-0	2-1	0-0	3-2	3-0	1-1	2-1	1-0	0-0	2-0	*	1-1	2-1	2-0	1-3	2-1	2-0	0-1	1-3	3-2	3-3
Hampton	1-1	1-1	1-1	1-0	3-2	1-2	0-2	2-1	6-0	2-1	2-4	2-0	*	0-1	0-0	1-1	6-3	0-0	2-1	1-1	0-5	2-1
Harrow	2-3	3-3	2-4	0-2	2-3	2-4	1-3	5-0	2-0	2-4	0-3	0-0	0-1	*	0-2	1-3	1-1	0-1	0-3	1-2	2-6	1-6
Hendon	0-1	1-3	1-2	1-3	2-1	1-2	1-2	0-1	0-1	2-0	1-1	1-0	0-1	0-1	*	1-0	2-2	2-0	1-1	1-0	1-0	4-3
Heybridge	1-2	5-1	1-1	2-3	0-2	1-1	0-7	2-3	2-2	4-2	1-2	1-1	1-3	1-1	1-6	*	3-1	1-1	2-0	3-3	0-2	2-0
Hitchin	0-3	0-1	3-0	2-3	4-1	1-1	2-3	1-0	3-0	1-2	0-4	0-2	3-0	4-2	3-0	1-0	*	0-0	1-0	0-3	2-4	0-2
Kingstonian	2-1	1-1	3-0	4-1	1-1	1-1	2-2	1-0	3-0	0-2	0-1	2-3	1-0	3-1	3-0	1-2	2-2	*	1-0	1-5	4-2	1-1
Maidenhead	1-2	2-2	2-1	0-2	2-0	0-2	2-0	0-4	0-1	0-1	0-3	2-1	4-2	3-1	1-0	1-0	2-2	0-1	*	1-3	2-1	2-2
Purfleet	2-1	0-0	1-1	1-1	0-1	3-2	2-2	3-1	5-1	1-0	2-0	1-3	3-0	1-0	2-0	3-1	3-1	1-1	5-2	*	0-1	1-1
StAlbans	0-3	2-0	0-0	0-0	1-0	3-1	2-1	3-1	5-0	1-1	2-1	2-1	1-3	1-0	1-1	3-1	1-2	2-2	1-0	0-1	*	2-0
SuttonUtd	2-0	2-1	2-2	1-1	2-2	3-1	1-1	0-1	2-0	1-1	2-2	2-0	2-0	1-1	2-1	4-1	2-4	0-0	2-1	0-0	1-1	*

Sponsored by Stan James

SCOTTISH PREMIER LEAGUE 2001-2002 RESULTS

	Aberd'n	Celtic	Dundee	D'dee U	D'fermline	Hearts	Hibernian	Kilmarn'ck	Livingston	M'therwell	Rangers	St J'stone
Aberdeen	*	2-0	0-1	4-0	2-1	3-2	2-0	1-1	2-0	4-2	0-1	1-0
Celtic	1-0	*	3-1	5-1	5-0	2-0	3-1	2-0	3-2	5-1	1-1	2-1
Dundee	2-3	1-4	*	1-0	2-2	1-1	1-0	1-2	1-0	2-0	0-0	3-0
Dundee Utd	1-1	0-4	0-3	*	3-2	0-2	1-2	0-2	2-0	2-0	1-6	1-0
Dunfermline	1-0	0-0	2-0	1-1	*	0-1	3-1	2-0	0-0	1-1	0-1	2-1
Hearts	1-0	0-4	1-4	2-0	2-0	*	1-2	2-0	1-3	3-1	5-2	2-1
Hibernian	2-0	3-4	1-1	1-2	1-1	1-2	*	2-1	2-3	3-1	1-0	1-2
Kilmarnock	3-1	0-1	0-2	2-2	5-1	3-3	2-2	*	0-3	1-5	0-2	3-0
Livingston	0-0	2-2	1-3	0-1	2-0	2-0	1-1	0-1	*	2-0	0-2	2-1
Motherwell	3-2	1-2	0-4	4-2	1-0	1-2	2-0	3-1	3-1	*	2-2	1-2
Rangers	2-0	2-0	0-2	1-1	2-1	2-0	2-0	3-1	5-0	3-0	*	3-0
St Johnstone	1-1	1-2	0-2	0-1	0-1	0-2	0-1	1-0	3-0	0-2	0-2	*

BELL'S SCOTTISH FIRST DIVISION 2001-2002 RESULTS

	Airdrie	Arbroath	Ayr	Clyde	Falkirk	Inverness	Partick	Raith	Ross Co.	St Mirren
Airdrie	*	2-0	2-1	3-1	2-1	1-0	1-1	1-0	0-2	0-0
Arbroath	0-6	*	0-2	0-0	0-1	1-0	1-3	2-2	1-1	0-3
Ayr	1-3	1-0	*	0-0	0-0	2-2	1-1	1-1	2-0	4-1
Clyde	0-1	0-3	2-2	*	2-3	1-1	3-1	1-2	3-0	3-1
Falkirk	2-2	1-2	1-2	1-6	*	0-0	1-4	2-1	1-4	3-2
Inverness	1-2	1-0	0-2	5-1	3-2	*	3-0	5-0	1-1	4-2
Partick	1-1	1-1	2-1	2-1	3-0	5-1	*	1-0	0-0	3-3
Raith	2-1	2-2	3-1	0-0	5-2	5-1	1-2	*	0-1	1-0
Ross County	0-1	4-1	1-1	0-1	4-2	1-2	0-1	3-2	*	4-1
St Mirren	2-1	0-0	0-1	1-0	0-0	1-1	0-2	1-0	1-1	*

BELL'S SCOTTISH SECOND DIVISION 2001-2002 RESULTS

(Home \ Away)	Alloa	Berwick	Clydebank	Cowdenb'th	Forfar	Hamilton	Morton	Queen of Sth	Stenhsmuir	Stranraer
Alloa	*	1-1	2-2	1-0	2-1	2-2	4-0	4-1	4-0	2-2
Berwick	0-4	*	0-2	2-5	0-2	0-2	0-0	1-0	1-1	4-1
Clydebank	1-1	1-2	*	3-2	1-0	3-2	3-2	0-1	3-2	1-3
Cowdenbeath	1-2	1-1	2-1	*	1-2	2-1	1-1	1-2	2-4	2-2
Forfar	4-1	0-0	1-2	0-0	*	1-4	2-1	0-3	2-0	1-1
Hamilton	1-0	3-1	2-0	1-0	1-1	*	1-4	1-1	0-0	3-2
Morton	0-0	3-2	3-1	0-2	1-3	0-0	*	2-2	4-1	0-1
Queen of Sth	0-1	2-2	1-2	2-1	1-2	3-1	6-5	*	1-0	2-2
Stenhsmuir	1-0	3-0	0-0	0-1	0-0	0-3	4-0	1-4	*	3-1
Stranraer	1-1	2-2	0-2	3-0	0-3	3-2	0-0	2-2	1-0	*

BELL'S SCOTTISH THIRD DIVISION 2001-2002 RESULTS

(Home \ Away)	Albion	Brechin	Dumbarton	East Fife	Elgin	E. Stirling	Montrose	Peterhead	Queen's Park	Stirling
Albion	*	0-0	1-2	1-1	0-2	2-2	0-0	2-1	2-1	2-0
Brechin	4-1	*	0-1	6-0	3-2	1-0	2-0	4-3	5-0	3-1
Dumbarton	2-0	1-2	*	2-0	3-1	2-2	0-1	3-0	2-1	4-1
East Fife	0-0	2-3	1-0	*	4-1	3-0	2-0	1-2	1-4	1-1
Elgin	2-0	0-0	2-0	1-1	*	0-1	1-0	4-1	0-1	2-3
E. Stirling	1-2	1-2	3-4	2-0	0-3	*	2-1	2-3	3-1	3-0
Montrose	0-2	1-2	0-0	1-1	1-0	0-2	*	0-3	3-1	1-3
Peterhead	0-2	0-0	4-2	4-0	1-3	2-0	3-1	*	1-2	5-1
Queen's Park	0-3	1-2	1-3	0-2	3-0	2-3	0-1	2-2	*	0-0
Stirling	0-3	2-2	2-1	4-5	3-1	1-1	0-1	2-1	3-2	*

Sponsored by Stan James

FINAL

ARSENAL	2-0	CHELSEA

(AT THE MILLENNIUM STADIUM)

SEMI-FINALS

MIDDLESBRO	0-1	ARSENAL
FULHAM	0-1	CHELSEA

SIXTH ROUND

WBA	0-1	FULHAM
NEWCASTLE	1-1	ARSENAL
SPURS	0-4	CHELSEA
MIDDLESBRO	3-0	EVERTON

REPLAY

ARSENAL	3-0	NEWCASTLE

FIFTH ROUND

TOTTENHAM	4-0	TRANMERE
NEWCASTLE	1-0	MAN CITY
ARSENAL	5-2	GILLINGHAM
CHELSEA	3-1	PRESTON
MIDDLESBRO	1-0	BLACKBURN
EVERTON	0-0	CREWE
WALSALL	1-2	FULHAM
WBA	1-0	CHELTENHAM

REPLAY

CREWE	1-2	EVERTON

FOURTH ROUND

PRESTON	2-1	SHEFFIELD UTD
ROTHERHAM	2-4	CREWE
CHARLTON	1-2	WALSALL
TRANMERE	3-1	CARDIFF CITY
GILLINGHAM	1-0	BRISTOL ROV
YORK CITY	0-2	FULHAM
PETERBORO	2-4	NEWCASTLE
TOTTENHAM	4-0	BOLTON
CHELSEA	1-1	WEST HAM
MILLWALL	0-1	BLACKBURN
CHELTENHAM	2-1	BURNLEY
EVERTON	4-1	L. ORIENT
WBA	1-0	LEICESTER
MIDDLESBRO	2-0	MAN UTD
IPSWICH	1-4	MAN CITY
ARSENAL	1-0	LIVERPOOL

THIRD ROUND

STOCKPORT	1-3	BOLTON
MIDDLESBRO	2-0	WIMBLEDON
WATFORD	2-4	ARSENAL
MAN CITY	2-0	SWINDON
STOKE	0-1	EVERTON
FULHAM	1-0	WYCOMBE
CHARLTON	2-1	BLACKPOOL
SHEFF UTD	1-0	NOTTM FOREST
LEICESTER	2-1	MANSFIELD
SOUTHEND	1-3	TRANMERE

DERBY	1-3	BRISTOL ROV
BRIGHTON	0-2	PRESTON
GRIMSBY	0-1	YORK
ROTHERHAM	2-1	SOUTHAMPTON
BURNLEY	4-1	CANVEY IS
MILLWALL	2-1	SCUNTHORPE
CHELTENHAM	2-1	OLDHAM
PETERBORO	2-0	DARLINGTON
WALSALL	2-0	BRADFORD
CHELSEA	4-0	NORWICH
MACCLESFIELD	0-3	WEST HAM
DAG & RED	1-4	IPSWICH
PORTSMOUTH	1-4	L. ORIENT
LIVERPOOL	3-0	BIRMINGHAM
COVENTRY	0-2	TOTTENHAM
CARDIFF	2-1	LEEDS
BLACKBURN	3-1	BLACKBURN
SUNDERLAND	1-2	WEST BROM
NEWCASTLE	2-0	C. PALACE
ASTON VILLA	2-3	MAN UTD
CREWE	2-1	SHEFF WED
WOLVES	0-1	GILLINGHAM

SECOND ROUND

ALTRINCHAM	1-2	DARLINGTON
BLACKPOOL	2-0	ROCHDALE
BRIGHTON	2-1	RUSHDEN
CANVEY IS	1-0	NORTHAMPTON
CARDIFF	3-0	PORT VALE
CHESTERFIELD	1-1	SOUTHEND
EXETER	0-0	DAGENHAM
HALIFAX	1-1	STOKE
HINCKLEY	0-2	CHELTENHAM
HULL	2-3	OLDHAM
L. ORIENT	2-1	LINCOLN
MACCLESFIELD	4-1	SWANSEA
MANSFIELD	4-0	HUDDERSFIELD
PETERBROUGH	1-0	BOURNEMOUTH
PLYMOUTH	1-1	BRISTOL ROV
SCUNTHORPE	3-2	BRENTFORD
SWINDON	3-2	HEREFORD
TRANMERE	6-1	CARLISLE
WYCOMBE	3-0	NOTTS CO.
YORK	2-0	READING

REPLAYS

STOKE	3-0	HALIFAX
BRISTOL ROV	3-2	PLYMOUTH
SOUTHEND	2-0	CHESTERFIELD
DAGENHAM	3-0	EXETER

FIRST ROUND

HAYES	3-4	WYCOMBE
ALDERSHOT	0-0	BRISTOL ROV
ALTRINCHAM	1-1	LANCASTER
BARNET	0-0	CARLISLE

196

GET IN: The Gunners celebrate after Cup triumph over Chelsea

BEDFORD	0-0	PETERBORO
BLACKPOOL	2-2	NEWPORT
BOURNEMOUTH	3-0	WORKSOP
BRENTFORD	1-0	MORECAMBE
BRIGHTON	1-0	SHREWSBURY
BRISTOL CITY	0-1	L. ORIENT
CAMBRIDGE UTD	1-1	NOTTS CO.
COLCHESTER	0-0	YORK
DAG & RED	1-0	SOUTHPORT
DONCASTER	2-3	SCUNTHORPE
EXETER	3-0	CAMBRIDGE C.
GRAYS	1-2	HINCKLEY
HALIFAX	2-1	FARNBORO
HEREFORD	1-0	WREXHAM
HUDDERSFIELD	2-1	GRAVESEND
KETTERING	1-6	CHELTENHAM
KIDDERMINSTR	0-1	DARLINGTON
LEWES	0-2	STOKE
LINCOLN CITY	1-1	BURY
MACCLESFIELD	2-2	FOREST GREEN
MANSFIELD	1-0	OXFORD UTD
NORTHWICH	2-5	HULL
OLDHAM	1-1	BARROW
PORT VALE	3-0	AYLESBURY
READING	1-0	WELLING
SOUTHEND	3-2	LUTON
STALYBRIDGE	0-3	CHESTERFIELD
SWANSEA	4-0	QPR

SWINDON	3-1	HARTLEPOOL
TAMWORTH	1-1	ROCHDALE
TIVERTON	1-3	CARDIFF
TORQUAY	1-2	NORTHAMPTON
TRANMERE	4-1	BRIGG TOWN
WHITBY	1-1	PLYMOUTH
WIGAN	0-1	CANVEY IS
WORCESTER	0-1	RUSHDEN

REPLAYS

BARROW	0-1	OLDHAM
BRISTOL ROVERS	1-0	ALDERSHOT
BURY	1-1	LINCOLN CITY
(AET - LINCOLN WON 3-2 ON PENS)		
CARLISLE UTD	1-0	BARNET
LANCASTER	1-4	ALTRINCHAM
(AET)		
NOTTS COUNTY	2-0	CAMBRIDGE UTD
PLYMOUTH	3-2	WHITBY
PETERBORO	2-1	BEDFORD
ROCHDALE	1-0	TAMWORTH
YORK	2-2	COLCHESTER
(AET - YORK WON 3-2 ON PENS)		
FOREST GREEN	1-1	MACCLESFIELD
(AET - MACCLESFIELD WON 11-10 ON		
PENALTIES)		
NEWPORT	1-4	BLACKPOOL
(AET)		

Sponsored by Stan James

FINAL

BLACKBURN	2-1	TOTTENHAM

(AT THE MILLENNIUM STADIUM)

SEMI-FINAL (TWO LEGS)

TOTTENHAM	6-3	CHELSEA
BLACKBURN	6-3	SHEFF WED

QUARTER-FINAL

BLACKBURN	4-0	ARSENAL
CHELSEA	1-0	NEWCASTLE
SHEFF WED	4-0	WATFORD
TOTTENHAM	6-0	BOLTON

FOURTH ROUND

LEEDS UTD	0-2	CHELSEA
ASTON VILLA	0-1	SHEFF WED
FULHAM	1-2	TOTTENHAM
BLACKBURN	2-0	MAN CITY
ARSENAL	2-0	GRIMSBY
BOLTON	2-2	SOUTHAMPTON

(AET, BOLTON WON 6-5 PENS)

WATFORD	3-2	CHARLTON
NEWCASTLE	4-1	IPSWICH

THIRD ROUND

WEST BROM	0-1	CHARLTON
BOLTON	1-0	NOTTM FOREST
COVENTRY	0-2	CHELSEA
GILLINGHAM	0-2	SOUTHAMPTON
SHEFF WED	2-2	C. PALACE

(AET, SHEFF WED WON 3-1 ON PENS)

FULHAM	5-2	DERBY
WATFORD	4-1	BRADFORD
BLACKBURN	2-1	MIDDLESBRO
LIVERPOOL	1-2	GRIMSBY
ASTON VILLA	1-0	READING
LEICESTER	0-6	LEEDS
CREWE	2-3	IPSWICH
BARNSLEY	0-1	NEWCASTLE
ARSENAL	4-0	MAN UTD
MAN CITY	6-0	BIRMINGHAM
TRANMERE	0-4	TOTTENHAM

SECOND ROUND

BLACKPOOL	0-1	LEICESTER
ROTHERHAM	0-4	BRADFORD
NOTTS COUNTY	2-4	MAN CITY
PETERBORO	2-2	COVENTRY

(AET, COVENTRY WON 4-3 ON PENS)

BRIGHTON	0-3	SO'TON
CREWE	2-0	RUSHDEN
MIDDLESBRO	3-1	NORTHAMPTON
WBA	2-0	SWINDON
ROCHDALE	2-2	FULHAM

(AET, FULHAM WON 4-2 ON PENS)

READING	0-0	WEST HAM

(AET, READING WON 6-5 ON PENS)

GRIMSBY	3-3	SHEFF UTD

(AET, GRIMSBY WON 4-2 ON PENS)

COLCHESTER	1-3	BARNSLEY
GILLINGHAM	2-1	MILLWALL
TRANMERE	4-1	PRESTON
BOLTON	4-3	WALSALL
NOTTM FOR	1-1	STOCKPORT

(AET, FOREST WON 8-7 ON PENS)

DERBY	3-0	HULL
NEWCASTLE UTD	4-1	BRENTFORD
BRISTOL ROV	0-3	BIRMINGHAM
SPURS	2-0	TORQUAY
BRISTOL CITY	2-3	WATFORD
BLACKBURN	2-0	OLDHAM
CHARLTON	2-0	PORT VALE
EVERTON	1-1	C. PALACE

(AET, C.PALACE WON 5-4 ON PENS)

SHEFF WED	4-2	SUNDERLAND

FIRST ROUND

KIDDERMSTER	2-3	PRESTON
MANSFIELD	3-4	NOTTS CO.
PORT VALE	2-1	CHESTERFIELD
DARLINGTON	0-1	SHEFF UTD
BURNLEY	2-3	RUSHDEN
HARTLEPOOL	0-2	NOTTM FOR
BARNSLEY	2-0	HALIFAX
WREXHAM	2-3	HULL
STOCKPORT	3-0	CARLISLE
SCUNTHORPE	0-2	ROTHERHAM
BURY	1-3	SHEFF WED
STOKE	0-0	OLDHAM

(AET, OLDHAM WON 6-5 ON PENS)

HUDDERSFIELD	0-1	ROCHDALE
BLACKPOOL	3-2	WIGAN
MACCLESFIELD	1-2	BRADFORD
GRIMSBY	2-1	LINCOLN
YORK	2-2	CREWE

(AET, CREWE WON 6-5 ON PENS)

TRANMERE	3-1	SHREWSBURY
WOLVES	1-2	SWINDON
EXETER	0-1	WALSALL
MILLWALL	2-1	CARDIFF
CAMBRIDGES	1-1	WEST BROM

(AET, WBA WON 4-3 ON PENS)

BRISTOL CITY	2-1	CHELTENHAM
SWANSEA	0-1	PETERBORO
BIRMINGHAM	3-0	SOUTHEND
OXFORD	1-2	GILLINGHAM
L. ORIENT	2-4	C. PALACE
WYCOMBE	0-1	BRISTOL ROV
NORTHAMPTON	2-1	QPR
BOURNEMOUTH	0-2	TORQUAY
WATFORD	1-0	PLYMOUTH
BRENTFORD	1-0	NORWICH
BRIGHTON	2-1	WIMBLEDON
PORTSMOUTH	1-2	COLCHESTER
READING	4-0	LUTON

Sponsored by Stan James

FINAL

CELTIC	2-3	RANGERS

(AT HAMPDEN PARK)

SEMI-FINAL

AYR UNITED	0-3	CELTIC
RANGERS	3-0	PARTICK

FIFTH ROUND

FORFAR	0-6	RANGERS
DUNDEE UTD	2-2	AYR UNITED
ABERDEEN	0-2	CELTIC
PATICK	2-2	INVERNESS CT

REPLAY

AYR UNITED	2-0	DUNDEE UTD
INVERNESS CT	0-1	PARTICK

FOURTH ROUND

DUNDEE UTD	4-0	HAMILTON
PARTICK	1-1	DUNDEE
CLYDE	1-2	FORFAR
HEARTS	1-3	INVERNESS CT
RANGERS	4-1	HIBERNIAN
AYR UTD	3-0	DUNFERMLINE
KILMARNOCK	0-2	CELTIC
ABERDEEN	2-0	LIVINGSTON

THIRD ROUND

ARBROATH	0-2	INVERNESS CT
ALBION	1-4	LIVINGSTON
ALLOA	0-5	CELTIC
BERWICK	0-0	RANGERS
CLYDE	1-0	ST MIRREN
DEVERONVALE	0-6	AYR
DUNDEE	1-1	FALKIRK
DUNDEE UTD	3-0	FORRES
DUNFERMLINE	3-1	MOTHERWELL
GALA	0-5	FORFAR
HAMILTON	1-0	RAITH
HEARTS	2-1	ROSS COUNTY
KILMARNOCK	3-1	AIRDRIE
EAST FIFE	2-4	PARTICK
ST JOHNSTONE	0-2	ABERDEEN
STRANRAER	0-0	HIBERNIAN

REPLAY

RANGERS	3-0	BERWICK
FALKIRK	0-1	DUNDEE
HIBERNIAN	4-0	STRANRAER

SECOND ROUND

BRECHIN	0-1	ALBION
E. STIRLING	1-1	FORRES
DEVERONVALE	0-0	SPARTANS
BERWICK	1-0	COWDENBEATH

ROVERS: A Worthy triumph

QUEEN'S PARK	0-0	EAST FIFE
ALLOA	1-0	QOTS
CLYDEBANK	0-1	STRANRAER
FORFAR	2-0	THREAVE
HAMILTON	4-0	MONTROSE
GALA	1-0	STIRLING

REPLAY

FORRES	3-1	EAST STIRLING
SPARTANS	1-2	DEVERONVALE
E FIFE	2-2	QUEEN'S PARK

(E FIFE WIN 4-2 ON PENS)

FIRST ROUND

MORTON	1-2	QOTS
STIRLING	2-1	BUCKIE THISTLE
WICK	2-3	THREAVE
TARFF ROV	1-4	MONTROSE
ALBION	0-0	ELGIN CITY
BRECHIN	4-0	STEN'MUIR
ALLOA	3-1	DUMBARTON
CLYDEBANK	1-0	PETERHEAD

REPLAY

ELGIN	0-1	ALBION

FINAL
| RANGERS | 4-0 | AYR |

SEMI-FINAL
| RANGERS | 2-1 | CELTIC (AET) |
| HIBERNIAN | 0-1 | AYR (AET) |

QUARTER-FINAL
LIVINGSTON	0-2	CELTIC
ROSS COUNTY	1-2	RANGERS
AYR UNITED	5-1	INVERNESS CT
HIBERNIAN	2-0	DUNDEE UTD

THIRD ROUND
RANGERS	3-0	AIRDRIE
RAITH	0-2	HIBERNIAN
DUNFERMLINE	1-1	INVERNESS CT
(INVERNESS WIN 1-4 ON PENS)		
DUNDEE UTD	3-2	ST JOHNSTONE
ABERDEEN	1-6	LIVINGSTON
ROSS COUNTY	2-1	DUNDEE
AYR	0-0	KILMARNOCK
(AYR WIN 5-4 ON PENS)		
CELTIC	8-0	STIRLING

SECOND ROUND
DUNFERMLINE	3-0	ALLOA
HAMILTON	0-2	DUNDEE
FALKIRK	0-2	RAITH
AIRDRIE	2-1	MOTHERWELL
AYR	4-0	STRANRAER
QOTS	1-2	ABERDEEN
INVERNESS	3-3	PARTICK
(PARTICK WON 4-2 ON PENS)		
STIRLING	2-1	ST MIRREN
LIVINGSTON	3-0	EAST FIFE
ROSS COUNTY	0-0	HEARTS
(ROSS WON 5-4 ON PENS)		
DUNDEE UTD	3-0	DUMBARTON
CLYDE	1-2	ST JOHNSTONE

FIRST ROUND
BERWICK	0-3	PARTICK
RAITH ROVERS	1-0	MONTROSE
STIRLING	3-2	COWDENBEATH
ALLOA	4-0	PETERHEAD
FORFAR	1-2	FALKIRK
EAST STIRLING	0-3	QOTS
CLYDE	2-2	STEN'MUIR
(CLYDE WIN 4-2 ON PENS)		
AIRDRIE	3-0	MORTON
EAST FIFE	1-0	ARBROATH
QUEEN'S PARK	0-1	HAMILTON
ELGIN CITY	2-3	STRANRAER
ALBION ROVERS	0-2	INVERNESS CT
DUMBARTON	2-0	CLYDEBANK
ROSS COUNTY	3-0	BRECHIN

UEFA Cup
2001-2002

FINAL
| FEYENOORD | 3 - 2 | B. DORTMUND |

SEMI-FINAL
AC MILAN	3 - 1	B. DORTMUND
FEYENOORD	2 - 2	INTER MILAN
FIRST LEG		
B. DORTMUND	4 - 0	AC MILAN
INTER MILAN	0 - 1	FEYENOORD

QUARTER-FINAL
AC MILAN	2 - 0	H TEL AVIV
B. DORTMUND	4 - 0	S. LIBEREC
FEYENOORD	1 - 1	EINDHOVEN
VALENCIA	0 - 1	INTER MILAN
FIRST LEG		
H. TEL AVIV	1 - 0	AC MILAN
INTER MILAN	1 - 1	VALENCIA
PSV EINDHOVEN	1 - 1	FEYENOORD
S. LIBEREC	0 - 0	B. DORTMUND

FOURTH ROUND
AC MILAN	0 - 1	RODA JC
AEK ATHENS	2 - 2	INTER MILAN
B. DORTMUND	0 - 0	LILLE
FEYENOORD	3 - 2	RANGERS
LEEDS	0 - 1	EINDHOVEN
PARMA	1 - 2	H. TEL AVIV
SERVETTE	2 - 2	VALENCIA
S. LIBEREC	4 - 1	LYON
FIRST LEG		
H. TEL AVIV	0 - 0	PARMA
INTER MILAN	3 - 1	AEK ATHENS
LILLE	1 - 1	B. DORTMUND
LYON	1 - 1	S. LIBEREC
PSV EINDHOVEN	0 - 0	LEEDS
RANGERS	1 - 1	FEYENOORD
RODA JC	0 - 1	AC MILAN
VALENCIA	3 - 0	SERVETTE

THIRD ROUND
BRONDBY	0 - 3	PARMA
CELTIC	1 - 0	VALENCIA
FC LOVECH	1 - 1	AEK ATHENS
FREIBURG	2 - 2	FEYENOORD
HERTHA	0 - 3	SERVETTE
INTER MILAN	4 - 1	IPSWICH
LEEDS	2 - 2	ZURICH
LILLE	2 - 0	FIORENTINA
LYON	3 - 0	FC BRUGES
MALLORCA	1 - 2	S.LIBEREC
EINDHOVEN	4 - 1	SALONIKA
PARIS ST-G.	0 - 0	RANGERS
S. LISBON	1 - 1	AC MILAN
B. DORTMUND	1 - 0	COPENHAGEN
L MOSCOW	0 - 1	H. TEL AVIV
RODA JC	2 - 0	BORDEAUX
FIRST LEG		
AC MILAN	2 - 0	S. LISBON

Sponsored by Stan James

GOING DUTCH: Feyenoord celebrate their UEFA Cup triumph

AEK ATHENS	3 - 2	FC LOVECH		ST GALLEN	1 - 4	FREIBURG
FC BRUGES	4 - 1	LYON		STANDARD LIEGE	0 - 2	BORDEAUX
COPENHAGEN	0 - 1	B. DORTMUND		TIROL INNSBRUCK	2 - 2	FIORENTINA
FEYENOORD	1 - 0	FREIBURG		TROYES	3 - 2	LEEDS
FIORENTINA	0 - 1	LILLE		VALENCIA	6 - 1	L. WARSAW
GRASSHOPPERS	1 - 2	LEEDS		AEK ATHENS	3 - 2	OSIJEK
IPSWICH	1 - 0	INTER MILAN		FC LOVECH	0 - 0	UNION BERLIN
SALONIKA	3 - 2	EINDHOVEN		WISLA KRAKOW	1 - 0	INTER MILAN
PARMA	1 - 1	BRONDBY				

FIRST LEG

RANGERS	0 - 0	PARIS ST-G.		AC MILAN	2 - 0	CSKA SOFIA
SERVETTE	0 - 0	HERTHA		BORDEAUX	2 - 0	S. LIEGE
SLOVAN LIBEREC	3 - 1	MALLORCA		CSKA KIEV	0 - 2	FC BRUGES
VALENCIA	1 - 0	CELTIC		CELTA VIGO	3 - 1	S. LIBEREC
BORDEAUX	1 - 0	RODA JC		FC COPENHAGEN	0 - 0	AJAX
HAPOEL TEL AVIV	2 - 1	L MOSCOW		FC UNION BERLIN	0 - 2	FC LOVECH
				FC UTRECHT	1 - 3	PARMA

SECOND ROUND

				FIORENTINA	2 - 0	T. INNSBRUCK
AJAX	0 - 1	COPENHAGEN		FREIBURG	0 - 1	ST GALLEN
BRONDBY	5 - 0	VARTEKS		GRASSHOPPERS	4 - 1	FC TWENTE
CSKA SOFIA	0 - 1	AC MILAN		HALMSTADS	0 - 1	SP. LISBON
CHELSEA	1 - 1	H. TEL AVIV		H. TEL AVIV	2 - 0	CHELSEA
D. PRIBRAM	2 - 2	SALONIKA		INTER MILAN	2 - 0	W. KRAKOW
D. MOSCOW	1 - 4	RANGERS		IPSWICH	0 - 0	HEL'BORGS
FC BRUGES	5 - 0	CSKA KIEV		LEEDS	4 - 2	TROYES
FC TWENTE	4 - 2	ZURICH		LEGIA WARSAW	1 - 1	VALENCIA
HELSINGBORGS	1 - 3	IPSWICH		OSIJEK	1 - 2	AEK ATHENS
HERTHA BERLIN	2 - 0	V. STAVANGER		PAOK SALONIKA	6 - 1	D. PRIBRAM
M. TEL AVIV	2 - 1	RODA JC		PARIS ST-G.	4 - 0	RAPID VIENNA
PARMA	0 - 0	FC UTRECHT		RANGERS	3 - 1	D. MOSCOW
RAPID VIENNA	2 - 2	PARIS ST-G.		REAL ZARAGOZA	0 - 0	SERVETTE
SERVETTE	1 - 0	R.ZARAGOZA		VARTEKS	3 - 1	BRONDBY
SLOVAN LIBEREC	3 - 0	CELTA VIGO		RODA JC	4 - 1	M. TEL AVIV
SP. LISBON	6 - 1	HALMSTADS		V. STAVANGER	0 - 1	HERTHA

Sponsored by Stan James

Champions League 2001-2002

FINAL
LEVERKUSEN	1 - 2	REAL MADRID

SEMI-FINAL
REAL MADRID	1 - 1	BARCELONA
LEVERKUSEN	1 - 1	MAN UTD

FIRST LEG
MAN UTD	2 - 2	LEVERKUSEN
BARCELONA	0 - 2	REAL MADRID

QUARTER-FINAL
MAN UTD	3 - 2	DEPORTIVO
REAL MADRID	2 - 0	B. MUNICH
LEVERKUSEN	4 - 2	LIVERPOOL
BARCELONA	3 - 1	PANA'IKOS

FIRST LEG
LIVERPOOL	1 - 0	LEVERKUSEN
P'THINAIKOS	1 - 0	BARCELONA
B. MUNICH	2 - 1	REAL MADRID
DEPORTIVO	0 - 2	MAN UTD

2ND STAGE GROUP A
B. MUNICH	2 - 1	NANTES
BOAVISTA	0 - 3	MAN UTD
MAN UTD	0 - 0	B. MUNICH
NANTES	1 - 1	BOAVISTA
B. MUNICH	1 - 0	BOAVISTA
MAN UTD	5 - 1	NANTES
BOAVISTA	0 - 0	B. MUNICH
NANTES	1 - 1	MAN UTD
MAN UTD	3 - 0	BOAVISTA
NANTES	0 - 1	B. MUNICH
B. MUNICH	1 - 1	MAN UTD
BOAVISTA	1 - 0	NANTES

2ND STAGE GROUP B
GALATASARAY	0 - 1	BARCELONA
LIVERPOOL	2 - 0	ROMA
BARCELONA	0 - 0	LIVERPOOL
ROMA	1 - 1	GALATASARAY
GALATASARAY	1 - 1	LIVERPOOL
ROMA	3 - 0	BARCELONA
BARCELONA	1 - 1	ROMA
LIVERPOOL	0 - 0	GALATASARAY
BARCELONA	2 - 2	GALATASARAY
ROMA	0 - 0	LIVERPOOL
GALATASARAY	1 - 1	ROMA
LIVERPOOL	1 - 3	BARCELONA

2ND STAGE GROUP C
P'THINAIKOS	2 - 2	REAL MADRID
S PRAGUE	2 - 0	PORTO
PORTO	2 - 1	PANA'IKOS
REAL MADRID	3 - 0	S. PRAGUE
P'THINAIKOS	2 - 1	S. PRAGUE
PORTO	1 - 2	REAL MADRID
REAL MADRID	1 - 0	PORTO
S. PRAGUE	0 - 2	PANA'IKOS
PORTO	0 - 1	S. PRAGUE
REAL MADRID	3 - 0	PANA'IKOS
P'THINAIKOS	0 - 0	PORTO
S. PRAGUE	2 - 3	REAL MADRID

2ND STAGE GROUP D
DEPORTIVO	1 - 3	LEVERKUSEN
JUVENTUS	1 - 0	ARSENAL
ARSENAL	0 - 2	DEPORTIVO
LEVERKUSEN	3 - 1	JUVENTUS
ARSENAL	4 - 1	LEVERKUSEN
DEPORTIVO	2 - 0	JUVENTUS
LEVERKUSEN	1 - 1	ARSENAL
JUVENTUS	0 - 0	DEPORTIVO
ARSENAL	3 - 1	JUVENTUS
LEVERKUSEN	3 - 0	DEPORTIVO
JUVENTUS	4 - 0	LEVERKUSEN
DEPORTIVO	2 - 0	ARSENAL

1ST STAGE GROUP A
L. MOSCOW	2 - 0	REAL MADRID
ROMA	1 - 1	ANDERLECHT
ANDERLECHT	1 - 5	L. MOSCOW
REAL MADRID	1 - 1	ROMA
ANDERLECHT	0 - 2	REAL MADRID
L. MOSCOW	0 - 1	ROMA
REAL MADRID	4 - 1	ANDERLECHT
ROMA	2 - 1	L. MOSCOW
ANDERLECHT	0 - 0	ROMA
REAL MADRID	4 - 0	L. MOSCOW
L. MOSCOW	1 - 1	ANDERLECHT
ROMA	1 - 2	REAL MADRID

1ST STAGE GROUP B
DYNAMO KIEV	1 - 0	BOAVISTA
LIVERPOOL	2 - 0	B. DORTMUND
B. DORTMUND	1 - 0	D. KIEV
BOAVISTA	1 - 1	LIVERPOOL
B. DORTMUND	2 - 1	BOAVISTA
DYNAMO KIEV	1 - 2	LIVERPOOL
BOAVISTA	2 - 1	B. DORTMUND
LIVERPOOL	1 - 0	DYNAMO KIEV
B. DORTMUND	0 - 0	LIVERPOOL
BOAVISTA	3 - 1	DYNAMO KIEV
DYNAMO KIEV	2 - 2	B. DORTMUND
LIVERPOOL	1 - 1	BOAVISTA

1ST STAGE GROUP C
MALLORCA	1 - 0	PANA'IKOS
SCHALKE	3 - 1	ARSENAL
ARSENAL	3 - 1	MALLORCA
P'THINAIKOS	2 - 0	SCHALKE
ARSENAL	2 - 1	PANA'IKOS
MALLORCA	0 - 4	SCHALKE
P'THINAIKOS	1 - 0	ARSENAL
SCHALKE	0 - 1	MALLORCA
ARSENAL	3 - 2	SCHALKE
P'THINAIKOS	2 - 0	MALLORCA
MALLORCA	1 - 0	ARSENAL
SCHALKE	0 - 2	PANA'IKOS

1ST STAGE GROUP D
GALATASARAY	2 - 0	EINDHOVEN
NANTES	1 - 0	LAZIO
LAZIO	1 - 0	GALATASARAY
PSV	0 - 0	NANTES
GALATASARAY	0 - 0	NANTES
LAZIO	2 - 1	EINDHOVEN
NANTES	0 - 1	GALATASARAY
PSV	1 - 0	LAZIO
LAZIO	1 - 3	NANTES
PSV	3 - 1	GALATASARAY
GALATASARAY	1 - 0	LAZIO
NANTES	4 - 1	EINDHOVEN

Sponsored by Stan James

1ST STAGE GROUP E

CELTIC	4 - 3	JUVENTUS
PORTO	1 - 0	ROSENBORG
JUVENTUS	3 - 1	PORTO
ROSENBORG	2 - 0	CELTIC
JUVENTUS	1 - 0	ROSENBORG
PORTO	3 - 0	CELTIC
CELTIC	1 - 0	ROSENBORG
PORTO	0 - 0	JUVENTUS
CELTIC	1 - 0	PORTO
ROSENBORG	1 - 1	JUVENTUS
JUVENTUS	3 - 2	CELTIC
ROSENBORG	1 - 2	PORTO

1ST STAGE GROUP F

LEVERKUSEN	2 - 4	LYON
BARCELONA	1 - 0	FENERBAHCE
FENERBAHCE	1 - 2	B. LEVERKUSEN
LYON	2 - 3	BARCELONA
BARCELONA	2 - 1	B. LEVERKUSEN
LYON	3 - 1	FENERBAHCE
LEVERKUSEN	2 - 1	FENERBAHCE
BARCELONA	2 - 0	LYON
LEVERKUSEN	2 - 1	BARCELONA
FENERBAHCE	0 - 1	LYON
FENERBAHCE	0 - 3	BARCELONA
LYON	0 - 1	B. LEVERKUSEN

1ST STAGE GROUP G

LILLE	1 - 1	MAN UTD
OLYMPIAKOS	1 - 1	DEPORTIVO
DEPORTIVO	1 - 1	LILLE
MAN UTD	3 - 0	OLYMPIAKOS
MAN UTD	2 - 3	DEPORTIVO
OLYMPIAKOS	2 - 1	LILLE
LILLE	1 - 1	DEPORTIVO
OLYMPIAKOS	0 - 2	MAN UTD
DEPORTIVO	2 - 1	MAN UTD
LILLE	3 - 1	OLYMPIAKOS
DEPORTIVO	2 - 2	OLYMPIAKOS
MAN UTD	1 - 0	LILLE

1ST STAGE GROUP H

FEYENOORD	2 - 1	S. MOSCOW
S. PRAGUE	0 - 1	B. MUNICH
B. MUNICH	3 - 1	FEYENOORD
S. MOSCOW	2 - 2	S. PRAGUE
B. MUNICH	5 - 1	S. MOSCOW
FEYENOORD	0 - 2	S. PRAGUE
FEYENOORD	2 - 2	B. MUNICH
S. PRAGUE	2 - 0	S. MOSCOW
S. PRAGUE	4 - 0	FEYENOORD
S. MOSCOW	1 - 3	B. MUNICH
B. MUNICH	0 - 0	S. PRAGUE
S. MOSCOW	2 - 2	FEYENOORD

OLE, OLE, OLE, OLE: Spanish giants Madrid are kings of Europe
Sponsored by Stan James

203

FINAL BRITISH 2001/2002 DRAWS CHART

X = Score draw
O = 0-0 draw

V = Void match
* = Pools panel

Pools No	Aug 11	Aug 18	Aug 25	Sep 1	Sep 8	Sep 15	Sep 22	Sep 29	Oct 6	Oct 13	Oct 20	Oct 27	Nov 3	Nov 10	Nov 17	Nov 24	Dec 1	Dec 8	Dec 15	Dec 22	Dec 29	Jan 5	Jan 12	Jan 19	Jan 26	Feb 2	Feb 9	Feb 16	Feb 23	Mar 2	Mar 9	Mar 16	Mar 23	Mar 30	Apr 6	Apr 13	Apr 20	Apr 27	O	X
1	-	-	-	X	-	*	X	-	*	-	-	X	-	X	-	*	0	0	-	-	*	0	-	-	X	-	-	-	*	X	X	-	-	-	X	-	-	*	3	8
2	-	-	-	*	0	-	-	-	-	0	X	-	-	*	X	-	0	-	-	-	-	X	X	*	-	-	-	-	-	X	-	-	-	-	X	X	-	*	3	7
3	-	-	X	*	0	-	-	*	-	X	-	-	-	-	-	X	-	-	-	-	X	0	X	*	0	-	-	-	-	-	-	-	-	-	-	-	X		3	5
4	-	-	0	X	*	X	-	0	-	-	0	-	-	-	*	-	-	X	X	-	-	X	-	*	-	-	-	X	-	-	X	0	-	-	-	X	-		4	8
5	X	-	-	*	-	-	-	-	-	-	*	-	V	-	*	-	-	*	-	-	-	*	-	-	-	-	-	0	-	-	X	-	-	-	-	-	*		1	2
6	-	-	-	*	-	-	-	-	-	X	-	-	X	-	-	-	-	X	*	-	-	*	-	X	-	*	-	X	X	-	-	-	-	-	-	-	0		0	6
7	-	-	0	-	*	-	-	X	-	-	-	0	-	0	X	-	-	X	-	-	X	*	-	X	-	-	-	-	-	0	X	X	X	-	X	-	-	-	4	9
8	-	0	-	0	*	-	V	-	-	X	-	-	-	X	-	-	-	-	-	*	-	X	-	*	0	-	0	-	X	-	-	-	X	-	-	*	-		4	5
9	-	X	-	*	X	-	-	0	0	-	X	-	-	0	*	-	-	X	-	X	-	*	-	X	-	-	-	-	-	-	-	-	-	-	-	-	-		3	7
10	X	-	-	*	-	0	-	-	*	-	-	-	-	-	-	-	0	-	-	-	-	-	X	-	X	-	-	X	-	-	-	-	-	-	-	*	X	-	2	5
11	-	-	-	*	-	-	-	*	-	X	-	-	X	-	-	-	0	-	0	0	-	-	X	0	-	-	-	X	-	-	-	X	-	-	X	-		4	6
12	0	-	-	X	-	-	-	*	-	X	-	X	-	X	-	-	-	-	-	0	0	-	*	X	-	-	X	-	-	0	-	-	-	-	*		4	7
13	-	-	-	-	-	-	-	*	-	-	-	*	-	-	X	-	-	X	-	-	0	-	-	X	-	-	X	-	0	X	-		2	6
14	-	-	-	-	-	-	-	*	-	-	X	-	-	0	-	-	-	0	*	-	-	X	-	-	X	-		2	3
15	-	X	-	-	-	X	-	*	-	-	0	-	X	X	X	X	-	-	*	-	X	-	-	-	X	-	-	-	-	-	0		1	7
16	-	0	-	X	-	X	-	0	0	*	-	-	V	-	-	-	-	X	-	0	0	-	X	0	0	-	0	-	0	X	-	-	0		9	5
17	-	-	*	-	X	X	-	V	-	-	-	-	-	-	X	X	-	-	-	X	-	-	X	-	-		0	6
18	0	-	X	0	X	-	X	-	-	-	-	-	-	-	-	-	0	-	-	X	-	-	X	-	0	-	-		4	5
19	-	-	-	-	-	-	X	-	X	-	-	0	-	X	-	-	-	X	X	-	-	0	-	-	-	X	X	-		2	7
20	X	-	X	X	0	-	-	X	-	-	X	-	X	-	X	-	X	-	0	*	-	-	X	X	-	-	0		2	11
21	X	-	X	-	-	-	*	-	-	X	-	0	-	X	X	X	X	-	-	-	X	-	-	-	X		1	8
22	-	-	0	*	-	-	-	-	X	-	-	X	-	X	-	*	-	X	X	-	X	0	-	-	-	0	-	-		3	6

Mathmo takes abacus to new summer games

TWO new games were launched this summer and both need careful scrutiny. We'll take Camelot's Lotto Hotpicks first, then Littlewoods' Premier Challenge where you have to predict the results of ten top games. I'm afraid anyone asking me for Lotto Hotpick "plans" is told, "We don't do plans for that, it's rubbish."

Winning £40 for picking two Lotto numbers, £450 for three and £7,000 for four might seem a lot, but rest assured that in time Camelot should pay out less than half of what they take. Ironically, even the bookies' awful lotto games are better value.

The real odds against netting two numbers are 77-1 yet Camelot are paying 39-1; for three numbers the odds are 920-1 (Camelot – 449-1) and the odds against getting four are 14,124-1

(Camelot – 6,999-1). If you want to play a three-of-four number Lotto game, then do Prizebuster 3 or Prizebuster 4 with Littlewoods. For coupons, contact Collectors, call free on 0800 490 000, or play on line at www.bet247.co.uk. The average payout in 2001 was £100 more than Camelot's fixed prize and peaked at £2,800.

If you use a consecutive pair plus higher numbers, your win should be above average if your numbers come up.

The average Prizebuster 4 payout in 2001 was £2k above Camelot's deal – £9,100, and twice in 2002 it's hit the maximum £25,000. There's a consolation prize of £20 or more for getting three right, too.

Which brings me to Premier Challenge, a game

Sponsored by Stan James

now attached to the regular coupon. Littlewoods have made this simple, at the price of making it dull.

A ten-match acca. is hardly an attractive bet, especially when your stake is fixed at £1 and you can only do up to four entries with no perming.

Eight bankers with two 2-way is the maximum possible and even then you have to write out all four combinations. Why isn't it designed like a Placepot ticket so that perms are possible, increasing the interest and the pool?

Unlike a ten-fold with the bookie, however, there are consolation prizes for eight or nine correct and with the top prize capped at £10,000, money will sometimes cascade down into these second and third dividends.

On weeks when there are shock results or lots of draws and the bookies clean up, too, the top prize could go to lines with one or even two wrong.

To win £10k on this therefore, eccentric forecasting, going against form and using four or five draws is the key.

Sponsored by Stan James

Sponsored by Stan James